CAMBRIDGE TEXTS IN THE HISTORY OF PHILOSOPHY

LA METTRIE

Machine Man and Other Writings

CAMBRIDGE TEXTS IN THE HISTORY OF PHILOSOPHY

The main obective of Cambridge Texts in the History of Philosophy is to expand the range, variety and quality of texts in the history of philosophy which are available in English. The series includes texts by familiar names (such as Descartes and Kant) and also by less well-known authors. Wherever possible, texts are published in complete and unabridged form, and translations are specially commissioned for the series. Each volume contains a critical introduction together with a guide to further reading and any necessary glossaries and textual apparatus. The volumes are designed for student use at undergraduate and postgraduate level and will be of interest not only to students of philosophy, but also to a wider audience of readers in the history of science, the history of theology and the history of ideas.

For a list of titles published in the series, please see end of book.

JULIEN OFFRAY DE LA METTRIE

Machine Man and Other Writings

TRANSLATED AND EDITED BY

ANN THOMSON

University of Caen

Published by the Press Syndicate of the University of Cambridge
The Pitt Building, Trumpington Street, Cambridge CB2 1RP
40 West 20th Street, New York, NY 10011–4211, USA
10 Stamford Road, Oakleigh, Melbourne 3166, Australia

First published 1996

Printed in Great Britain at Bell & Bain Ltd, Glasgow

A catalogue record for this book is available from the British Library

Library of Congress cataloguing in publication data

La Mettrie, Julien Offray de, 1709–1751.
[Selections. English. 1996]
Julien Offray de La Mettrie: Machine Man and other writings/ [edited by] Ann Thomson.
p. cm. – (Cambridge texts in the history of philosophy)
Includes bibliographical references and index.
1. Materialism. 2. Mechanism (Philosophy).
I. Thomson, Ann. II. Title. III. Series.
B2062.E5 1996
3194–dc20 95–14609 CIP

ISBN 0 521 47258 X hardback
ISBN 0 521 47849 9 paperback

CE

Contents

Foreword

None of La Mettrie's works appeared under his own name, and the precise attribution of works to him still presents problems. The texts which here accompany *Machine Man* represent the most important of his philosophical works, and are beyond doubt by La Mettrie. *Machine Man* is given here complete (but without the polemical dedication to Haller), as are the shorter works, *Man as Plant*, *The System of Epicurus* and *Preliminary Discourse*. As for the two longer works, *Treatise on the Soul* and *Anti-Seneca*, the first half of each is included here, as in both cases it provides the essential arguments. La Mettrie's *Philosophical Works* contained one other, partly satirical text, *Animals More than Machines*, which has been omitted from the present volume.

Apart from *Machine Man*, which was translated into English soon after its publication, and retranslated in 1912, together with extracts from the *Natural History of the Soul* (*Treatise on the Soul*), the other works have never before appeared in English.

The translation of the title *L'Homme machine* since the eighteenth century has been *Man a Machine*, but it was felt by the series editor that a modern translation was called for. *Machine Man* corresponds most closely to La Mettrie's provocative French title; for *L'Homme plante*, however, *Man as Plant* was considered to be more appropriate, as here the author is making a fanciful comparison, which is not the case in the former work. Consequently, the symmetry of the two French titles is not preserved in the new English titles.

All the texts have been translated for the present volume. Translating La Mettrie presents certain problems in view of his playful and sometimes punning style. It should be noted in particular that the word 'esprit' in French, a key term which occurs frequently in his writing, can sometimes refer to the mind, but at others to intelligence, wit, etc. Thus a certain word play is here lost in translation. I have chosen, in nearly all cases, to translate 'homme' by 'man' rather than 'human', as in my opinion, this reflects more accurately what was in the mind of an eighteenth-century thinker like La Mettrie; it also enables the reader to see when he himself chooses to use 'human' instead of 'man'.

I should like to emphasise my debt to those who have published annotated editions of various of La Mettrie's works: A. Vartanian (*L'Homme machine*), J. Falvey (*Anti-Senèque*) and T. Verbeek (*Traité de l'âme*). In addition, my thanks go to those who reread parts of the translation and made useful comments: Valerie Burling, Wynne Hellegouarc'h, Fiona MacPhail and Nina and Tommy Thomson.

Introduction

La Mettrie is known mainly for *L'Homme machine* or *Machine Man*, a work whose title has rung out as a provocation since its publication in Holland in 1747. This was doubtless the effect sought by the author; like the majority of his works, it has little of a formal treatise and is mainly a polemical work addressed to the general reading public of educated people. Because of this, it seems to have been quite widely distributed for most of the eighteenth century, although since the end of the century, it has been more often referred to than read, a fact which has paradoxically increased its scandalous reputation. In any case, the life of its author, Julien Offray de La Mettrie, was such that it could only increase the aura of scandal surrounding his work. A medical doctor who wrote both satires against his colleagues and irreligious philosophical works, he was forced to leave his native France and then Holland before finding refuge at the court of Frederick II of Prussia, where he continued to write 'scandalous' works developing amoral conclusions drawn from his uncompromising materialism, which aroused condemnation even among those who had not been shocked by his earlier works. He died, in 1751, of what was commonly described as indigestion.[1]

He was writing at a turning-point in the mid-eighteenth century, when the intellectual scene was dominated by Voltaire, when the works of Buffon, Montesquieu, Rousseau and Diderot were beginning to be published and the *Encyclopédie* project was getting under way, and he was very conscious of this new self-conscious philosophical party critical of many aspects of the Old Régime. Prussia was by no means an intellectual backwater, as Frederick attracted many scientists, in addition to French men of letters such as Maupertuis, Voltaire and d'Argens; nevertheless, La Mettrie seems to have felt his exile as a hard blow and attempted, thanks to Voltaire's intervention, to obtain permission to return to France. The publication of his philosophical works in Berlin in 1750 seems to have been partly a way of showing that he was involved in the new movement, and even the fact that

[1] For the events of his life, see the Chronology.

he chose to call each of the texts contained in the volume a contribution to the 'natural history of man' can be seen as a reference to Buffon's *Natural History*, whose first volumes had just been published. His death, in 1751, meant that he did not take part in the activity around the *Encyclopédie*, and the Philosophes of the second half of the century all dissociated themselves from someone with such an unsavoury reputation who could easily be accused of undermining morality and the foundations of society. Materialists such as Diderot or d'Holbach shared many of his ideas, and Diderot's *Dalembert's Dream* or *Refutation of Helvétius*, in particular (neither of which was published at the time), bear many affinities with La Mettrie's ideas. Nevertheless, La Mettrie's writings undermined their attempts to provide a non-religious basis for morality; this led to attacks on him, in d'Holbach's *The System of Nature* and in Diderot's *Essay on the Reigns of Claudius and Nero*, for his moral theories and his view of the philosopher as someone writing only for an élite, whose speculations do not take acount of the needs of society. He was thus denounced as a 'lunatic' by those who were in part indebted to him, and his reputation suffered an eclipse.[2]

Recently, interest in La Mettrie's works has been aroused, including among those studying brain functioning, but attention still tends to be paid mainly to *Machine Man*. However, for a clear understanding of the author's aim and the implications of the issues he discussed, it is necessary to look also at his other main philosophical works, which either laid down the bases for the discussion in his most famous work or developed in a different way some of the issues raised there. They enable us to see more clearly what La Mettrie considered to be the main aspects of his materialism, which remained constant despite changes in emphasis or formulation and even a certain amount of incoherence. This, together with his often satirical intention and the fact that he was concerned less with philosophical consistency than with expounding a thoroughgoing materialism, has led to differences of interpretation. In addition, many of the problems raised by his writings remain obscure to the modern reader and need to be placed in the context in which they were written. La Mettrie was contributing to certain long-standing debates but, at the same time, he was very much aware of new developments in intellectual life, which were reported in the journals that he read assiduously, as did all educated people. Indeed, his writings often seem to have been sparked off by recent publications. He reacts, even if it is often in a superficial manner, to the latest scientific discoveries and to the important publications that were of interest to the educated, but not necessarily specialist, reading public he was addressing.

This does not mean that he was simply a curious amateur. La Mettrie was a practising medical doctor and, however much he may have considered that his

2 See in particular *Système de la Nature*, (2 vols., 'Londres', 1770), Bk, II ch. 12 and Diderot, *Essai sur la vie de Sénèque le philosophe, sur ses écrits et sur les règnes de Claude et de Néron* (2 vols., 'Londres', 1782), vol. 2, pp. 29–32. For further details, see my *Materialism and Society in the Mid-Eighteenth Century* (Geneva, 1981), pp. 181ff.

medical studies were insufficient, for him the study of medicine seems to have been extremely important, as he emphasises throughout his writings. His first published works were medical and included pamphlets on the conflict between doctors and surgeons, original works based on his own observations (as a practitioner in Brittany and as a military doctor) and translations of the great Leiden teacher Hermann Boerhaave, whose pupil he claimed to be after having spent a couple of years in Leiden. La Mettrie considered his philosophical works to be an extension of his medical concerns and he never failed to remind the reader that he was approaching philosophical subjects from a medical standpoint. Thus, when taking part in current philosophical debates his inspiration tends to be eclectic, and his arguments frequently rely on medical data. But before looking at these arguments, we first need to clarify the issues which were the subject of debate.

La Mettrie's starting-point is the question of the soul. His treatment of this subject lies at the intersection of several different debates and traditions; as a result, he does not always approach the issue from the same point of view, and his use of terms can lead to confusion. On the one hand, there was speculation on the animal soul in the wake of the controversy over Cartesian animal machines. The theory was espoused in its literal sense by philosophers such as Malebranche but others refuted it, fearing that it might simply be extended to humans – which La Mettrie of course claims to be doing, even implying that this had been Descartes' own intention and that, had Descartes been free to write what he believed, he would have extended his theory to humans. An alternative view posited, with the Gassendists, the existence of different types of soul, the animals possessing an inferior, material soul. This theory was adopted by two late seventeenth-century medical writers to whom La Mettrie was particularly indebted. The first was the Englishman Thomas Willis, who did important work on the anatomy of the brain. He published in 1672 *De anima brutorum* (translated in 1683 as *Two Discourses Concerning the Soul of Brutes*), in which, referring to the Lucretian tradition and to Gassendi, he develops the theory of a corporeal fiery soul extended throughout the bodies of animals and humans, while insisting on the existence of a second higher, rational soul in humans. Willis was followed by the Frenchman Guillaume Lamy, a follower of Gassendi who likewise situated himself in the Epicurean tradition. In *Anatomical Discourses* (1675) and *Explication mécanique et physique des fonctions de l'âme sensitive* (*Mechanical and Physical Explanation of the Functions of the Sensitive Soul*, 1678), Lamy explained the functioning of the human senses, passions and will by a material sensitive soul, while being careful to avoid talking about intellectual faculties and to claim that faith teaches us the existence of an immortal spiritual soul. La Mettrie's discussion of the question in *Natural History of the Soul* (later *Treatise on the Soul*) in 1745 adopts the same prudent approach and is in the tradition of these late seventeenth-century Epicureans who challenged the Cartesian theory of the soul. But La Mettrie finally throws off all prudence in *Machine Man* and, abandoning the theory of a separate sensitive or animal soul, challenges religious orthodoxy by openly denying any separate immortal soul in humans as in animals.

For La Mettrie is also a representative of the current of antireligious thought which, in the late seventeenth and early eighteenth centuries, called into doubt many doctrines of the Christian churches and in particular their teaching on the existence of an immortal, immaterial soul. Lamy's works, with their open Epicureanism and antifinalism, were also part of this current, although on the question of the soul he was careful to make concessions to religious orthodoxy, preferring to proceed by insinuation. There were many such coded references to the question in 'Libertin' writings,[3] linked to what is generally called the clandestine tradition. For there existed a large number of heterodox and antireligious works which circulated unofficially throughout the century, many of which originated in the late seventeenth or early years of the eighteenth century. These works, sometimes printed illegally in France, Holland or elsewhere (although many circulated in manuscript form alone), cast doubt on many aspects of Christian teaching. They often listed the opinions of a variety of religious and classical sources and used for their own purposes arguments taken from theologians or thinkers like Malebranche, but they also drew on elements forming a common fund of seventeenth-century or earlier Pyrrhonian, or sceptical, writing, or on the works of Locke, Hobbes, Toland or other English freethinkers. The result was often a patchwork of different passages joined together in a way that was not always coherent, similar to that found, to a lesser extent, in much of La Mettrie's *Treatise on the Soul*.[4] La Mettrie seems to have known these works well, as he refers to some of them and traces of others can be found in his writings, and there is no doubt that his own publications must also be situated in the context of this clandestine tradition, some of whose techniques he borrowed, at least as long as he was in France.

The question of the human soul was particularly discussed by these clandestine treatises; indeed, the titles of several of them refer to a material or mortal soul. Amongst them was Voltaire's letter on Locke from the *Philosophical Letters* (1734), which circulated separately as a 'Letter on the soul', which La Mettrie had read. Locke's hypothesis that God might 'superadd to matter a faculty of thinking' gave rise to great controversy in Britain concerning materialism and the nature of the soul,[5] which continued to rage at the time that La Mettrie was writing; but although he refers to the hypothesis, other works seem to have been more important for him. One of them was perhaps the most famous of the clandestine treatises, dating from

[3] This term refers to the seventeenth-century group of irreligious thinkers and their followers; see R. Pintard, *Le libertinage érudit dans la première moitié du 17ème siècle* (Paris, 1943). On the influence of their antireligious thought and their methods, in particular the use of coded references for insiders, see O. Bloch, 'L'héritage libertin dans le matérialisme des Lumières', *Dix-huitième Siècle*, 24 (1992), pp. 73–82.

[4] See Verbeek's critical edition of this work, and in particular his study of its sources.

[5] Locke, *An Essay Concerning Human Understanding*, Bk. IV, ch. 3, §6. On the controversy in England, see J. Yolton, *Thinking Matter* (Oxford, 1983).

the turn of the century, which circulated in various versions under the title either of *Traité des trois imposteurs* (*The Three Impostors*) or of *L'esprit de Spinosa* (*The Spirit of Spinoza*). This patchwork of ideas taken partly from Spinoza but also from the Libertin tradition, criticises final causes, posits the existence of a material God and questions the existence of an immortal soul. It adopts the theory of a fiery soul – a very subtle fluid or tenuous matter, part of the soul of the world – taken from the Paduan school, but in a passage copied from Lamy's sixth *Anatomical Discourse*. It was therefore a form of atheism and materialism that this work propagated under the aegis of Spinoza and that was called, in the early part of the eighteenth century, Spinozism. In several of his philosophical works, La Mettrie claims for himself the label 'Spinozist', equating it with both materialism and determinism, or the belief that the individual is not free but is determined by bodily states. 'Man' is therefore a 'machine' in the sense of being an automaton. This opinion is clearly spelled out in the exposition of Spinoza's philosophy provided by La Mettrie in the *Summary of the Systems* (§vii), annexed to his *Treatise on the Soul* in 1750, where he writes: 'The author of *Machine Man* seems to have written his book on purpose to defend this sad truth' (that the human being is an automaton).

La Mettrie's materialism was therefore, for him, equivalent to the Spinozism spread by the clandestine tradition. But, on the specific issue of the soul, the materialism of the clandestine treatises took different forms. On the one hand, it was possible, as in the *Three Impostors*, to posit with the Epicureans the existence of a material soul or subtle matter, which is then used to explain all the intellectual functions; but on the other, one could deny the existence of any sort of soul, material or otherwise, and affirm simply that thought and the other mental processes are the result of a particular organisation of matter in the brain.[6] Although La Mettrie seems at times tempted by the former theory in the *Treatise on the Soul* and also, in *Machine Man*, identifies the Hippocratic 'ενορμών or elemental force with the soul, it is the latter explanation that he finally adopts; indeed, he is careful to situate this elemental force in the brain.

It is clear from what has just been said that the nature of matter and its properties was therefore an issue of great importance, and it is this question that La Mettrie tackles unsuccessfully at the beginning of his *Treatise on the Soul* (using Aristotelian categories), and to which he returns in *Machine Man*. La Mettrie tries to show that matter possesses motive force and sensitivity, but the question for him, as for Diderot in his commentary on Helvétius in the 1770s, is whether they are inherent in its smallest particles or are the result of a particular organisation of matter. On this issue, La Mettrie prudently restricts himself to saying, in the *Treatise*, ch. VI, and *Machine Man*, that they are only observed in organised matter. But there was also the further question of how this sensitive matter could explain intellectual functions, for he is consistent in his claim that if observed matter can be seen to

[6] See A. Vartanian, 'Quelques réflexions sur le concept d'âme dans la littérature clandestine', *Le Matérialisme du XVIIIe siècle et la littérature clandestine*, ed. O. Bloch (Paris, 1982), pp. 149–65.

possess the capacity to move, one can deduce the capacity to feel and therefore to think. For him, the question of vital force and that of intelligence are inextricably linked, although he distinguishes life and movement from intelligence and is suspicious of the idea of a soul spread throughout the body, which runs the danger of 'spiritualising matter' rather than 'materialising the soul'. However, his approach to these questions evolves. La Mettrie's speculation concerning the soul and the functioning of the human organism had first been expressed in comments he added to his translation of Albrecht von Haller's annotated edition of Boerhaave's *Institutions*;[7] the *Natural History of the Soul* developed from these comments and draws on Boerhaave's writings, while adopting a different philosophical standpoint. In this work, as we have seen, he uses the theory of a sensitive soul but he discusses its seat in the brain in a manner that is very much indebted to his proclaimed master, Boerhaave, the leading representative of the iatromechanist school. This school, strongly influenced by Cartesian physiology, described the workings of the body in terms of mechanical principles and posited that the soul receives sensations by means of animal spirits moving through the nerves, which were hollow cylinders. The precise seat of the immaterial soul, where it received these sensations, was open to debate and various parts of the brain were proposed.

The iatromechanist theory posed great problems for the explanation of vital phenomena and was challenged by the animism of the German G. E. Stahl (in particular in *Theoria medica vera* (*True Medical Theory*), 1708), who defined the principle of movement in the body as the immaterial soul, which directed all of the body's actions. La Mettrie's denunciation of Stahl's theories runs as a leitmotiv throughout his works, medical as well as philosophical. Iatromechanists, to avoid such solutions, appealed to various explanations of motive force in matter, using dynamic theories inspired by Leibniz or making use of forms of subtle matter or of an innate vital principle. La Mettrie's speculations were also made against the background of new developments in physiological theory, for at precisely the time when he was writing, Haller was developing his theory of irritability, which posited the existence of a force inherent in muscle fibres. Although the theory was only developed fully from 1752, indications were given in Haller's comments on Boerhaave's *Institutions*. Such speculation about the source of vital functions was soon to lead to the development of vitalism (which was to influence Diderot's materialism).[8] La Mettrie, in *Machine Man*, gives examples to demonstrate the existence of life in the smallest parts of the body (or what he calls their 'natural oscillation'), from which he deduces that a certain organisation of matter in the brain produces thought. Finally, however, he freely admits his ignorance as to

7 La Mettrie translated Boerhaave's *Institutiones rei medicae*, as annotated by A. von Haller in his *Praelectiones academicae* (1739–44), and published them under the title of *Institutions de médecine de M. Hermann Boerhaave* (Paris, 1743–50).

8 On these developments in physiology, see F. Duchesneau, *La Physiologie des Lumières* (The Hague, 1982).

exactly how organised matter acquires the faculty of thought (although he is consistent in limiting intelligence to the brain), because the essential point for him is to deny the existence of an immaterial and immortal soul, which follows from the acceptance of a dynamic view of matter. He seems at times favourable to any theory which could explain intellectual phenomena in terms of matter alone. This is what constitutes his materialism or, as he also says, Spinozism.

An aspect of this materialism is the denial not only of human freedom but also of the existence of absolute moral values. Good and evil are created by religion for the needs of society and have no other validity. Although this conclusion is not drawn in *Machine Man*, La Mettrie expounded it immediately afterwards in his *Anti-Seneca* in a way which was no longer acceptable to those Philosophes who were trying to found a secular morality. Here again we see that, despite his concern to keep up to date on scientific and intellectual developments, La Mettrie's outlook and many of the important influences on him look back to the seventeenth century. In the early eighteenth-century literary dispute between the Ancients and the Moderns, he is in general on the side of the Ancients, and he is also largely in the Epicurean tradition, as he frequently affirms. This separates him from the Philosophes who were coming to the fore at the time of his death and who, as we have seen, rejected any association with him. More details of the contradictions engendered by his position at a moment of transition will emerge from a discussion of the individual works presented here. In order to see the progression of his thinking on the central issues, I shall begin with his first philosophical work.

Treatise on the Soul

The *Treatise on the Soul* (chs. I–X of which are included here), published in 1750, is an amended version of the *Natural History of the Soul*, first published in 1745. The 1745 text already seems to have been recast several times, drawing on different, sometimes incompatible, sources, which leads to a certain confusion and even contradictions. The work's unavowed aim is to show that all those faculties which are attributed to the workings of the soul can be explained by matter alone, and thus that there is no need to posit an immaterial soul; for this La Mettrie adopts the threefold Scholastic division of the soul into the vegetative, sensitive and reasonable souls, each responsible for different faculties. He is here following the lead of Willis and Lamy, who claimed not to be discussing the rational soul of man. The *Treatise* begins with a discussion of matter (chs. I–VII) in which La Mettrie attempts to show that it possesses the faculty to move and consequently to feel; this discussion calls on a variety of philosophical traditions, notably the Scholastic, and on Madame du Châtelet's exposition of the philosophy of Leibniz and Wolff in *Physical Institutions* (1740), and it is generally rather confused. La Mettrie finally admits ignorance as to the nature of matter and arrives at the conclusion that organised, observable matter possesses the faculty to feel. He then proceeds, in chapters VIII–IX, to a discussion

workings of the senses and the brain, La Mettrie does not wish to repeat them in *Machine Man*, but goes on to draw the conclusions of these explanations in a more radical way than he had done before. His physiological explanations in the *Treatise* are largely drawn from the medical writings of Boerhaave and also from Haller's commentaries on Boerhaave. Certain passages are even taken directly from this work, but La Mettrie is not particularly concerned with fidelity to the original and gives them a materialistic colouring, as he had already done in a more timid way in his translation of Boerhaave/Haller, for he clearly shows that the soul which receives sensations in the brain is material.[10] This materialistic aim was in contradiction with Boerhaave's dualism. Haller's angry reaction, accusing him of plagiarism, was no doubt partly prompted by his fear of being associated with La Mettrie's materialistic conclusions, and was probably what incited La Mettrie to dedicate *Machine Man* to him in a provocative manner.

Machine Man

In *Machine Man*, written in Holland, where La Mettrie had sought refuge after the scandal of his *Natural History of the Soul*, his attempt to explain all the workings of the human body in terms of matter alone is now clearly avowed. It relies to a large extent on examples of comparative anatomy, showing the similarities between humans and animals. The title, 'machine man', refers specifically to the Cartesian hypothesis that animals are mere machines without a soul, and La Mettrie claims that what he is doing is simply applying the Cartesian hypothesis to humans; he shows repeatedly that whatever applies to animals applies equally to humans. Athough he does not attempt, in his text, to demonstrate that humans are no more than animals in the Cartesian sense, his title and his invocation of Cartesian authority for what he was doing were enough to ensure the work's immediate notoriety. The arguments concerning animal soul had been examined in detail by Pierre Bayle in his *Dictionary*[11] article 'Rorarius', in which he pointed out clearly the dangers of the different theories and of their extension to humans; if the existence of a material soul in animals is accepted, there is no reason why the souls of humans should be any different, even though to deny souls to animals and to claim that they were mere machines, as did the Cartesians, was not a solution, as nothing would prevent the same thing being said of humans. It is clear that La Mettrie is adopting Bayle's reasoning and insisting on the comparison between humans and animals, given the similarity of their organisation. Indeed, he gives many examples of intelligence in animals, in the tradition of Montaigne. This line of argument was taken up again in his *Animals More than Machines* (1750). There

[10] For details, see Verbeek's critical edition of the *Traité*. On the translation of Haller, see also my, 'La Mettrie, lecteur et traducteur de Boerhaave', *Dix-huitième Siècle*, 23 (1991), pp. 23–9.

[11] *Dictionnaire historique et critique*, first published Rotterdam, 1696, went through numerous editions in the late seventeenth and early eighteenth centuries.

of the soul which concentrates mainly on the sensitive soul, common to humans and animals. He describes the mechanism of sensation (ch. X), relying on the theory of animal spirits which transmit sense impressions to the brain; this enables him to show that the (sensitive) soul is material, and is identified with the *sensorium commune*, or termination of the nerves (generally considered to be the seat of the soul), in turn identified with the brain as a whole. It is here that the extract in the present volume ends. Having shown that the sensitive principle is material, he then goes on (chs. XI–XII) to describe the different faculties of the sensitive soul, managing to include almost everything. These chapters contain discussion of contemporary literature and writers. He admits (ch. XIII) the existence of a rational soul responsible for intellectual faculties, whose existence is taught to us by faith (ch. XIV), but its role is reduced to such an extent as to be practically meaningless. The work finishes (ch. XV) with a series of stories proving that all our ideas come from the senses. Here, the obvious reference is Locke who was to have such an influence on Condillac, Helvétius and others. Indeed, in *Machine Man*, La Mettrie accuses himself of aping Locke in this work. However, it shows less his influence than that of the Aristotelians or Gassendi.[9] The *Treatise of the Soul* was accompanied by a *Summary of the Systems*, composed of developments of what were notes in the 1745 version; La Mettrie summarises the philosophies of Descartes, Malebranche, Leibniz, Wolff, Locke, Boerhaave and Spinoza, and gives a review of different opinions concerning the soul (like that found in many clandestine manuscripts), intended to insist on its materiality. The paragraph on Locke implies that he was only reviving the ancient axiom that there is nothing in the mind which was not formerly in the senses, and seems to be taken mainly from secondary sources, including Voltaire.

The work is not devoid of a polemical aim, in particular in its rejection of the Cartesian conception of the soul and of animal machines, and it also contains a number of satirical elements. But it mainly attempts to provide detailed explanations of how matter can explain all natural phenomena, including intellectual activity. La Mettrie gives details concerning the mechanism of the sensations and the workings of the brain which are absent from *Machine Man*. In the *Treatise on the Soul* the animal spirits play an important role in his discussion of the mechanism of sensations and of the sensorium. La Mettrie here follows Boerhaave's definition of animal spirits and of the nerves as hollow tubes containing little globules which transmit sensation to the brain by means of physical contact. This seems to be abandoned in *Machine Man* where there is no clear model of the workings of the animal spirits and where they seem to be used much more as a metaphor. For it is the conclusion of the *Treatise* that is important, namely that 'the soul depends essentially on the organs of the body, with which it is formed, grows and declines'. Perhaps realising the rather unsatisfactory nature of his explanations of the

[9] See Verbeek's critical edition, in particular vol. 2, pp. 86ff.

has been much discussion of the extent to which La Mettrie's remarks in *Machine Man* can be taken at their face value, and whether he was in fact extending Descartes' analysis to humans, thus abandoning the hostility shown in the *Treatise on the Soul.*[12] This is not the place to go into this complex issue, beyond pointing out that Cartesian 'animal-machines' constitute an important element in the intellectual backdrop to his thinking, whether he was reacting against the theory or claiming to adopt it.

His polemical beginning, rejecting all the existing philosophical systems which claim to explain human nature and the soul and attacking the theologians, is typical of irreligious works. Proclaiming that one should be guided by observation and experiment alone, La Mettrie gives a long series of medical examples proving the dependence of the 'soul' on bodily states. He then moves on to the teaching of comparative anatomy, an important field for Boerhaave's school, and in particular to the comparison of the brains of humans and animals, and of the behaviour that results. He claims that it would be possible to teach an ape to speak, in which case nothing would distinguish it from a human, for, like the Cartesians, he insists on the importance of language. His discussion of the imagination is intended to show that the brain is not simply a passive organ, as it had appeared in the *Treatise on the Soul*, but is also creative; its capacities depend on its organisation and the education it has received. Coming back to the subject of animals, he shows the superiority of their instinct, and that they have a moral sense, like humans; if we deny moral sense in animals, then we must deny it in humans as well. The question of a knowledge of natural law in humans and animals (a subject on which he adopts a different position in *Anti-Seneca*) leads to a long discussion of the existence of God. Here La Mettrie is mainly replying to the deistic arguments of Diderot in *Philosophical Thoughts* (1746), parts of which, in turn, were a reply to La Mettrie's *Natural History of the Soul*, which did not prevent Diderot's work being attributed to La Mettrie. Here La Mettrie does not openly reject the existence of God, but his criticism of Diderot's position and the doubts he raises show clearly enough his atheistic position.

He then returns to the dependence of mental on bodily states, with another series of experimental observations intended to show that each part of living matter possesses its own innate force. As we have already seen, the explanation of vital phenomena was an important problem for physiologists, but La Mettrie linked it to the explanation of intellectual functions and considered it to be a vital step in his demonstration that there is no need for a soul. He here makes use of the theory of

[12] A. Vartanian, in particular, in his important critical edition of *L'Homme machine*, which should be consulted for more detailed information on the issues and scientists referred to in this work, emphasises La Mettrie's Cartesianism; he sees in this text a rejection of a Lockean position adopted in the *Treatise on the Soul.* This opinion has been contested by myself and Verbeek. See also L. C. Rosenfield, *From Beast-Machine to Man-Machine: Animal Soul in French Letters from Descartes to La Mettrie* (New York, 1941), and H. Kirkinen, *Les Origines de la conception moderne de l'homme machine* (Helsinki, 1960)

irritability developed by Haller, for whom it meant the capacity of a fibre to shorten when subject to an external stimulus and who specifically applied it to muscle fibres. Haller distinguished it from sensitivity, by which he meant the capacity to transmit sensations to the brain. But La Mettrie applies it to all fibres and links it to theories of the existence of a motive force and sensitivity in all matter, and even with theories of a material soul throughout nature. This shows that his main aim is not to develop a scientific explanation of the workings of the human 'machine', but to use any evidence to deny the need for a soul.

From involuntary movements he moves on to an explanation of voluntary movements, by means of animal spirits directed by a material principle in the brain. Thus he is able to postulate the 'material unity of man', backed up by examples showing how the will depends on bodily states. He uses the comparison, common at the time, and which he seems to have taken directly from a clandestine text called *Le philosophe* (*The Philosopher*),[13] between the human body and a machine or watch, in which there is a mainspring driving the rest; however, he puts it to a different use, explaining that each small cog has its own moving principle, as matter is self-moved. This is his main affirmation, and is part of what he means by declaring that humans are machines. He admits his ignorance as to the detailed workings of this machine, and in particular as to how matter acquires the faculty of movement. After further examples concerning reproduction and the development of the foetus (a debate to which he was to return in *Man as Plant*), in which the similarity of humans and animals is again emphasised, La Mettrie ends with an uncompromising declaration of materialism – that only matter exists in the universe – and defiance of the theologians.

It is clear that the main aim of this work is to expound a materialistic philosophy, consisting in the claim that matter is both self-moved and sensitive, which for La Mettrie is enough to deduce that a particular organisation of it produces thought; matter is therefore sufficient to explain all existing phenomena. He is much more forthright than he had been in 1745, no longer attempts a detailed description of the workings of the brain or the functioning of the animal spirits and abandons the search for the *sensorium commune*. Instead, *Machine Man* proposes a certain number of metaphors and a declaration of principle and is, to a large extent, a polemical work directed mainly against those who defended the existence of an immaterial soul, whether theologians or physiologists like Stahl. The sympathy he shows for all those who seem to support, or who could be enlisted in favour of, his position leads to a lack of clarity in his use of certain concepts, but not in his main argument, which provoked a scandal even greater, no doubt, than the one he intended.

[13] Frequently attributed to the grammarian C. Chesneau Dumarsais, it was published in 1743 and later formed the basis of the *Encyclopédie* article 'Philosophe'. See H. Dieckmann, *Le Philosophe: Texts and Interpretation* (St Louis, 1948).

Man as Plant

The title of this work seems to have been chosen in order to exploit the impact made by *Machine Man*. It provides a description of the workings of the human body based on a comparison with the organisation of plants, in an attempt to show the uniformity of the animal and vegetable kingdoms. The first chapter describes human organisation in terms of the parts of plants, with particular reference to reproduction, and concludes with a Latin description of the human being in Linnaean terminology, which was omitted from the final version, in 1750. In the second chapter, La Mettrie moves on to the differences between animals and plants, in which much space is devoted to a demonstration that there is no need of a soul to explain the functioning of plants. He then introduces the subject of polyps, whose particular form of reproduction had been recently discovered by the Genevan naturalist, Abraham Trembley, and had created a great stir in scientific circles. They were considered to be transitional beings between the vegetable and animal kingdoms. La Mettrie had been particularly interested in Trembley's discoveries, referred to in *Machine Man*, as they presented problems for the existence of the soul. But they also seemed to show the continuity in nature, and the subject leads La Mettrie on to the question of the great chain of being, a widespread idea in the eighteenth century, which is developed in the final chapter.[14] La Mettrie's interest here in this topos is to insist on the uniformity of all living beings and to insist, as he had done in *Machine Man*, on the similarities between humans and animals and on the claim that human superiority is only the result of physical organisation. The end of *Man as Plant* is thus rather similar to *Machine Man* and specifically refers to the debate on animal souls.

This work enables La Mettrie to discuss some questions that he had not hitherto gone into. In addition to insisting on the conclusions of *Machine Man*, he draws on much recent work on botany, particularly Needham's microscopic observations, which had revived interest in plant reproduction.[15] La Mettrie joins the debate on animal reproduction, already mentioned towards the end of *Machine Man*, which centred on the role played by the eggs and the sperm and on whether both parents participated in the formation of the foetus; new theories of reproduction were throwing doubt on the preformationist theory, still defended by scientists such as Réaumur or, afterwards, Bonnet, who postulated that all animals had been created together and that future animals already existed completely in either the spermatozoid or the egg. Maupertuis' *Vénus physique* (*Physical Venus*, 1745) contained a comprehensive discussion of the different theories and most recent research on the question of reproduction; he developed a theory of reproduction based on attraction (to which La Mettrie also refers quite favourably in *Machine Man*), which explained

14 On this subject, see A. O. Lovejoy, *The Great Chain of Being* (Cambridge, Mass., 1936).

15 John Turberville Needham, *An Account of Some New Microscopical Discoveries* (London, 1745). It was translated into French in 1747.

the formation of the foetus by the coming together of different elements in the seminal fluids of both the mother and the father, and reduced the role of the spermatozoa. La Mettrie favours preformation, and he does not follow Maupertuis, but seems to adopt the view of those who believed that the sperm alone produced the individual and that the egg simply nourished it. This position was in fact stated with more force in *Machine Man*. He comes back to the question of reproduction, from a slightly different angle, in *The System of Epicurus*.

The System of Epicurus

The final version of *The System of Epicurus* is composed of ninety-four paragraphs of somewhat disorganised reflections, inspired by Lucretius's poem *De rerum natura*, on themes that La Mettrie had not always developed elsewhere. It is interesting to note that Diderot's *Letters on the Blind*, published in 1749, included developments taken from Lucretius which were very similar to some of those by La Mettrie. But two recently published works mentioned in the text can only have served as a stimulus to these reflections. The first three volumes of Buffon's *Natural History*, contained a discussion of the origin of animals and reproduction, and Benoît de Maillet's *Telliamed*, which had circulated in manuscript form before being published in 1748, developed the theory that all animal life had originally come from the sea. The original title of La Mettrie's work, 'reflections on the origin of animals' doubtless reflects this contemporary debate. This, together with the reference to Montesquieu's newly published *Spirit of the Laws*, also shows how he was reacting to recent developments in French intellectual circles.

After the author's initial protestations concerning our ignorance of nature, *The System of Epicurus* first of all develops the Lucretian theme that the existence of all things is due to the chance development of grains floating in the air (§V–XIX) and, like Lamy and others, he refuses any form of teleology (§XX–XXVII). His insistence on the dependence of human reason on bodily organisation and the comparison with the faculties of animals (§XVIII–XLVIII) repeat the themes already developed in *Machine Man*, while he also refers to what he has already written in the *Treatise on the Soul* and *Man a Plant*, mixed with reflections concerning our ignorance of nature. La Mettrie then moves on to reflections on death and the need to expect it stoically (§XLIXI–LXXIV), followed by a reaction against this philosophy, with an affirmation of the joys of living, and essentially sensual pleasures. These remarks possibly constitute a partial reply to Maupertuis' *Essai de philosophie morale* (*Essay on Moral Philosophy*, 1749), discussed below. The work terminates with praise for Frederick II, at whose court he had found refuge (§LXXVI–XCIV).

These Epicurean musings, which are often very personal and, ironically enough, refer to La Mettrie's own death, which was to follow soon afterwards, also concern the pleasures of life, in a similar vein to those found in his work entitled *L'Ecole de la volupte´* (*The School of Sensuality*).[16] The personal reflections are consciously modelled on those of Montaigne, to whom there are several references and whom La Mettrie seems to have consistently considered as one of his models. Those on the origin of animals are not particularly original, as they follow Lucretius, and his rejection of teleology, which is one of their main points of emphasis, put him clearly in the Epicurean tradition of the Libertins, whose importance for La Mettrie we have already seen. Some of the remarks found here are developed at much greater length in a work which La Mettrie considered to be extremely important, but which was not included in the volume of philosophical works published in 1750; this is *Anti-Seneca.*

Anti-Seneca

Also known as *On Happiness*, this work, rewritten several times after its first publication in 1748, shows that La Mettrie's interest had moved to the moral consequences that could be drawn from his materialism. He believed, on his arrival at Frederick's court in 1748, that he would have greater freedom to write as he wished without fearing religious censorship. This did not turn out to be completely true, but he was able to publish his moral philosophy, which for him was important as he considered it to follow directly from his materialism. It is precisely this moral teaching that so much shocked his contemporaries, to the extent that he was disowned by all the eighteenth-century materialists, and even those who in the nineteenth century attempted to rehabilitate him, like Lange, ignored this compromising work.[17]

It was originally an introduction to a translation made by La Mettrie of Seneca's *On the Happy Life*, in which he rejected Seneca's teaching and proclaimed once again his Epicureanism. He shows clearly the influence of seventeenth-century sceptics, in particular La Mothe le Vayer, whose *De la vertu des payens* (*The Virtue of the Pagans*), is mentioned several times and which even seems to have been a source for some of his information concerning the Stoics. The idea of writing such a translation was apparently suggested to La Mettrie by his friend and compatriot from Saint-Malo, P. L. Moreau de Maupertuis, President of the Berlin Science Academy, who was largely responsible for Frederick's invitation to La Mettrie to come to Potsdam. Maupertuis, possibly shocked by La Mettrie's work, published his own *Essay on Moral Philosophy*, obviously from a very different standpoint from that of La Mettrie. Maupertuis insisted on intellectual pleasures inspired by justice and truth, reminded his readers of the unpleasant side-effects of indulgence in sensual pleasures, affirmed human liberty and defended the philosophy of the

[16] Published in 1746 with no indication of publisher or place. Originally called *La Volupte´* (first edition unknown). In 1751 it was reworked as *L'Art de jouïr* ('Cythère', 1751).

[17] F. A. Lange, *History of Materialism and Criticism of its Present Importance* (London, 1879–81; original German ed., 1860).

Stoics. In turn, La Mettrie added in the 1750 edition of the *Anti-Seneca* several references to Maupertuis' work, although his praise for it was removed from the 1751 edition.

After the initial rejection of Seneca's philosophy, La Mettrie discusses the sources of happiness, which he divides into internal and external; it is mainly the internal source that he develops, or in other words the individual's own physical organisation which, as he had shown in *Machine Man*, determines the intellect. His examples of the way bodily states (including those induced by drugs or alcohol) influence mental and emotional ones are in line with his proclaimed materialism. As there is no afterlife or immortal soul, we should only live for the present, and the only virtues that can exist are those dictated by the needs of society. Good and evil do not exist absolutely, and our knowledge of them does not come from an innate awareness of natural law (as La Mettrie seemed to believe in *Machine Man*) but from education, as can be seen from the different moral values found in different countries. The remorse we feel for our actions is not natural, but simply the result of our education and childhood conditioning. Referring to examples already given in *Machine Man*, La Mettrie shows that people are not free when they commit crimes, but are pushed by physical states over which they have no control. As remorse is useless to society and merely makes people suffer needlessly, we should try to free people from it, instead of condemning them for following the dictates of nature. Education is the only way to correct defects and teach behaviour required by society, but its effect is limited and temporary as the organisation is stronger. The relative influence of education and the individual's physical organisation was later to become an issue between Diderot and Helvétius, and in the former's remarks on Helvétius's two works, *On the Mind* (1758) and the posthumously published *On Man*, Diderot particularly criticises the importance accorded by Helvétius to education and shares La Mettrie's opinion concerning the way humans are determined by their physical constitution and bodily states.

La Mettrie's change of opinion concerning natural law may be attributed to a clandestine work called *L'examen de la religion* (*Examination of Religion*), to which he refers.[18] This deistic work contains a chapter denying the existence of absolute moral values and attributing remorse to education. It had circulated for some time in manuscript form but there had recently been several editions of it, including one by Voss in Potsdam, and it was the object of articles in several journals, particularly in Germany. La Mettrie may therefore only just have come to know the work (unless he was attempting to give publicity to a work printed by his own publisher). It is also interesting that La Mettrie refers here to Hobbes, who had hitherto been absent from his works. His attention may have been drawn to the English

[18] It is found in many different manuscript forms and was published several times, from 1719 onwards; see A. Fairbairn and B. E. Schwarzbach, 'The *Examen de la religion*: A Bibliographical Note', *Studies on Voltaire and the Eighteenth Century*, 249 (1987), pp. 91–145 and my 'L'*Examen de la religion*', *Filosofie e religione nella letteratura clandestina*, ed. G. Canziani (Milan, 1994), pp. 35–72.

philosopher by Diderot's translation of Shaftesbury's *Inquiry Concerning Virtue, or Merit*, published in 1745, which had been attributed to La Mettrie himself, for it is unlikely that he was directly influenced by the works of Hobbes. La Mettrie's argument may also be partly directed against this work, in which not only is virtue seen to be natural and a source of happiness but, in addition, education is said to be more effective in instilling virtue than is the fear of punishment.[19]

The extract from the *Anti-Seneca* given in the present volume ends here. In the remaining part, La Mettrie discusses other sources of happiness, such as intellectual pleasures, wealth, indulgence in sensual pleasures, or even crime. It is here a passage occurs which has frequently been quoted as proof of his total cynicism: he admits that it is possible for those with certain physical organisations to find pleasure in the worst form of crime and debauchery (provided they can free themselves from remorse). They can be punished by society but not condemned absolutely and no form of moralising can prevent them acting in this way. Seen from a medical standpoint, the only reaction towards them is compassion, although society needs to punish them. In the different versions of this work, the endings vary, but the main thrust, that all our actions are dictated by our physical make-up, does not change.

It is easy to see why, despite La Mettrie's protestations of innocence, his amoral position should have shocked so many and why he could not include it in the volume of his philosophical works published in 1750. As it draws the extreme conclusions from a materialistic point of view, it is not surprising that later materialists should have attempted to distance themselves from the work and its author, despite the fact that in some unpublished writings, particularly in his letter to Landois of 1756, Diderot comes very near to the same position, denying human liberty and affirming that in that case 'there is no vice or virtue, nothing that must be rewarded or punished'.[20] The accusations that he was sapping the foundations of society by destroying morality led La Mettrie to see the need to write a defence of his philosophical opinions and broach the subject of the philosopher's relation to society which he had avoided, preferring to follow only what he considered to be the truth shown by observation of nature.

Preliminary Discourse

La Mettrie's defence of his philosophy was elaborated in the *Preliminary Discourse* placed at the head of his philosophical works published in 1750. All his books had attracted criticism and condemnation, both from various authorities and from writers in journals and elsewhere; La Mettrie reacted to this criticism, but he did

19 *Essai sur le mérite et la vertu* (Amsterdam, 1745), in Diderot, *Œuvres complètes*, Hermann (Paris, 1975–), vol. 1, pp. 350ff.

20 'Lettre à Monsieur Landois', *Correspondance*, ed. G. Roth, (6 vols., Paris, 1955–61), vol. 2, pp. 209–17.

not undertake a systematic defence of his writings until 1750, probably because he was then at the Prussian court and dependent on Frederick's protection. The main line of attack on his works concerned the danger they posed to society by undermining religious belief, but articles on the *Anti-Seneca* published in periodicals in France, Britain and Germany (including several by Haller) went further, accusing him of actively inciting to crime. His main aim in the *Preliminary Discourse* is thus both to reaffirm his materialism and to show that his philosophy is not dangerous, because the object of philosophy is totally separate from that of morality and religion; philosophy is concerned with the search for the truth, while the aim of morality and religion is to protect society. He distinguishes philosophers in their ivory towers, who do not attempt to influence people's behaviour and whose truths are reserved for an élite, from religious fanatics who are much more dangerous. This socially conformist argument, similar to that used by Voltaire, had already been evoked in his conclusion of the *Natural History of the Soul* in 1745. He also shows that, as citizens, philosophers abide by the needs of society whatever they may secretly think of established religion and morality. Following in the Libertin tradition, he presents philosophers as individuals with a superior organisation which sets them apart from the people and leads them to practise social virtues. Here he borrows from the clandestine work *The Philosopher*, but this does not mean that his conclusions are the same as those of its author, for whom philosophy is inseparable from the needs of society. La Mettrie also appeals to Bayle's arguments in the *Thoughts on the Comet* (1681), showing that a society of atheists is perfectly viable. These arguments had been recently revived by both Diderot, in his translation of Shaftesbury, and by Montesquieu's *Spirit of the Laws*.[21] La Mettrie's attempt to place himself within a current of thought which was coming to dominate intellectual life becomes even clearer in the second part of the *Preliminary Discourse* where, unconcerned about possible contradictions in his argument, he claims to show how philosophy can be useful to society, giving examples of many fields in which it has a contribution to make. He appeals to philosophers to publish the truth without fear, referring to the recent examples of Diderot, imprisoned in the Vincennes fort, and Toussaint, who fled to Holland after the condemnation of his *Moeurs* (*Morals*, 1748). He ends with another appeal to Frederick II to continue to protect persecuted thinkers. This latter part of the work makes it clear that La Mettrie was determined to show he was part of the movement centring around the *Encyclopédie*, however different his denial of an innate knowledge of virtue may have been from their opinions. In view of La Mettrie's unambiguous declarations at the beginning of the work, reaffirming the amoral conclusions of his *Anti-Seneca* and insisting that the subject of philosophy is totally distinct from society and is even antithetical to the needs of society, it is hardly surprising that the reaction of

[21] *Essai sur le mérite et la vertu*, pp. 343–4; *Spirit of the Laws*, Bk. XXIV, ch. 2.

the Philosophes was unanimously hostile. The volume was apparently banned by the King and withdrawn from sale.

La Mettrie was considered as a liability who could only do harm to the Philosophes' cause, as he had drawn extreme conclusions from positions shared with other people, which could make this philosophy appear as dangerous for society. And indeed, in the second half of the century, the opponents of the Philosophes consistently used quotations from La Mettrie's works against them. La Mettrie undermined the attempts of Diderot and d'Holbach to show that natural and social morality coincide. This led to the violent condemnations of La Mettrie's moral and social writings, despite (or because of) the fact that in some of his works not destined for publication Diderot reached positions in many ways similar to those of La Mettrie. Indeed, his awareness of the problems posed by such opinions can be seen in *Rameau's Nephew*. But the condemnations did not prevent La Mettrie's philosophical works being republished throughout the eighteenth century (the last edition being in 1796), with a peak in the 1770s, as interest in them was reawakened by the publication of *The System of Nature* in 1770. The modernity of many of his insights and the uncompromising nature of his materialism, which led him to draw unpalatable conclusions, have also meant that his works continue to be of interest. But he was also in many ways a man of the first half of the century with roots firmly in the previous century, particularly in his conception of the role of the philosopher in society. The contradictions apparent in the *Preliminary Discourse* are evidence of the fact that it was written at a moment of transition between the old conception of the role of the 'philosophe' and the new. It is possible that, in view of his eagerness to participate in the new intellectual movement, he might have altered his conservative social stance had he lived longer and been able to return to France, but that is merely speculation.

Chronology

1709 Birth of La Mettrie in Saint-Malo in Brittany
1725 Attends Harcourt College in Paris
1733 Receives the degree of Doctor of Medicine in Reims
1733–4 Attends lectures in Leiden
1735 First published work, a translation of Boerhaave on venereal disease
1734 Starts medical practice in Saint-Malo
1740–8 War of the Austrian Succession
1742 Goes to Paris; doctor to the Duke of Grammont and the French Guards; participates in military campaigns
1743 Publishes *Observations de médecine pratique* (*Observations on Practical Medicine*); begins publication of his translation of Boerhaave's *Institutions* with Haller's commentary
1744 Siege of Freiburg; La Mettrie nearly dies of a fever. Publication of Trembley's *Memoirs on a Type of Freshwater Polyp*
1745 Battle of Fontenoy; Duke of Grammont killed; La Mettrie put in charge of military hospitals in Flanders. Publishes *Natural History of the Soul*; it is immediately seized by the police. Publication of Maupertuis' *Physical Venus* and Diderot's translation of Shaftesbury's *Inquiry Concerning Virtue, or Merit*
1746 *Natural History of the Soul* condemned by the Paris Parlement to be burned, together with Diderot's *Philosophical Thoughts*. Forced to leave for Holland. Publishes *Politique du médecin de Machiavel* (*Machiavellian Policy of Doctors*), criticising the medical profession
1747 Publication of *Machine Man* in Leiden; the publisher Luzac condemned by the religious authorities. Diderot and d'Alembert become the editors of the *Encyclopédie*
1748 La Mettrie forced to flee; goes to Potsdam as 'lecteur' and physician at the court of Frederick II; becomes member of Berlin Academy of Sciences. Publishes first version of *Anti-Seneca, Man as Plant* and the first two

volumes of his medical satire *L'Ouvrage de Pénélope* (*Penelope's Work*). Publication of Montesquieu's *Spirit of the Laws*

1749 Publishes *Physical Reflexions on the Origin of Animals*. Publication of first three volumes of Buffon's *Natural History*, Maupertuis' *Essay on Moral Philosophy* and Diderot's *Letter on the Blind*

1750 Publishes *Philosophical Works* and third volume of *Penelope's Work*. Publication of the 'Prospectus' of the *Encyclopédie*

1751 Publishes *Medical Works*. Death of La Mettrie. Publication of first volume of the *Encyclopédie*

Further reading

La Mettrie's works are to be found in various eighteenth-century editions, of which the most reliable is the first edition: *Œuvres philosophiques* ('Londres, J. Nourse, 1751'; in fact published by Etienne de Bourdeaux in Berlin in 1750). This edition has been republished as the first volume of La Mettrie's *Œuvres philosophiques* in the series 'Corpus des Œuvres de philosophie de langue française' (Paris, Fayard, 1987); the second volume contains several other works, for some of which the attribution to La Mettrie is doubtful. His most important works have been published in critical editions, which should be consulted: A. Vartanian, *La Mettrie's l'Homme machine, a Study in the Origins of an Idea* (Princeton, Princeton University Press, 1960); J. Falvey, *Critical Edition of 'Discours sur le Bonheur'*, Studies on Voltaire and the Eighteenth Century', no. 134 (Banbury, Voltaire Foundation, 1975); A. Thomson, *Materialism and Society in the Mid-Eighteenth Century: La Mettrie's 'Discours préliminaire'* (Geneva, Droz, 1981); T. Verbeek, *Traité de l'Ame de La Mettrie* (2 vols., Utrecht, OMI/Grafisch Bedrijf, 1988). All of these editions contain studies of La Mettrie's life and thought and provide good starting-points for a deeper study of the philosopher.

A recent work is useful for the medical background: K. Wellman, *La Mettrie: Medicine, Philosophy, and Enlightenment* (Durham and London, Duke University Press, 1992), while the only biography is P. Lemée, *Julien Offray de La Mettrie* (Mortain, 'Le Mortainais', 1954), which contains a list of all his works. Several books can be consulted for the intellectual context in which La Mettrie's works were written: for the debate over animal soul and animal machines, see L. C. Rosenfield, *From Beast-Machine to Man-Machine: Animal Soul in French Letters from Descartes to La Mettrie* (New York, Oxford University Press, 1941) and H. Kirkinen, *Les Origines de la conception moderne de l'homme machine*, 'Annales Academiae Scientarum Fennicae', B, 122 (Helsinki, Suomalainen tiedeakatemia, 1960) while the scientific background is best understood from J. Roger, *Les Sciences de la vie dans la pensée française du XVIIIe siècle* (Paris, A. Colin, 1963). But see also A. Vartanian, 'Trembley's Polyp, La Mettrie and 18th-century French Materialism', *Journal of the History of Ideas*, 3, no. 3 (June 1950) and L. J. Rather, *Mind and Body in Eighteenth Century Medicine* (London, Wellcome Institute, 1965). Eighteenth-century physiology is studied in great detail in F. Duchesneau, *La Physiologie des Lumières* (The Hague, M. Nijhoff, 1982).

On clandestine irreligious writings, the classic work is I. O.Wade, *The Clandestine Organisation and Diffusion of Philosophic Ideas in France, 1715–1750* (Princeton, Princeton University Press, 1938), but for more recent work see, for example, J. S. Spink, *French Free-Thought from Gassendi to Voltaire* (London, Athlone Press, 1960), and *Le Matérialisme du XVIIIe siècle et la littérature clandestine*, ed. O. Bloch (Paris, Vrin, 1982). On materialism in general, see O. Bloch, *Le matérialisme* (Paris, P.U.F., 1985) and the number of *Dix-huitième Siècle* devoted to 'Le Matérialisme des Lumières' (no. 24, 1992). For particular influences, see P. Rétat, *Le Dictionnaire de Bayle et la lutte philosophique au XVIIIe siècle* (Paris, Les Belles Lettres, 1981); J. Yolton, *Locke and French Materialism* (Oxford, Clarendon Press, 1991); *Spinoza au XVIIIe siècle*, ed. O. Bloch, (Paris, Klincksieck, 1990) (all of which include studies of La Mettrie). See also J. A. Perkins, 'Diderot and La Mettrie', *Studies on Voltaire and the Eighteenth Century*, 10 (1959), 49–100, and A. Vartanian, 'La Mettrie and Diderot revisited: an intertextual encounter', *Diderot Studies*, 21 (1983), 55–97. La Mettrie's relationship with Maupertuis is discussed in D. Beeson, *Maupertuis: An Intellectual Biography*, 'Studies on Voltaire and the Eighteenth Century', 229 (Oxford, Voltaire Foundation, 1992) .

The journal *Corpus* (Paris) has published a special issue on La Mettrie (no. 5/6, 1987). Apart from articles included in the above volumes, other recent studies are: D. Leduc-Fayette, 'La Mettrie et Descartes', *Europe* (October 1978) 37–48, and 'La Mettrie et le "labyrinth de l'homme" ', *Revue philosophique de la France et de l'Etranger*, no. 105 (1980), 343–64; L. Honoré, 'The Philosophical Satire of La Mettrie', *Studies on Voltaire and the Eighteenth Century*, 215 (1982), 175–222, and 216 (1983), 203–28; A. Thomson, 'L'unité matérielle de l'homme chez La Mettrie et Diderot', *Colloque international Diderot*, ed. A. M. Chouillet (Paris, Aux Amateurs de Livres, 1985), 61–8, 'L'Homme-machine, mythe ou métaphore?', *Dix-huitième Siècle*, 20 (1988), 367–76, 'La Mettrie, Lecteur et traducteur de Boerhaave', *Dix-huitième Siècle*, 23 (1991), 23–9; and A. Vartanian, 'Le Frère de Maupertuis et l'homme machine', *Dix-huitième Siècle*, 14 (1982), 305–23.

Machine Man

Note on the text

L'Homme machine was first published anonymously by Elie Luzac in Leiden, towards the end of 1747, but dated 1748. Luzac added his own preface justifying the publication of the book. Two other editions, also dated 1748, are listed by Vartanian, and La Mettrie made a final revision of the work for his *Philosophical Works* in 1750. This last state of the text, used by Vartanian for his critical edition of *L'Homme machine*, 1960, is the one used for this translation. All editions contain La Mettrie's provocative dedication to Haller, which has been omitted here. The first three editions of the work also contained on the title page five lines of verse from Voltaire's 'Epître à Monsieur de Genonville', which were omitted in 1750. Editions of *L'Homme machine* were published by J. Assézat in Paris in 1865, and by M. Solovine in 1921, and there have been several cheap modern French editions of the work, the most recent of them with an introduction and notes by P. L. Assoun, Paris, 1981. An English translation, attributing the authorship to the Marquis d'Argens, was published as *Man a Machine* in London by W. Owen in 1749, and reprinted in 1750 giving the author as La Mettrie; another English translation with the same title, by G. C. Bussey, was published in Chicago by The Open Court in 1912 and reprinted in 1927 and 1943.

In this and the following texts, La Mettrie's footnotes are indicated by letters and the editor's by arabic numerals.

For a wise man, it is not enough to study nature and the truth; he must dare to proclaim it for the benefit of the small number of those who are willing and able to think; for the others, who are the willing slaves of prejudice, are no more capable of reaching the truth than are frogs of flying.

The philosophers' systems concerning the human soul can, in my opinion, be reduced to two: the first, and the oldest, is the system of materialism, and the second is that of spiritualism.

Those metaphysicians who have implied that matter might well possess the faculty of thinking did not dishonour their reason. Why? Because they had the advantage (for in this case it is one) of expressing themselves badly. To ask whether matter, considered only in itself, can think is like asking whether matter can indicate the time. We can already see that we shall avoid the rock on which Mr Locke unfortunately foundered.[1]

The Leibnizians with their *monads* have constructed an incomprehensible hypothesis. They have spiritualised matter rather than materialising the soul. How can we define a being whose nature is absolutely unknown to us?

Descartes and all the Cartesians, among whom the followers of Malebranche have long been included,[2] made the same mistake. They admitted two distinct substances in man as if they had seen and counted them.

The wisest have said that the soul could not be known otherwise than by the light of faith; yet as rational beings they believed they could retain the right to examine what the Scriptures meant by the word *spirit*, which is used when speaking of the human soul. And if in their research they disagree with the theologians on this point, are the theologians any more in agreement with each other on all the other points?

Here, in a few words, is the result of all their reflections.

If there is a God, he is the creator of nature as much as of revelation; he gave us the one to explain the other, and reason to reconcile them.

To mistrust the knowledge we can gain from studying living bodies is to see nature and revelation as two mutually destructive opposites, and consequently to dare to affirm an absurdity, namely that God contradicts himself in his different works and deceives us.

If there is a revelation, it cannot belie nature. It is through nature alone that we can discover the meaning of the words of the Gospel, which can only be truly interpreted by experience. Previous commentators have only confused the truth, as we can judge from the author of the *Spectacle of Nature*. 'It is surprising', he says (referring to Mr Locke) 'that a man who debases our soul so far as to consider it to

1 A reference to Locke's hypothesis concerning thinking matter in *An Essay Concerning Human Understanding*, Bk. IV, ch. 3, §6, discussed by Voltaire in the thirteenth *Lettre philosophique* (London, 1734).

2 The followers of Malebranche included Bernard Lamy, Henri Lelevel, Y. M. André, A. Baxter, J. Norris and S. Gerdil, none of whom is named by La Mettrie.

be made of clay, dares to set up reason as the judge and sovereign arbiter of the mysteries of faith; for', he adds 'what an astonishing idea of Christianity would we have if we attempted to follow reason?'[3]

Apart from the fact that these reflections throw no light on the question of faith, they constitute such frivolous objections to the method of those who believe they can interpret the holy books that I am almost ashamed to waste time refuting them.

1. The excellence of reason does not depend on a grand meaningless word (immateriality) but on its force, its extent or its acuteness. Thus a 'soul of clay' which discovers as if at a glance the relationships and consequences of an infinite number of ideas which are difficult to grasp would obviously be preferable to a silly, stupid soul made of the most precious elements. A true philosopher does not blush, like Pliny, at our miserable origin.[4] What seems to be base is here the most precious object, on which nature seems to have expended the most art and effort. But since man, even if he came from an apparently even baser source, would nevertheless be the most perfect of all beings, whatever the origin of his soul, if it is pure, noble and sublime, it is a splendid soul which makes whosoever is endowed with it admirable.

Mr Pluche's second mode of reasoning seems to me to be flawed, even in his system which smacks a little of fanaticism; for if we have a conception of faith which is contrary to the clearest principles and the most incontrovertible truths, we should believe, for the honour of revelation and its author, that this conception is false and that we do not yet know the meaning of the Scriptures.

Either everything – both nature itself and revelation – is illusion, or experience alone can justify faith. But could anything be more ridiculous than our author? I can imagine hearing a Peripatetician say 'We must not believe Toricelli's experiment for if we did, if we abandoned nature's abhorrence of a vacuum, what an amazing philosophy we would have!'[5]

I have shown how flawed Mr Pluche's reasoning is[a] in order to show, first, that if there is a revelation it is insufficiently proven by the authority of the Church alone, without being examined by reason, as is claimed by all those who fear reason; and second in order to shield from attack the method of those who wish to follow the path I am showing them and to interpret what is supernatural and incomprehensible in itself by the light each of us has received from nature.

Thus, experience and observation alone should guide us here. They are found in abundance in the annals of physicians who were philosophers, not in those of philosophers who were not physicians. Physicians have explored and thrown light on the labyrinth of man; they alone have revealed the springs hidden under

[a] His mistake is obviously that he begs the question.

[3] Abbé N. Pluche, *Spectacle de la Nature* (8 vols., Paris, 1732–50), vol. 5, pp. 176–7.

[4] See the quotation from Pliny at the beginning of *The System of Epicurus* and note.

[5] E. Toricelli's experiment of 1643 showed that mercury rose in a tube according to measurable parameters, thus discrediting the explanation that nature abhors a vacuum.

coverings which keep so many marvels from our gaze. They alone, calmly contemplating our soul, have caught it a thousand times unawares, in its misery and its grandeur, without either despising it in one state or admiring it in the other. Once again, these are the only natural philosophers who have the right to speak on this subject. What could the others, in particular the theologians, tell us? Is it not ridiculous to hear them shamelessly pronouncing on a subject they are incapable of understanding, from which, on the contrary, they have been deflected by obscure studies that have led them into a thousand prejudices and, in a word, fanaticism, which adds to their ignorance of the mechanism of our bodies?

But although we have chosen the best guides, we shall still find many thorns and obstacles in our path.

Man is a machine constructed in such a way that it is impossible first of all to have a clear idea of it and consequently to define it. That is why all the greatest philosophers' *a priori* research, in which they tried, as it were, to use the wings of the mind, have failed. Hence it is only *a posteriori*, or by trying as it were to disentangle the soul from the body's organs, that we can, not necessarily discover with certainty the true nature of man, but reach the greatest possible degree of probability on the subject.

Therefore let us take up the staff of experience and ignore the history of all the futile opinions of philosophers. To be blind and to believe that one can do without this staff is the height of blindness. How right a modern author is to say that it is nothing but vanity which prevents one from using secondary causes to the same effect as primary ones![6] We can, and even should, admire all of those great geniuses – Descartes, Malebranche, Leibniz, Wolff, etc. – in their most futile labours; but pray, what fruits have we derived from their profound meditations and all their works? So let us begin, by seeing not what people have thought, but what we should think for the sake of an untroubled life.

To each different temperament there corresponds a different mind, character and habits. Even Galen knew this truth, which Descartes developed, going as far as to say that medicine alone could change minds and habits by changing the body.[7] It is true that if we take melancholy, bile, phlegm, blood and so on, the different nature, quantity and combination of these humours make each man into a different man.

In sickness, sometimes the soul disappears and gives no sign of life and sometimes it is so transported by fury that it appears to be doubled; sometimes imbecility is dissipated and convalescence turns an idiot into a clever man. Sometimes the finest genius becomes stupid and no longer knows himself; farewell all that splendid knowledge acquired at such cost and with so much effort!

Here we see a paralytic asking if his leg is in his bed; there a soldier who thinks he still has his arm, which has been cut off. The memory of former sensations and

6 This was La Mettrie himself in *Natural History of the Soul* (1745).

7 Descartes expounded this idea in the *Discourse on Method*, Bk. VI.

of the place to which his soul attached them creates the illusion and his type of delirium. It is enough to speak to him of the missing part, for him to remember it and feel all its movements, with a sort of displeasure in his imagination which it is impossible to describe.

One man cries like a baby at the approach of death, while another jokes. What would have changed the bravery of Canus Julius, Seneca or Petronius into fear or cowardice? An obstruction in the pancreas or the liver, or a blockage in the portal vein. Why? Because the imagination is blocked together with the organs, and this is what gives rise to all the remarkable phenomena of hysteria and hypochondria.

What more can I say on the subject of those who imagine they have been changed into werewolves, cocks or vampires, or who believe that they are being sucked by the dead? Why waste time on those who believe that their nose or other members are made of glass and who have to be advised to sleep on straw for fear of breaking, so that they recover their use and their true flesh when the straw is set alight in order to make them afraid of being burnt. This fear has sometimes cured paralysis. I ought to pass rapidly over facts which everyone knows.

Nor shall I spend more time on details concerning the effects of sleep. See that tired soldier, snoring in the trench to the sound of a hundred cannons! His soul hears nothing, his sleep is a perfect apoplexy. A bomb is about to crush him and he will perhaps feel the blow less than an insect under one's foot.

On the other hand, that man devoured by jealousy, hatred, greed or ambition can find no rest. The quietest place, the most refreshing and soothing drinks are all useless for those who have not freed their souls from the torment of the passions.

The soul and the body fall asleep together. As the blood's movement is calmed, a sweet feeling of peace and calm spreads throughout the machine. The soul feels itself lazily becoming heavy together with the eyelids, and relaxing together with the brain fibres. It thus slowly becomes as if paralysed, together with all the body's muscles. They can no longer hold up the weight of their head, while the soul can no longer bear the burden of thought. When it is asleep, it is as if it did not exist.

If the circulation is too rapid, the soul cannot sleep; if the soul is too agitated, the blood cannot calm down; it gallops through the veins with an audible sound. These are the two reciprocal causes of insomnia. A single fright in our dreams makes the heart beat twice as fiercely, and tears us from the need or the sweetness of sleep as would a sharp pain or a pressing need. Finally, as only the cessation of the soul's functions brings sleep, there exists, even during waking (which is then only a half-waking), a sort of very frequent little sleep of the soul, or day-dreams, which prove that the soul does not always wait for the body in order to go to sleep. For if it is not completely asleep, how close it is! Since it is unable to pick out a single object which it has noticed at all, among the great mass of confused ideas which, like so many clouds, fill as it were the atmosphere of our brains.

Opium is so closely related to the sleep it brings that we cannot ignore it here. This remedy inebriates, as do wine or coffee, etc., each in its own way, according to the dose. It makes man happy in a state that would seem to be the tomb of feeling, as it is the image of death. What sweet lethargy! The soul would like never to leave it. It was prey to the greatest pain and now it only feels the pleasure of no longer suffering and of enjoying the most charming tranquillity. Opium even changes the will; it forces the soul, which wanted to stay awake and enjoy itself, to go to bed despite itself. I shall not discuss the history of poisons.

It is by lashing the imagination that coffee, the antidote to wine, dissipates our headaches and our sorrows without, like wine, saving them up for the morrow.

Let us observe the soul in its other needs.

The human body is a machine which winds itself up, a living picture of perpetual motion. Food maintains what is aroused by fever. Without it, the soul languishes, becomes furious and dies dejected. It is like a candle whose light flares up just as it is going out. But if you feed the body, pour into its pipes vigorous sugars and strong liquors, then the soul becomes as generous as they are and arms itself with proud courage, and the soldier who would have fled if given water becomes ferocious and gaily runs to his death to the sound of drums. In the same way hot water agitates the blood while cold water calms it.

How powerful a meal is! Joy revives in a sad heart; it enters the souls of the diners who give vent to it in the charming songs for which the French are known. Only the melancholy man is cast down, and the studious man is no longer fit to study.

Raw meat makes animals ferocious, and men would become equally so with the same food. This ferocity gives rise in the soul to pride, hatred, contempt for other nations, insubordination and other feelings which deprave the character, in the same way as coarse food makes for a heavy, dense mind whose favourite attributes are laziness and indolence.

Mr Pope well knew the power of greed, when he said:

Catius is ever moral, ever grave,
Thinks who endures a knave, is next a knave,
Save just at dinner – then prefers, no doubt,
A rogue with ven'son to a saint without.

He says elsewhere:

See the same man, in vigour, in the gout;
Alone, in company; in place, or out;
Early at business, and at hazard late;
Mad at a fox-chase, wise at a debate;
Drunk at a borough, civil at a ball;
Friendly at Hackney, faithless at Whitehall.[8]

In Switzerland we knew a bailiff called Mr Steiguer from Wittighofen; when

[8] A. Pope, *Moral Essays*, Epistle I, ll. 177–80, 71–6.

fasting he was the most upright and even indulgent of judges, but woe to the poor wretches who found themselves in the dock when he had feasted! He was capable of hanging the innocent as well as the guilty.

We think, and we are even honest citizens, only in the same way as we are lively or brave; it all depends on the way our machine is constructed. One could say at times that the soul is to be found in our stomach and that when Van Helmont placed its seat in the pylorus, his only mistake was to take the part for the whole.[9]

To what excesses cruel hunger can push us! There is no more respect for the bowels to which we owe or have given life; we tear them voraciously apart, we feast on them horribly and, in the fury which carries us away, the weakest always falls prey to the strongest.

Pregnancy, that rival desired by those with chlorosis, is not content with bringing most frequently in its wake the depraved tastes which accompany these two states; it sometimes makes the soul execute the most atrocious plots, the effects of a sudden mania which smothers even the law of nature. Thus the brain, the mind's womb, is perverted, in its way, together with that of the body.

What other kind of fury is to be found in the man or woman tormented by continence and good health! This shy, retiring young girl has not only lost all shame and modesty; she now considers incest merely as a flighty woman considers adultery. If her needs are not promptly assuaged, they will not be confined to the mere accidents of uterine passion, mania, etc., and the unfortunate woman will die of an affliction for which there are so many doctors.

We need only to have eyes to see the necessary influence of age on reason. The soul follows the body's progression, as it does that of education. In the fair sex, the soul also follows the delicacy of the temperament; hence the tenderness, affection and lively feelings based on passion rather than on reason, the prejudices and superstition whose deep imprint can scarcely be erased, etc. In men, on the contrary, whose brains and nerves have the firmness of all solids, the mind, like the features, is more lively. Education, which women lack, further reinforces their souls. With such help from nature and art, how could they not be more grateful, generous, constant in friendship, firm in adversity, etc.? But, following more or less the idea of the author of the *Letters on Physiognomy*,[10] those who combine grace of mind and body with almost all the tenderest and most delicate feelings of the heart should not envy the twofold strength which seems to have been given to man; for the one exists only in order to be all the more affected by the attractions of beauty, and the other only to minister all the better to their pleasures.

You do not need to be as great a physiognomist as this author to guess the quality of a mind from the face or the features when they are particularly marked,

9 J. B.Van Helmont situated the Archeus or soul (part of the soul of the world) in the upper opening of the stomach, not in the pylorus; see his *Ortus medicinae* (Amsterdam, 1648).

10 See Abbé J. Pernetti, *Lettres philosophiques sur les physionomies* (The Hague, 1746), which interpreted character through facial traits and was considered to lend weight to materialistic arguments.

any more than you need to be a great physician to recognise an illness accompanied by its obvious symptoms. Examine the portraits of Locke, Steele, Boerhaave, Maupertuis, etc.: you will not be at all surprised to see that they have strong features and eagle eyes. Look at numerous others, and you will always be able to distinguish the superficial from the great genius and even often the honest man from the rogue.

History provides a memorable example of the power of the air. The famous Duke of Guise was so convinced that Henry III, who had had him in his power so many times, would never dare to assassinate him, that he left for Blois. When Chancellor Chiverny heard that he had gone, he cried: 'he is a doomed man'. When events justified his fatal prediction, he was asked the reason for it. 'I have known the King for twenty years', he said. 'He is naturally good and even weak, but I have noticed that when it is cold, a trifle makes him impatient and furious.'

Some people's minds are heavy and stupid, while others' are lively, light and penetrating. What is the cause of this, other than, in part, the food they eat, their fathers' seed[b] and the chaos of different elements swimming in the immensity of the air? The mind, like the body, has its epidemics and its scurvy.

Such is the power of the climate that a man who changes climates feels the effects despite himself. He is like a wandering plant which has transplanted itself; if the climate is not the same, it is normal that the plant should decline or improve.

In addition, we take everything – gestures, accents, etc. – from those we live with, in the same way as the eyelid blinks under the threat of a blow that is foreseen, or as the body of a spectator imitates mechanically, and despite himself, all the movements of a good mime.

What I have just said proves that the best company for a thinking man is his own, if he cannot find any like himself. The mind gets out of practice in the company of those who have none, through lack of exercise; in tennis, we return the ball badly when it is badly served. I prefer an intelligent man with no education to one who has had a bad education, providing he is still young enough. A badly trained mind is like an actor who has been spoilt by provincial theatres.

The different states of the soul are thus always related to those of the body. But in order to demonstrate better the extent of this dependence and its causes, let us use comparative anatomy here; let us open up the entrails of men and animals. How can we know human nature if we have not been enlightened by an accurate comparison of the structures of men and animals!

In general, the form and composition of the quadruped's brain is more or less the same as man's. Everywhere we find the same shape and the same arrangement, with one essential difference: man, of all the animals, is the one with the largest and the most convoluted brain, in relation to the volume of his body. Next come the ape, beaver, elephant, dog, fox, cat, etc.; these are the animals that are most like

[b] The history of animals and men proves the influence of the father's seed on the minds and bodies of their children.

man, for we can also see in them the same graduated analogy concerning the corpus callosum, in which Lancisi placed the seat of the soul before the late M. de la Peyronie, who however illustrated this opinion with a mass of experiments.[11]

After all the quadrupeds, those who have the most brain are the birds. Fish have big heads, but they are empty of sense, like those of many men. They have no corpus callosum and very little brain, which is totally lacking in insects.

I shall not indulge in greater detail concerning nature's variety, nor in speculation since both are infinite, as can be judged from a simple reading of Willis's treatises, *The Anatomy of the Brain and Nerves* and *Two Discourses Concerning the Soul of Brutes*.[12]

I shall simply draw the following obvious conclusions from these incontrovertible observations: (1) the more ferocious animals are, the less brain they have; (2) this organ seems to grow, as it were, in relation to their docility; (3) here we see a singular condition eternally imposed by nature, that what is gained on the side of intelligence is lost on the side of instinct. Which is greater, the gain or the loss?

But do not think that I am thereby claiming that the volume of the brain alone is enough to indicate an animal's degree of docility; quantity must also correspond to quality, and the solids and fluids must be in the right balance to ensure health.

If, as is generally observed, the idiot does not lack a brain, this organ tends to suffer from a bad consistency; for example, it is too soft. It is the same for lunatics; the defects of their brains are not always hidden from our investigations. But if the causes of idiocy, madness, etc. are not obvious, how can we hope to find the causes of the differences between minds? They would escape the gaze of a Lynx or an Argus. 'A trifle, a tiny fibre, something that the most subtle anatomical study cannot discover' would have made fools of both Erasmus and Fontenelle, who observes as much himself in one of his best *Dialogues*.[13]

Apart from the softness of the brain marrow in children, puppies and birds, Willis remarks that the corpora striata are obliterated and discoloured in all these animals, and that the streaks are as imperfectly formed as in paralytics. He adds, which is true, that man has a very large pons varolii and then, decreasing progressively, come the ape and the other animals mentioned above, while the calf, ox, wolf, sheep, pig, etc. – in which this part's volume is very small – have very big nates and testes.[14]

However discreet and reserved we may be about the conclusions we can draw from such observations and many others, concerning the sort of inconstancy of

[11] See G. Lancisi, *Dissertatio altera de sede cogitantis animae*, in G. Fantoni, *Observationem anatomicomedicarum* (Venice, 1743), and F. G. de La Peyronie's paper read to the Académie des Sciences in 1741: 'Observations par lesquelles on tâche de découvrir la partie du cerveau où l'âme exerce ses fonctions.'

[12] T. Willis, *Cerebri anatome: cui accessit nervorum descriptio et usus* (London, 1664) and *De anima brutorum* (London, 1672); see Introduction, pp. x.

[13] B. Le Bovier de Fontenelle, *Nouveaux dialogues des morts* (Paris, 1683), 'Charles V et Erasme'. See *Œuvres diverses* (8 vols., Paris, 1715), vol. 1, p. 202.

[14] These are the optic lobes in the brain.

vessels and nerves, etc., nevertheless such variety cannot be the result of nature's meaningless games. They prove at least the need for a good and ample organisation, since in the whole animal world the soul becomes firmer together with the body and acquires wisdom as it gains strength.

Let us stop for a moment to consider different animals' capacity to learn. The best conceived analogy no doubt leads the mind to believe that the causes we have mentioned produce all the differences between them and us, although we must admit that our feeble understanding, limited to the crudest observations, cannot see the ties linking the cause and its effects. It is a sort of *harmony* that philosophers will never understand.

Among the animals, some learn to talk and sing; they can remember tunes and copy all the notes as precisely as musicians can. Others, while displaying more intelligence, like the monkey, cannot manage it. Why so, unless it is due to a defect in the speech organs?

But is this defect so inbuilt that it cannot be remedied? In a word, would it be absolutely impossible to teach this animal a language? I do not think so.

I would take the great ape in preference to any other, until chance leads us to discover another species more similar to ours, for there is no reason to believe that one cannot exist in as yet unknown regions. This animal bears such a strong resemblance to us that naturalists have called it the 'wild man' or the 'man of the woods'.[15] I would take one following the criteria of Amman's schoolchildren,[16] that is to say I should like it to be neither too young nor too old; for those brought to Europe are usually too old. I would choose the one with the cleverest physiognomy, who best confirmed this promise in a thousand little tests. Finally, as I do not consider myself worthy of being its tutor, I would send it to the school of the excellent teacher whom I have just mentioned, or of another equally skilful one, should he exist.

You know, from Amman's book and from all those who have translated his method,[c] all the miracles he has wrought on children born deaf, whose eyes he has, as he himself explains, turned into ears, and how quickly he has taught them to hear, talk, read and write. I agree that a deaf person's eyes see better and are more intelligent than those of one who is not, because the loss of one member or sense can increase the force or the penetration of another. But the ape can see and hear, he understands what he hears and sees; he apprehends so perfectly the signs made to him, that at any other game or exercise I have no doubt that he would surpass Amman's pupils. Why then should the education of apes be impossible? Why could he not, if given sufficient care and attention, imitate, like the deaf, the sounds

[c] The author of the *Natural History of the Soul*, etc.

[15] La Mettrie means the orang-utan, concerning which there was much speculation in the eighteenth century, in particular E. Tyson, *Orang-outang, sive homo sylvestris* (London, 1699).

[16] J. C. Amman developed a method of teaching deaf-mutes, which La Mettrie discusses in the *Treatise on the Soul*, ch. XV, story no. 4.

needed for pronunciation? I do not presume to decide whether the ape's speech organs will never be able to articulate anything whatever we do, but such an absolute impossibility would surprise me, in view of the close analogy between ape and man, and the fact that there is no animal so far known whose interior and exterior bears such a striking resemblance to man. Mr Locke, who was certainly never suspected of being credulous, had no difficulty in believing a story told by Sir William Temple in his *Memoirs* about a parrot who replied pertinently and had learnt, like us, to conduct a sort of coherent conversation.[17] I know that some have made fun of this great metaphysician,[d] but if someone had announced to the world that generation could happen without eggs and without women, would he have found many supporters? Yet Mr Trembley has discovered generation without mating, by simple segmentation. Surely Amman would also have been considered mad if he had boasted, before experimenting successfully, that he could teach pupils like his, and in such a short time? Yet his success has astounded the universe and, like the author of the History of Polyps,[19] he has achieved instant immortality. A man who owes the miracles he performs to his own genius is, to my mind, superior to one who owes his to chance. He who has discovered the art of embellishing the finest of the kingdoms, and of providing perfections it did not have, should be placed above a lazy inventor of futile systems or a laborious author of sterile discoveries. Those of Amman are of much greater worth; he has saved men from the mere instinct to which they seemed condemned; he has given them ideas, a mind and, in a word, a soul which they would never have had. How much greater this power is!

Let us not limit nature's resources; they are infinite, particularly when assisted by great skill.

Surely the same mechanism which opens the Eustachian tube in the deaf could unblock it in monkeys? Surely a beneficial desire to imitate their master's pronunciation could free the organs of speech in animals, which can imitate so many other signs with such skill and intelligence? I defy anyone to quote a single truly conclusive experiment which proves that my plan is impossible and ridiculous; what is more, the similarity of the ape's structure and functions is such that I hardly doubt at all that if this animal were perfectly trained, we would succeed in teaching him to utter sounds and consequently to learn a language. Then he would no longer be a wild man, nor an imperfect man, but a perfect man, a little man of the town, with as much substance or muscle for thinking and taking advantage of his education as we have.

[d] The author of the *History of the Soul.*[18]

[17] Locke, *Essay Concerning Human Understanding*, Bk. II, ch. 27, §8, quotes Temple, *Memoirs of What Passed in Christendom* (London, 1692).

[18] Ch. XV, story VII.

[19] A. Trembley's description in *Mémoires pour servir à l'histoire d'un genre de polypes d'eau douce* (Paris, 1744), of how polyps reproduce asexually by division caused a great stir as it seemed to pose serious questions about the nature of animals.

From animals to man there is no abrupt transition, as true philosophers will agree. What was man before he invented words and learnt languages? An animal of a particular species who, with much less natural instinct than the others, whose king he did not yet consider himself to be, was only distinguishable from the ape and other animals in the same way as the ape himself is; I mean by a physiognomy that indicated greater discernment. Reduced to the mere intuitive knowledge of the Leibnizians,[20] he saw only forms and colours, without being able to distinguish any of them; old or young, a perpetual child, he stuttered out his feelings and his needs like a starved or restless dog who wants to eat or go for a walk.

Words, languages, laws, science and arts came, and thanks to them the rough diamond of our minds was finally polished. Man was trained like an animal; he became an author in the same way as he became a porter. A mathematician learnt the most difficult proofs and calculations, as a monkey learnt to put on and take off his little hat or to ride his trained dog. Everything was done by signs; each species understood what it was able to understand, and that was how man acquired symbolic knowledge, as it is called by our German philosophers again.

As we can see, there is nothing simpler than the mechanism of our education! It all comes down to sounds, or words, which are transmitted from one person's mouth, through another's ear and into his brain, which receives at the same time through his eyes the shape of the bodies for which the words are the arbitrary signs.

But who was the first to speak? Who was the first tutor of the human race? Who invented the means to make the best use of our organism's aptitude for learning? I do not know; the names of those first welcome geniuses have been lost in the mists of time. But art is the child of nature, and nature must have long preceded it.

We must suppose that the men with the best organisms, those on whom nature had poured out its gifts, must have taught the others. They could not, for example, have heard a new sound, felt new feelings or been struck by all the different beautiful objects which form part of the enchanting spectacle of nature, without finding themselves in the same position as the famous deaf man from Chartres, whose story was first told by Fontenelle,[21] on hearing for the first time, at the age of forty, the astonishing sound of bells.

Would it then be absurd to believe that those first mortals tried, like that deaf man or like animals and dumb people (who are another sort of animals), to express their new feelings by movements dictated by the economy of their imagination and then, as a result, by spontaneous sounds particular to each animal; this was a natural expression of their surprise, joy, emotions or needs. For doubtless those whom nature endowed with more refined feelings were also given greater facility to express them.

[20] La Mettrie has misunderstood what Leibniz means by intuitive knowledge which, on the contrary, is the clearest and most certain type.

[21] See *L'Histoire de l'Académie royale des sciences* (Paris, 1703); La Mettrie recounts this story in the *Treatise on the Soul*, ch. XV, story I.

That is how I believe man used his feelings or his instinct to acquire his wits, and his wits to acquire knowledge. That is how, as far as I can grasp, the brain was filled with the ideas for whose reception nature had formed it. The one helped the other, and the smallest beginnings grew little by little until all of the objects in the universe were as easily perceived as a circle.

In the same way as a violin string or a harpsichord key vibrates and gives out a sound, so the strings of the brain, struck by rays of sound, are stimulated to give out or repeat the words which touch them. But such is the construction of this organ that, as soon as the eyes, which are properly formed for optics, have received the depiction of certain objects, the brain cannot but see their images and differences; and in the same way, when the signs for these differences have been marked or engraved on the brain, the soul has necessarily examined the relationships between them. This examination would have been impossible without the discovery of signs or the invention of languages. At the time when the universe was almost silent, the soul was, in respect of all these objects, like a man with no idea of proportions looking at a picture or a sculpture; he would not be able to distinguish anything, or like a little child (for then the soul was in its childhood) holding in its hand a certain number of little pieces of straw or wood, who sees them in general in a vague and superficial way without being able to count or differentiate them. But if a sort of ensign or flag is put, for example, on the piece of wood called a mast, and if another is put on another identical object, and the first numbered with the sign '1' and the second with the sign or number '2', then the child will be able to count them and so he will learn the whole of arithmetic. As soon as a figure seems to him to be equal to another by its *numerical* sign, he will conclude without difficulty that these are two different bodies, and that 1 and 1 make 2, that 2 and 2 make 4, etc.[e]

It is this real or apparent similarity of figures that is the fundamental basis of all truths and all our knowledge, amongst which it is evident that those whose signs are less simple and perceptible are more difficult to learn than others, as they need more genius to assimilate and combine the huge quantity of words which are used by the sciences I am speaking of to express their truths; whereas sciences which use figures or other small signs are easy to learn, and it is no doubt this ease, even more than the evidence of algebraic calculations, that has led to their success.

All the windy learning which inflates the balloon-like brains of our haughty pedants is therefore nothing but a mass of words and figures, which form all the traces in the head by means of which we discern and recall objects. All our ideas are aroused in the same way as a gardener who knows plants remembers all their Latin definitions when he sees them. These words and the figures they represent are so closely linked in the brain that it is quite rare for us to imagine an object without the name or sign attached to it.

[e] There are still people today who, through lack of a great number of signs, can only count up to twenty.

I always use the word 'imagine' because I believe that everything is imagined and that all the parts of the soul can be properly reduced to imagination alone, which forms them all, and thus that judgement, reason and memory are only parts of the soul which are in no way absolute but are veritable modifications of that sort of medullary screen on which the objects painted in the eye are projected as in a magic lantern.

But if such is the wonderful and incomprehensible result of the organisation of the brain, if everything is conceived by the imagination, if everything is explained by it, then why divide up the sensitive principle which thinks in man? Surely this constitutes a manifest contradiction for the supporters of the mind's simple nature? For something that is divided can no longer, without absurdity, be seen as indivisible. See where we are led by the abuse of language and the haphazard use of grand words like 'spirituality' and 'immateriality' etc. without their being understood, even by clever people.

Nothing is simpler than to prove a system which is founded, like this one, on each individual's intimate feelings and experience. If the imagination, or that fantastic part of the brain about whose nature we know as little as we do about its method of working, is naturally small or weak, then it will scarcely have the strength to compare the analogy or the similarity between its ideas; it will only be able to see what is in front of it or what affects it most vividly, and even then in what a way! But it is nevertheless true that the imagination alone perceives; it forms an idea of all objects, with the words and figures that characterise them; thus, once again, the imagination is the soul, because it plays all its roles. Thanks to the imagination, to its flattering touch, the cold skeleton of reason acquires living rosy flesh; thanks to it the sciences flourish, the arts are embellished, woods speak, echoes sigh, rocks weep, marble breathes and all inanimate objects come to life. It is, again, the imagination that adds to the tenderness of a loving heart the spicy attraction of sensuality. It makes it flower in the study of the philosopher or the dry-as-dust pedant, and it moulds scientists as well as orators and poets. It is stupidly criticised by some and distinguished in vain by others, but none of them knows it properly. It does not only follow in the train of the Graces and the fine arts; it does not only paint nature, but it can also measure her. It reasons, judges, penetrates, compares and analyses. Could it feel so well the beauty of the pictures that are drawn for it without understanding their relationships? No. In the same way as it cannot fall back on the pleasures of the senses without appreciating all their perfection or sensuality, so it cannot reflect on what it has conceived mechanically without constituting judgement itself.

The more the imagination or the feeblest genius is exercised, the more it takes on, as it were, corpulence, the more it grows, becomes vigorous, robust, vast and capable of thinking. Even the best organisation needs such exercise.

Man's first asset is his organisation. It is pointless for all moralists to refuse to place those qualities which are given by nature among the estimable qualities, preferring talents acquired by reflection and hard work. For where, pray, do cleverness, learning and virtue come from, if not from a disposition which makes us apt to become clever, learned and virtuous? And where does that disposition come from if not from nature? All our estimable qualities come from nature; to her we owe all that we are. Why then should I not esteem those who possess natural qualities as much as those whose brilliance comes from acquired, one might almost say borrowed, virtues? All merit, from whatever source, is worthy of esteem; we only need to know how to measure it. Wit, beauty, riches and nobility, although children of chance, all have value, like dexterity, knowledge, virtue, etc. Those whom nature has showered with her most precious gifts should pity those who have been refused them, but they can enjoy their superiority without vanity and with discernment. A beautiful woman who considers herself ugly would be as ridiculous as a clever man who believes himself stupid. Exaggerated modesty (a rare defect, it is true) is a sort of ingratitude towards nature. Honest pride on the contrary is the mark of a fine, great soul, indicated by manly traits, moulded as if by feeling.

If organisation is an asset, the first asset, and the source of all the others, then instruction is the second. Without it, the best constructed brain would be wasted, in the same way as without manners the most handsome man would simply be a crude peasant. But also what fruit would the most excellent school produce without a womb perfectly open to the admission or the conception of ideas? It is as impossible to give a single idea to a man deprived of all the senses as to give a child to a woman in whom nature was absent-minded enough to forget to make a vulva, as I have seen in one who had neither opening nor vagina nor womb, and whose marriage was annulled for that reason after ten years.

But if the brain is both well organised and well educated, it is like perfectly sown, fertile earth which produces a hundred-fold what it has received; or (to abandon the figurative style which is often necessary in order to express better what is felt and to add grace to truth itself) imagination, raised by art to the splendid, rare dignity of genius, seizes exactly all the relations of ideas it has conceived, embraces easily an amazing mass of objects and deduces from them a long chain of consequences, which are simply new relationships born from a comparison with the first ones, with which the soul finds a perfect similarity. Such is, in my opinion, the generation of the mind. I have used the word 'find', as earlier I used the epithet 'apparent' for the similarities between objects, not because I think that our senses always deceive us, as Father Malebranche claimed, nor that our eyes, naturally slightly inebriated, do not see objects as they really are – although microscopes prove this every day – but in order not to have any argument with the Pyrrhonians, the most outstanding of whom was Bayle.[22]

I would say about truth in general what Mr de Fontenelle said about some truths

22 Malebranche in Bk. I of *De la recherche de la vérité*. On P. Bayle, see pp. xvi and n. 11, xxiv.

in particular, namely that it must be sacrificed to suit society. I am so good natured that I avoid all disputes unless I want to enliven conversation. Cartesians will here attack us in vain in the name of innate ideas, but I will not expend a quarter of Mr Locke's efforts in refuting such fantasies.[23] What is the use of writing a long book in order to prove a doctrine which was set up as an axiom three thousand years ago?

Following the principles we have laid down and that we believe to be true, the person with the most imagination should be considered as having the most intelligence or genius, for all these words are synonymous; and once again it is shameful misuse that makes us believe that we are saying different things when we merely pronounce different words or different sounds, to which we attach no real idea or distinction.

The finest, the greatest or strongest imagination is therefore the most suitable for both science and art. I do not wish to decide whether one needs more intelligence to excel in the art of Aristotle or Descartes or in that of Euripedes or Sophocles, or if nature expended more effort in producing Newton than in creating Corneille (which I doubt very much). But it is certain that their different triumphs and immortal glory were only due to imagination, differently applied.

If someone is considered to have little judgement and much imagination, that means that their imagination, left too much to its own devices and almost always busy, as it were, looking at itself in the mirror of its own feelings, is not sufficiently used to examining closely these feelings themselves and is more taken up with the traces or images than with their truth or likeness.

It is true that the springs of the imagination are so lively that if the attention, the key or mother of science, does not intervene, imagination can only glimpse or touch the surface of objects.

Look at that bird on the branch: it always seems ready to take flight. The imagination is the same, always carried away by the vortex of the blood and the spirits; one wave leaves a trace, which is erased by the following one. The soul runs after them, often in vain. It must expect to regret those it was not quick enough to seize and keep. Thus the imagination, in the true likeness of time, is perpetually destroyed and renewed.

Such is the chaos and the perpetual rapid succession of our ideas; they pursue each other as one billow pushes another, so that unless the imagination uses part of its muscles, so to speak, to balance on the brain's strings, in order to support itself for a while on an object that is about to flee and to prevent itself from falling onto another, which it is not yet the moment to contemplate, it will never be worthy of being called judgement. It will express vividly what it has felt vividly; it will form orators, musicians, painters, poets and not a single philosopher. On the contrary, if from childhood the imagination has been accustomed to restraining itself and not

[23] Particularly in Bk. I of *Essay Concerning Human Understanding*.

being carried away by its own recklessness, which only creates brilliant enthusiasts, if it has been accustomed to stopping and containing its ideas and to turning them in every direction in order to look at all sides of an object, then the imagination will be ready to judge and, thanks to its reasoning, will take in the greatest range of objects; and its liveliness, which is always so promising in children and which only needs to be disciplined by study and exercise, will become only far-seeing perspicacity, without which little scientific progress can be made.

These are the simple foundations on which the structure of logic has been built. Nature laid them for all the human race, but some have profited from them, while others have misused them.

Despite all of man's prerogatives over animals, to put him in the same class as them is to do him a great honour. It is true that up to a certain age he is more of an animal than they are because he is born with less instinct.

Which animal would die of hunger in the middle of a river of milk? Man alone. Like the old child mentioned by a modern author who cites Arnobius,[24] he knows neither that some food is good for him, nor that water can drown him, nor that fire can reduce him to powder. Shine candlelight in a child's eyes for the first time, and he will automatically stretch out his fingers to it, as if to discover the nature of this new phenomenon he sees; he will learn to his cost how dangerous it is, but he will not be caught out a second time.

Or put him with an animal on the edge of a cliff; only he will fall. He will drown while the other will swim away. At the age of fourteen or fifteen he hardly glimpses the great pleasures that await him in the reproduction of his species; he is already an adolescent, but he does not know what to do in a game that nature teaches animals so quickly; he hides as if ashamed of feeling pleasure and of being created in order to be happy, while animals glory in being cynical. Having no education, they have no prejudices. But, again, look at that dog and that child who have both lost their master on the highway: the child is crying and he does not know which way to turn, while the dog, which uses its sense of smell better than the other uses his reason, will soon find him.

Therefore nature made us to be beneath the animals, or at least in order to show up all the better the miracles worked by education, which alone can remove us from that level and finally lift us above them. But can the same distinction be extended to the deaf, those born blind, idiots, lunatics, wild men or those raised in the woods with animals; to those whose hypochondria has doomed their imagination; or to all those brutes in human form who only display the crudest instincts? No, all those who are men only in body but not in mind do not deserve a special class.

We do not mean to ignore the objections that can be made against our opinion in support of the primal distinction between man and animals. There is, it is said, a

[24] In *Treatise on the Soul*, ch. xv, § vii, 'Belle conjecture d'Arnobe', La Mettrie quotes the description given by Arnobius in *Adversus gentes*, of an experiment allowing a child to grow up with no human contact or sensory stimulation.

law of nature in man, a knowledge of good and evil, that has not been engraved on the hearts of animals.

But is this objection, or rather this assertion, founded on experience, without which a philosopher is entitled to reject any opinion? Is there a single experiment to convince us that man alone has been accorded a ray of light refused to all other animals? If there is not, we cannot know what happens inside them, and even inside other men, any more than we can avoid feeling what happens inside our own being. We know that we think and that we feel remorse, as an inner feeling forces us to admit only too well; but this feeling inside us is insufficient to enable us to judge remorse in others. That is why we must believe either what other men tell us or the same evident external signs that we have noticed in ourselves when we feel the same pangs of conscience.

But to decide whether animals that cannot speak have received a knowledge of the law of nature, we must for the same reason rely on the signs that I have just mentioned, supposing they exist. The facts seem to prove it. A dog which bites its master, who was annoying it, seems to repent the moment afterwards; it appears sad, upset, not daring to show itself and admitting its guilt by its cringing, humble attitude. History provides us with the famous example of a lion which refused to tear to pieces a man who had been thrown to it, because it recognised him as his benefactor. How one could wish that man himself always showed the same gratitude for kindness and the same respect for humanity! We would no longer have to fear ungrateful wretches or wars, which are the scourge of the human race and the true agents of destruction of the law of nature.

But a being to whom nature has given such a precocious, enlightened instinct, who judges, combines, reasons and deliberates as far as the sphere of its activity extends and allows; a being in whom kindness inspires devotion and whom harsh treatment incites to leave and try a better master; a being constructed like us, behaving the same way, feeling the same passions, the same pains and the same pleasures to a greater or lesser degree according to the power of its imagination and the delicacy of its nerves; surely such a being demonstrates clearly that it feels its wrongdoing and ours, that it distinguishes good from evil and that in short it is aware of what it is doing? How could its soul, which exhibits the same joys, the same mortification, the same disconcertment as ours, not feel repugnance at the sight of a fellow creature being torn to pieces or after having itself dismembered it without pity? Given this, we must suppose that animals have not been denied the precious gift in question; for, since they give us undeniable signs of both repentance and intelligence, why is it absurd to think that beings, machines almost as perfect as ourselves, were made like us to think and to feel nature's promptings?

It is no use objecting that animals are for the most part ferocious beings, incapable of appreciating the harm they do; for can all men distinguish any better vice from virtue? Ferocity exists in our species as in theirs. Men who are in the barbaric habit of infringing the law of nature feel fewer pangs than those who do so for the first time and are not hardened by bad examples. Animals are also like men in that both can be temperamentally more or less ferocious and that they become even more so in the company of those who are. But a sweet-natured and peaceful animal living with other similar animals on bland food will be opposed to blood and massacres; it will be secretly ashamed of having spilt blood, with perhaps the difference that, since for them everything is sacrificed to needs, pleasures and comfort, which they enjoy more than we do, their remorse does not apparently have to be as strong as ours because we are not in as great a need as they are. Habit blunts and perhaps even stifles remorse, as it does pleasure.

But suppose for a moment that I am wrong and that it is impossible for almost the whole of the universe to be mistaken on this subject while I alone am right. I grant that even the most excellent animals do not know the difference between moral right and wrong, that they have no remembrance of the care they have been given or the kindness they have been shown and no awareness of their own virtues; that, for example, the lion which I, like so many other people, have mentioned does not remember having refused to take the life of the man thrown to it in a spectacle that was more inhuman than all the lions, tigers and bears that exist, while our fellow-countrymen fight, Swiss against Swiss,[25] brothers against brothers, spy on each other, chain each other up or kill each other without remorse because a prince is paying for these murders; and if I suppose that the law of nature was not given to animals, then what will be the consequence? Man is not moulded from a more precious clay; nature has only used one and the same dough, merely changing the yeast. So if animals do not repent of having transgressed the inner feeling I have spoken about, or rather if they are totally deprived of it, man must necessarily be in the same state, in which case farewell to the law of nature and all the fine treatises published about it! The whole animal kingdom would be generally deprived of it. But by the same token, if man cannot avoid admitting that, when his health allows him to be in control of himself, he can always distinguish people with probity, humanity and virtue from those who are neither humane nor virtuous nor honest, and that it is easy to distinguish vice from virtue by the mere pleasure or the very repulsion which seem to be their natural effects, then it follows that animals, made from the same matter and lacking perhaps only a degree of fermentation which would have made them the complete equals of men, must partake of the same prerogatives of animal nature. Thus there can be no soul, or sensitive substance, without remorse. The following reflection will reinforce the ones I have just presented.

The law of nature cannot be destroyed; its imprint in all animals is so strong that I do not doubt that even the most savage and ferocious of them experience moments of repentance. I believe that the wild girl from Châlons in Champagne must have suffered for her crime if she really did eat her sister. I think the same

[25] La Mettrie was pretending in this work to be a Swiss compatriot of Haller; the Swiss were traditionally mercenary soldiers.

thing about all those who commit even involuntary crimes, or ones dictated by their temperament: Gaston d'Orleans who could not help stealing; a woman who was afflicted by the same vice during her pregnancy and whose children inherited it; one who in the same condition ate her husband; another who cut her children's throats, salted their bodies and ate a piece every day like salt pork; a daughter of a cannibal highwayman who became one herself at the age of twelve although she had lost both parents at the age of one and had been brought up by respectable people ; to say nothing of the many other examples that fill the pages of our observers and which all prove that there exist a thousand hereditary vices and virtues that are passed on to children from their parents, as those of a wet-nurse are passed on to those she suckles.[26] I say then, and I admit, that these unlucky individuals do not for the most part realise immediately the enormity of their actions. Bulimia, for example, or canine hunger, can extinguish all feelings; it is a mania of the stomach that one is forced to satisfy. But when those women recover their senses and are so to speak sobered up, what remorse they feel when they remember how they have murdered what they held dearest! What punishment for an involuntary evil which they were unable to resist and of which they were not aware! But that is apparently not enough for the judges. One of the women I have mentioned was broken on the wheel and burnt, and the other was buried alive. I am aware of what is required by the interests of society. But it would no doubt be preferable if all judges were excellent medical doctors. Only they could distinguish the innocent criminal from the guilty one. If reason is the slave of depraved or frenzied senses, how can it govern them?

But if crime brings its own more or less cruel punishment, if the longest, most barbaric habit cannot completely extirpate repentance from the most callous of hearts, if they are harrowed by the very memory of what they have done, why terrify the imagination of weak minds by hell, ghosts and fiery precipices, which are even more unreal than Pascal's?[f] Why do we need to invent fables, as an honest Pope himself once said, in order to torment the very miserable beings that we put to death because we do not consider them to be punished enough by their own consciences, which are the first to torture them? I do not mean that all criminals are unjustly punished; I am only claiming that those whose wills are depraved and

f In a group of people or at meals he always needed a rampart of chairs or someone near him on his left to prevent him from seeing the terrifying depths into which he was sometimes afraid of falling, however much he knew it was a delusion. What a terrifying effect of the imagination or of an unusual circulation in one of the brain's lobes! He was a great man on one side but he was half mad on the other. Madness and wisdom each had their department or their lobe, separated by the *falx*. From which side did his great attachment to Port-Royal come?[27]

26 Moreau de Saint-Elier's *Traité de la communication des maladies et des passions* (The Hague, 1738), claimed that the nurse passed her vices to children in her milk. The wild girl was mentioned in the *Mercure de France* in 1731. For details concerning her and the others described here, see Vartanian's edition, pp. 222–6.

27 This example of Pascal is used in a different context in the *Treatise on the Soul*, p. 69, to show the effects of imagination.

whose consciences are slumbering are punished enough by remorse when they return to their senses. I would even say that I think nature should, in this case, have freed from remorse those unlucky creatures who are driven on by fatal necessity.

However much cruel pleasure the criminal, the wicked, the ungrateful and those who are impervious to nature – miserable tyrants who do not deserve to live – derive from their barbarity, they nevertheless experience calm moments of reflection when the avenging voice of conscience is heard, testifies against them and condemns them to be almost incessantly torn apart at their own hands. Those who torment men are tormented by their own selves, and the evils they suffer will be in proportion to those they have caused.

On the other hand, there is so much pleasure in doing good, in feeling and appreciating the kindness we receive, so much satisfaction in practising virtue, in being good-natured, humane, tender, charitable, compassionate and generous (this word alone includes all the virtues), that I hold that whoever is unlucky enough not to have been born virtuous has been punished enough.

We were not originally made to be wise and we have perhaps become so by a sort of misuse of our organic faculties, at the expense of the State which keeps a crowd of good-for-nothings whom vanity has honoured with the name of 'Philosophers'. Nature created us all solely to be happy – yes, all, from the worm crawling on the ground to the eagle soaring on high. That is why she gave all animals a portion of the law of nature which is more or less refined depending on how well-conditioned are the organs of each animal which possesses it.

How then should we define the law of nature? It is a feeling which teaches us what we should not do, by what we would not like to be done to us. Dare I add to this generally accepted idea that, in my opinion, this feeling is only a kind of fear or fright which is as salutary for the species as it is for the individual? For perhaps we only respect the purses and lives of others in order to protect our own goods, our honour and ourselves, like those Christian Ixions who only love God and embrace so many illusory virtues because they are afraid of Hell.[28]

You can see that the law of nature is only an inner feeling which once again belongs to the imagination, like all the others, including thought. As a result it obviously does not presuppose education, revelation or a legislator, unless you wish to confuse it with civil laws, in the ridiculous manner of theologians.

The weapons of fanaticism may destroy those who uphold these truths, but they will never destroy these truths themselves.

This does not mean that I question the existence of a supreme Being; on the contrary, it seems to me that the greatest degree of probability is in its favour. But as this existence does not prove the need for one religion any more than another, it is a theoretical truth which serves very little practical purpose. So that, as we can

[28] Ixion, who was in love with Juno, was deceived by Zeus, who showed him a cloud in the shape of Juno, which he embraced.

say after so much experience that religion does not imply perfect honesty, the same reasons allow us to think that atheism does not preclude it.

Who knows after all whether the reason for man's existence is not his existence itself? Perhaps he was thrown by chance on a point of the earth's surface without anyone being able to say how or why, but simply that he has to live and die, like mushrooms which appear from one day to the next, or flowers which grow beside ditches and cover walls.

We should not lose ourselves in infinity; we were not made to have the slightest idea of it, and we are absolutely incapable of tracing things back to their origin. In any case, it does not affect our peace of mind whether matter is eternal or was created and whether there is or is not a God. It is folly to torture ourselves so much about what we cannot know and what would not make us any happier if we did manage to know it.

But, they say, read all the works of Fénelon, Nieuwentijd, Abbadie, Derham, Ray and so on.[29] Well, what will they teach me? Or rather, what have they taught me? They are nothing but boring repetitions by zealous writers who add to each other only verbiage which is more likely to strengthen than undermine the foundations of atheism. The quantity of proofs drawn from the spectacle of nature does not give them any greater force. Either the structure of a finger, an ear, an eye or 'one of Malpighi's observations', alone proves everything – and no doubt better than 'Descartes and Malebranche' – or all the rest proves nothing.[30] It ought to be enough for Deists, and even Christians, to observe that in the whole animal kingdom the same purpose is achieved by an infinite number of different means, which are all nevertheless exactly geometrical. For what stronger weapons could there be to triumph over atheists? It is true that if my reason does not deceive me, man and the whole universe seem to have been destined for this unity of aims. Everything – the sun, the air, water, the organisation and form of bodies – is arranged in the eye as in a mirror which faithfully presents to the imagination the objets that are painted there, following the laws required by the infinite variety of bodies which are used for the purpose of seeing. We see everywhere ears of strikingly different shapes but this diverse construction of man, animals, birds or fish does not produce a different usage. All ears are so mathematically constructed that they all equally serve one single purpose, which is hearing. Is chance, the Deist asks, a great enough mathematician to vary thus at will the works it is supposed to

[29] All authors of apologetic works. Fénelon's main apologetic work was *Démonstration de l'existence de Dieu* (Paris, 1713); B. Nieuwentijd wrote *Het regt Gebruik der Werelt Beshouwingen* (Amsterdam, 1715), J. Abbadie, *Traité de la vérité de la religion chrétienne* (Rotterdam, 1684), W. Derham, *Physico-theology* (London, 1713) and J. Ray, *The Wisdom of God manifested in the Works of the Creation* (London, 1691).

[30] La Mettrie is here, and in the following pages, referring to the argument of, and sometimes quoting phrases from, Diderot's *Pensées philosophiques* (itself in part directed against La Mettrie's own *Natural History of the Soul*), which he names further on. M. Malpighi was famous for his microscopic observations of the skin and various organs.

have produced, without such diversity preventing it from achieving the same aim? He also points to the parts clearly contained in animals for future use: the butterfly in the caterpillar, man in the spermatozoa, a whole polyp in each of its parts, the valve in the *foromen ovale*, the lung in the foetus, teeth in their alveoli, bones in fluids which detach themselves and harden in an incomprehensible way. And as the supporters of this system forget nothing in their attempts to justify it and never tire of piling proof upon proof, they want to take advantage of everything, even the mind's weaknesses in certain cases. Look, they say, at Spinoza, Vanini, des Barreaux, Boindin, apostles who do more honour than harm to Deism.[31] Their unbelief only lasted as long as their health did, and the Deists add that it is rare for people not to renounce atheism as soon as their passions have weakened with the body which is their instrument.

That is certainly the most that can be said in favour of the existence of a God, although the last is a trifling argument, as such conversions are short-lived; the mind almost always returns to its former opinions and acts in consequence as soon as it recovers or rather renews its strength in that of the body. Anyway it is a lot more than is said by Doctor Diderot in his *Philosophical Thoughts*, a sublime work which would not convince an atheist.[32] Indeed, how can we answer a man who says: 'We do not know nature at all; causes hidden deep within her may have produced everything. Look in your turn at Trembley's polyp! Does it not contain inside it the causes of its own regeneration? Why then would it be absurd to believe that there exist physical causes for which everything was made and to which the whole chain of this vast universe is so necessarily linked and subordinated that nothing that happens could not have happened; that it is our absolutely invincible ignorance of these causes that has made us look to a God, who is not even a being of reason,[33] according to some? Thus, destroying chance does not mean proving the existence of a supreme Being, for there may be something else which is neither chance nor God; I mean nature, the study of which can as a result only produce unbelievers, as is proved by the manner of thinking of all its most successful observers.'

Therefore the 'weight of the Universe', far from 'crushing' a true atheist, will not affect him, and all the interminably repeated proofs of a Creator, which are far more highly esteemed than the way of thinking of our fellow beings, are only obvious, however far the argument is extended, to anti-Pyrrhonians or to those

[31] All celebrated unbelievers, who did not however all renounce their beliefs before dying. L. Vanini, an Italian philosopher, was burnt as a heretic at Toulouse in 1619; J. Vallée des Barreaux was a Libertin thinker and poet who retracted on his deathbed; N. Boindin, a noted freethinker, was still alive when La Mettrie wrote this.

[32] Diderot was not of course a medical doctor, but La Mettrie presumably thought so because of his translation (6 vols., Paris, 1745–8) of R. James's *Medicinal Dictionary* (3 vols., London, 1743–5).

[33] The expression 'être de raison' used by La Mettrie refers to Descartes' *Reply to the Second Objections*, where it is used to qualify the idea of God that is in us. See *Œuvres*, ed. C. Adam and P. Tannery (Paris, 1973), vol. IX–1, p. 106.

who have enough faith in their reason to think that they can judge on certain appearances; but, as you can see, atheists can counter with other absolutely opposing appearances which are perhaps just as strong. For if we listen to the naturalists again, they tell us that the same causes which enabled a chemist to create the first mirror by various chance compounds are used by nature to create clear water, which the simple shepherdess uses for the same purpose. They also tell us that the same movement which conserves the world could have created it; that each body occupies the place assigned to it by its nature; that the air had to surround the earth, for the same reason that iron and other metals are produced by its bowels; that the sun is as natural a product as that of electricity; that it was not made in order to heat the earth and all its inhabitants – whom it sometimes burns – any more than the rain was created in order to grow seeds – which it often spoils; that a mirror and water were not created to enable us to look at ourselves in them, any more than was any polished body with the same property; and that the eye is indeed a sort of looking-glass in which the soul can contemplate the images of objects as they are presented to it by those bodies. But they tell us that there is no proof that this organ was really created on purpose for such contemplation nor placed on purpose in its socket; and that Lucretius, Dr Lamy[34] and all past and present Epicureans might well be right when they claim that the eye sees only because it happens to be organised and placed as it is; and that, given the same rules of movement followed by nature in the generation and development of bodies, it was not possible for that wonderful organ to be organised and placed otherwise.

Those are the pros and cons, and a summary of the great reasons which will eternally divide philosophers: I am taking no sides.

> It is not in my power to decide so great a controversy between you.[35]

That is what I said to a French friend of mine who is as frank a Pyrrhonian as I am, a man of great worth who deserves a better fate. His reply was very curious. It is true, he said, that the pros and cons should not trouble the soul of a philosopher, who sees that nothing is demonstrated clearly enough to impose agreement and even that the indications proposed in favour of one side are immediately destroyed by those presented in favour of the other. Yet, he said, the universe will never be happy unless it is atheistic. Here are the reasons given by this abominable man. If atheism, he said, were generally accepted, all the branches of religion would be destroyed and their roots cut off. Result: no more theological wars, no more soldiers of religion, those dreadful soldiers! Nature, now infected by sacred poison, would regain its rights and its purity. Peaceful mortals, deaf to all other voices, would only follow the spontaneous promptings of their own individual being, which are the only ones that we ignore at our peril and which alone can lead us to happiness along the pleasant paths of virtue.

[34] On Guillaume Lamy, see Introduction, pp. x–xi.

[35] Virgil, *Bucolics*, Eclogue III.108: 'Non nostrum inter vos tantas componere lites.'

Such is the law of nature: whosoever observes it rigidly is a respectable man and deserves the confidence of the whole human race. Whosoever does not follow it scrupulously, however much he affects the specious trappings of another religion, is either a knave or a hypocrite, whom I distrust.

After that let the vain populace think differently, let them dare to claim that not to believe in revelation affects probity itself, that in short we need a religion other than that of nature, whatever it is! How miserable! How pitiful! And what a good opinion each person gives us of the religion he has embraced! We are not trying here to win the approbation of the rabble. He who erects in his heart altars to superstition was born to worship idols and not to appreciate virtue.

But since all the soul's faculties depend so much on the specific organisation of the brain and of the whole body that they are clearly nothing but that very organisation, the machine is perfectly explained! For after all even if man alone had received the law of nature as his heritage, would he be any less of a machine? Some wheels, a few springs more than in the most perfect animals, the brain proportionately closer to the heart and thus receiving more blood, the same gift of reason or – how do I know? – unknown causes would always have produced that delicate conscience which is so easily wounded, that remorse which is no more foreign to matter than is thought, and in short all of the differences that are supposed here. So does the organisation suffice to explain everything? Once again, yes. Since thought clearly develops with the organs, why should the matter which composes them not also be capable of remorse once it has acquired, with time, the faculty of feeling?

Thus the soul is merely a vain term of which we have no idea and which a good mind should use only to refer to that part of us which thinks. Given the slightest principle of movement, animate bodies will have everything they need to move, feel, think, repent and, in a word, behave in the physical sphere and in the moral sphere which depends on it.

None of this is mere supposition. Those who believe that all the difficulties have not yet been removed will find here a list of experiments which will completely satisfy them.

1. All animal flesh palpitates after death and the more cold-blooded the animal is and the less it perspires, the longer the flesh palpitates. Tortoises, lizards, snakes, etc. prove this.

2. When separated from the body, the muscles retract when they are pricked.

3. The bowels retain for a long time their peristaltic or vermicular movement.

4. A simple injection of warm water reanimates the heart and the muscles, according to Cowper.[36]

5. A frog's heart, particularly when left in the sun, or even better on a warm table or a plate, moves for an hour or more after having been removed from the body. If the movement seems to have vanished beyond recovery, you only need to prick the

[36] W. Cowper, *Myotomia reformata* (London, 1694).

heart and this hollow muscle still beats. Harvey has made the same observation concerning toads.[37]

6. Chancellor Bacon, a first-class author, speaks in his *History of Life and Death* of a man convicted of treason whose heart was torn out while he was still alive, and thrown into the flames; this muscle first leapt vertically to a height of one and a half feet, but then, losing force, it leapt less high each time, for seven or eight minutes.[38]

7. Take a chick still in its egg and tear out its heart: you will observe the same phenomena in more or less the same circumstances. The warmth of one's breath alone reanimates an animal on the point of death in a pneumatic engine.

The same experiments that we owe to Boyle and Steno[39] can be done on pigeons, dogs, rabbits, pieces of whose hearts move just like whole hearts. The same movement can be seen in the torn-off paws of moles.

8. Caterpillars, worms, spiders, flies and eels give rise to the same observations, and the movement in the cut-off parts increases in hot water because of the fire it contains.

9. A drunken soldier cut off the head of a turkey-cock with a sabre. The animal stayed upright, then it walked and ran; when it hit a wall it turned round, beat its wings, still running, and finally fell down. Even when it was on the ground, all this cock's muscles continued to move. That is what I saw, and it is easy to see more or less the same phenomena in kittens or puppies whose heads have been cut off.

10. Polyps do more than move after being cut up: within a week each piece generates a new animal. I am sorry for the way this affects the naturalists' theory of reproduction;[40] or rather I am pleased, because this discovery teaches us never to draw general conclusions, even from all the most decisive experiments ever known.

I have given many more facts than are needed to prove beyond all doubt that each tiny fibre or part of organised bodies moves according to its own principle, whose action does not depend, like voluntary movements, on the nerves; this is because the movements in question happen without the part which undergoes them being in contact with the circulation. Now, if this force can be observed even in the pieces of fibres, the heart, which is a particularly complex structure of fibres, must have the same property. I did not need Bacon's story to convince me of this. It was easy for me to deduce it from the perfect analogy in the structure of human and animal hearts, from the very mass of the former, in which this movement is hidden from sight only because it is stifled in it, and from the fact that everything is cold

[37] In fact concerning eels: W. Harvey, *De motu cordis et sanguinis in animalibus* (Frankfurt/Main, 1628).

[38] F. Bacon, *Historia vitae et mortis* (London, 1623), Intentiones, X, par. 32.

[39] See R. Boyle, *Some Considerations Touching the Usefulness of Experimental Natural Philosophy* (2 vols., Oxford, 1663), and N. Steno's experiments on animal hearts reported in *Bibliotheca anatomica* (Geneva, 1685); for details, see Vartanian's edition of *L'Homme machine*, p. 233.

[40] This is another reference to Trembley's discovery, which cast doubts on the theory of preformation, according to which an animal was contained completely in its father's sperm or its mother's egg. See also *Man as Plant*.

and flaccid in corpses. If dissections were practised on executed criminals while their bodies were still warm, we would see the same movements in their hearts that are observed in the facial muscles of decapitated people.

The principle of motion in whole bodies or in parts cut into pieces is such that it produces movements which are not, as has been thought, disordered, but completely regular, both in warm whole animals and in cold incomplete ones. Our opponents' only recourse is therefore to deny innumerable facts which can be easily verified by anyone.

If I were now asked where the seat of this innate force in our bodies is, I would reply that it is obviously situated in what the Ancients called the *Parenchyma*, or in the very substance of the parts, leaving aside the veins, arteries and nerves; in short, in the whole organisation of the body. Thus each part contains its own more or less vigorous springs, according to the extent to which it needs them.

Let us go into more details concerning these springs of the human machine. All the vital, animal, natural and automatic movements are carried out thanks to them. When the body draws back, struck with terror at the sight of an unexpected precipice, when the eyelids blink under the threat of a blow, as we have said, when the pupils contract in bright light to protect the retina and dilate to see objects in the dark, surely all this happens mechanically? When the skin's pores close in winter to prevent the cold penetrating inside the vessels; when the stomach heaves on being irritated by poison, by a certain amount of opium or by all emetics, etc.; when the heart, the arteries and the muscles contract during sleep in the same way as they do when awake; when the lung acts as perpetually active bellows, surely all this happens mechanically? When all the sphincters of the bladder, the rectum, etc. work; when the heart contracts more strongly than any other muscle; when the erector muscles make man's penis stand upright, like that of an animal, where it beats against its stomach, and even of a child, who is capable of an erection whenever that part is stimulated, surely all this happens mechanically? The last example, by the way, proves that this member has a singular spring, as yet little known, which produces effects which have not yet been very well explained despite all our knowledge of anatomy.

I shall not dwell any longer on all the little minor springs which everyone knows. But there is another more subtle and wonderful one, which drives them all. It is the source of all our feelings, all our pleasures, all our passions and all our thoughts; for the brain possesses muscles for thinking as the legs do for walking. I mean that instigating and impetuous principle which Hippocrates calls 'ενορμων (the soul).[41] This principle exists and has its seat in the brain at the origin of the nerves, by means of which it exerts its control over all the rest of the body. This explains

[41] In appealing to the Hippocratic notion of 'ενορμων or 'impetum faciens' La Mettrie may have been influenced by H. Gaub (*De regimine mentis*, Leyden, 1745), who later accused La Mettrie of giving his opinions a materialistic twist.

everything that can be explained, even the surprising effects of diseases of the imagination.

But in order not to become bogged down in a wealth and ill-understood profusion of details, we must limit ourselves to a small number of questions and reflections.

Why does the sight, or the mere idea, of a beautiful woman cause singular movements and desires in us? Does what happens then in certain organs come from the very nature of those organs? Not at all, but from the intercourse and sort of sympathy of those muscles with the imagination. All we have here is one spring, excited by the Ancients' 'beneplacitum' or by the sight of beauty, exciting another one, which was very drowsy when the imagination awoke it. And what can cause this except the riot and tumult of the blood and spirits, which gallop with extraordinary rapidity and swell the hollowed-out organs?

Since there is obviously communication between mother and child[g] and since it is hard to deny the facts reported by Tulpius and by other equally trustworthy writers (there is none more so),[42] we believe that it is by the same means that the foetus feels the effect of its mother's impetuous imagination, as soft wax receives all sorts of impressions, and that the same traces or desires of its mother can be imprinted on the foetus in a way which we do not understand, whatever Blondel and all his followers may say. Thus we here make amends to Father Malebranche, whose credulity was excessively mocked by authors who have not observed nature closely enough and wanted to subject it to their ideas.[43]

Look at the portrait of the famous A. Pope, the English Voltaire.[44] The efforts and nerves of his genius are etched on his physiognomy; it is totally convulsed, his eyes are starting out of their sockets and his eyebrows are lifted by the muscles of his forehead. Why? Because the source of his nerves is in labour and all his body must feel the effects of such a difficult birth. Where would all these phenomena come from if there were no internal string pulling thus on the outer ones? To admit the existence of a soul to explain them is tantamount to being reduced to the intervention of the Holy Ghost.

For if what thinks in my brain is not a part of that organ and thus of the whole body, why, when I am lying peacefully in my bed and I work out the plan of a book or follow an abstract line of reasoning, does my blood heat up? Why is the fever in my mind transmitted to my veins? Ask men of imagination, great poets, those who are enchanted by a well-expressed feeling or who are transported by exquisite taste

[g] At least through the vessels. Is it certain that there is none through the nerves?

[42] N. Tulpius, a Dutch anatomist; see the discussions of malformations in his *Observationes medicae* (Amsterdam, 1641).

[43] There was much discussion of the effect of the mother's imagination or strong emotions on the foetus, thought to explain certain malformations; Malebranche accepted this theory in his *De la recherche de la vérité*, Bk. II, Pt. 1, ch. 8, but it was strongly criticised by J. Blondel in *The Strength of Imagination in Pregnant Women Examined* (London, 1727).

[44] A. Pope, the English poet (1688–1744).

and the charms of nature, of truth or of virtue! You can judge the cause by its effects, by their enthusiasm and by what they tell you they have felt; from the harmony that a single anatomist, Borelli,[45] knew better than all the Leibnizians, you can discover the material unity of man. For if the tautness in the nerves which produces pain causes fever, by which the mind is disturbed and has no will left, and vice versa if an overactive mind disturbs the body and lights the fire of consumption which carried off Bayle at such an early age; if a particular titillation makes me want, forces me to desire ardently what I did not care about the moment before; if in turn certain traces in the brain excite the same lust and the same desires, why divide into two what is obviously only one? Protests based on the power of the will are vain. For every order it gives, it is forced a hundred times to obey. And what a miracle for the body to obey in its healthy state, because a torrent of blood and spirits come to force it, as the will has as its ministers an invisible legion of fluids moving quicker than a flash and always ready to serve it! But as the nerves exercise this power, they also thwart it. Can the best will and the most violent desires of an exhausted lover bring back his lost energy? Alas, no, and his will is the first to be punished because, given certain conditions, it is not within his power not to want pleasure. What I said before about paralysis, etc. is also relevant here.

You are surprised by jaundice! Do you not know that the colour of bodies depends on the colour of the lenses through which we look at them! Are you not aware that the hue of objects is that of the humours, at least for us, who are the vain playthings of a thousand illusions. But remove that hue of the eye's aqueous humour and make the bile flow through its natural filter: the soul will have new eyes and will no longer see yellow. Is sight not restored to the blind and hearing to the deaf in the same way, by removing a cataract or by injecting the Eustachian tube? How many people in ignorant times, who were perhaps merely clever charlatans, were thought to have performed great miracles! How splendid a soul and how powerful a will we have! It can act only as long as its bodily disposition allows and its tastes change with age and fever! Should we therefore be surprised that philosophers have always looked to the health of the body in order to preserve the health of the soul, that Pythagoras prescribed diet so carefully and that Plato forbade wine? The diet which suits the body is always the one that sensible doctors claim should come first when we wish to educate the mind and to raise it to a knowledge of truth and virtue, which are only vain noises amid the disorder of diseases and the uproar of the senses! Without the precepts of hygiene, Epictetus, Socrates, Plato, etc. would preach in vain: all moral teaching is fruitless for anyone who is not endowed with sobriety, the source of all the virtues, as intemperance is the source of all the vices.

What more is needed (and why should I allow myself to be led astray into the history of the passions, which can all be explained by Hippocrates's 'ενορμών) in

[45] G. A. Borelli, author of *De motu animalium* (Rome, 1681), was one of the founders of the iatromechanist school.

order to prove that man is only an animal or a construction made of springs which all wind each other up without us being able to tell at which point on the human circle nature began? If there is any difference between these springs, it comes from their position and a few degrees of strength, and never from their nature; consequently the soul is only a principle of motion or a tangible material part of the brain that we can, without fear of error, consider as a mainspring of the whole machine, which exercises a visible influence on all the others and even seems to have been made first. Thus all the others can be seen as an emanation of it, as we shall see from a few observations I shall quote, which were made on different embryos.

The natural oscillation, a property of our machine, possessed by every fibre and, so to say, every fibrous element, is like that of a clock in that it cannot always function. It must be renewed as it is depleted, given strength when it languishes, weakened when it is oppressed by too much strength and vigour. That is what constitutes the only true medicine.

The body is nothing but a clock whose clockmaker is new chyle. Nature's first care, when the chyle comes into the blood, is to stimulate in it a sort of fever which the chemists, who are obsessed by furnaces, must have taken for a sort of fermentation. This fever produces a greater filtration of the spirits, which then mechanically stimulate the muscles and the heart as if they were sent there on the orders of the will.

These are therefore the causes or the forces of life, which thus sustain for a hundred years the perpetual movement of solids and fluids and are equally necessary to both of them. But who can say whether the solids contribute more to this activity than the fluids and vice versa? All we know is that the action of the former would soon be destroyed without the help of the latter. The liquids incite and preserve the elasticity of the vessels, on which their own circulation depends, by their violent contact with them. That is why, after death, the natural springiness of each substance is still more or less strong, according to the vestiges of life, which it outlives so that it expires last of all. Thus it is true that this strength in the animal parts can be preserved and increased by the strength of the circulation, but it does not depend on it because, as we have seen, it does not need the member or organ to be whole!

I am aware that this opinion has not been to the taste of all scientists and that Stahl above all had only contempt for it. That great chemist wanted to persuade us that the soul alone was the cause of all our movements;[46] but that is the talk of a fanatic, not a philosopher.

In order to destroy Stahl's hypothesis, there is no need of all the efforts that I see have been made before me. One only needs to glance at a violinist. What suppleness! What agile fingers! His movements are so rapid that they hardly seem

[46] See G. E. Stahl, *Theoria medica vera* (Halle, 1708); on Stahl's animism and La Mettrie's hostility to it, see Introduction, p. xiii.

to follow one another. So I beg, or rather I defy the Stahlians, who know so well everything that our soul can do, to tell me how it could possibly execute so rapidly so many movements, happening so far from it in so many different places. It is like supposing that a flautist could play brilliant cadenzas on an infinite number of holes he does not know, on which he cannot even put his fingers.

But let us say, like Mr Hecquet,[47] that not everyone can go to Corinth. Why should Stahl not be even more blessed by nature as a man than as a chemist and practitioner? He must (the lucky mortal!) have been endowed with a different soul from the rest of men; a sovereign soul which, not content with having some control over the voluntary muscles, held without difficulty the reins of all the body's movements and could suspend, calm or arouse them at will! With such a despotic mistress, in whose hands lay, so to speak, the heartbeat and the laws of circulation, there is doubtless no fever, no pain, no repining and no shameful impotence or embarrassing uncontrollable erections. The soul decrees and the springs act, stiffen or go limp. How could those of Stahl's machine have broken down so soon? With such a great doctor in residence one should be immortal.

However Stahl was not alone in rejecting the principle of the oscillation of organised bodies. Greater minds than his did not adopt it in order to explain the heart's movement, the erection of the penis, etc. One has only to read Boerhaave's *Institutions of Medicine* to see what laborious and attractive systems that great man was forced to give birth to with the sweat of his great genius because he would not admit that the heart contained such striking power.[48]

Willis and Perrault,[49] who were lesser minds but careful observers of nature (which the famous Professor from Leiden really only knew from the writings of others and almost from second-hand information), seem to have preferred to posit a soul generally spread throughout the body rather than the principle which we are discussing. But in their hypothesis – which was Virgil's and that of all the Epicureans, and which the history of the polyp seems at first sight to support – the movements which survive after the death of the subject in which they are found come from a remnant of the soul, preserved in the parts which contract although they are no longer irritated by the blood and the spirits. From which we can see that these writers, whose solid works easily eclipse all the fables of philosophy, were only mistaken in the same way as those who accorded matter the faculty of thought; I mean that they expressed themselves badly, using obscure and meaningless terms. For what is this remnant of the soul but the Leibnizians' motive force, badly conveyed by such an expression, but which Perrault in particular really had an idea of. See his *Animal Mechanics*.

[47] P. Hecquet had been dean of the Paris Medical Faculty.

[48] H. Boerhaave, *Institutiones rei medicae* (Leiden, 1708) contains several discussions of the heart; see in particular §402–6.

[49] On Willis, see footnote 12. C. Perrault's *De la mécanique des animaux* (1680) in *Essais de physique* (4 vols., Paris, 1680–8), vol. 1, explained life by a soul existing throughout the body.

Now that it has been clearly demonstrated, against the Cartesians, the Stahlians, the Malebranchians and the theologians – who are hardly worthy of being mentioned here – that matter moves by itself not only when it is organised, as in a whole heart for example, but even when that organisation is destroyed, man's curiosity would like to know how a body, by the simple fact of being originally endowed with a breath of life, is as a result graced with the faculty of feeling and even of thought. And to satisfy this curiosity, good God, what efforts have been made by some philosophers and what nonsense I have been patient enough to read on this subject!

All that experience teaches us is that as long as some movement, however little, persists in one or several fibres, they only need to be pricked to awaken and animate this almost extinguished movement, as has been seen from the mass of experiments which I have quoted in order to disprove the various systems. Movement and feeling therefore invariably arouse each other in turn, both in whole bodies and in the same bodies when their structure is destroyed, to say nothing of certain plants which seem to exhibit the same combination of feeling and movement.

But in addition, how many excellent philosophers have demonstrated that thought is only a capacity to feel and that the rational soul is only the sensitive soul applied to the contemplation of ideas and to reasoning! This is proved by the simple fact that when feeling is extinguished, so is thought, as in apoplexy, lethargy, catalepsy, etc. Those who have said that the soul thinks just as much during soporific illnesses, despite not remembering the ideas it has had, have advanced a ridiculous claim.

Concerning this development, it is folly to waste one's time trying to discover its mechanism. The nature of movement is as unknown to us as is the nature of matter. There is no way of discovering how it comes to exist in matter unless, like the author of *The History of the Soul*, we revive the ancient incomprehensible doctrine of substantial forms![50] Hence I am as reconciled to my ignorance about how inert simple matter becomes active and composed of organs, as I am to the fact that I can only look at the sun through a red lens. And I am equally untroubled about the other incomprehensible wonders of nature, about the appearance of feeling and thought in a being who in the past seemed to our limited sight to be nothing but a lump of clay.

Simply admit that organised matter is endowed with a motive principle, which alone distinguishes it from unorganised matter (well, can we refuse to believe the most incontrovertible observations?), and that in animals everything is dictated by the diversity of this organisation, as I have sufficiently proved. That is enough to solve the riddle of substances and of man. We can see that there is only one substance in the universe and that man is the most perfect one. He is to the ape

50 La Mettrie is if course referring to his own *Treatise on the Soul.*

and the cleverest animals what Huygens's planetary clock is to one of Julien Leroy's watches. If it took more instruments, more cogs, more springs to show the movement of the planets than to show or tell the time, if it took Vaucanson[51] more artistry to make his flautist than his duck, he would have needed even more to make a speaking machine, which can no longer be considered impossible, particularly at the hands of a new Prometheus. Thus, in the same way, nature needed more artistry and machinery to construct and maintain a machine which could continue for a whole century to tell all the beats of the heart and the mind; for if we cannot tell the time from the pulse, it is at least the barometer of heat and liveliness, from which we can judge the nature of the soul. I am not mistaken; the human body is a clock but so huge and cleverly constructed that if the cog which tells the seconds happens to stop, the one which tells the minutes goes on turning, in the same way as the cog for the quarters continues to move, and so do the others, when the first ones are rusty or out of order for some reason and stop working. For we know that, in the same way, the obstruction of a few vessels is not enough to destroy or halt the main movement in the heart, which is like the mainspring of the machine. This is because, on the contrary, the fluids, which have diminished in volume, do not have so far to go and cover the distance all the more quickly, as if carried by a new current, because the strength of the heart has increased due to the resistance it meets with at the extremities of the vessels. When the optical nerve alone is compressed and no longer lets through the images of objects, we know that this loss of sight does not prevent the use of hearing, any more than the loss of hearing, when the *portio mollis* cannot work, implies the loss of sight. Again, in the same way we know that one person can hear without being able to say that he can hear (except after his attack is over), while another, who cannot hear but whose lingual nerves are free in the brain, recounts automatically all the dreams that come into his mind. Such phenomena do not surprise enlightened physicians. They know what to expect from man's nature; and, by the way, if we compare two doctors, the best and most trustworthy is always, in my opinion, the one who knows the most about the physics or the mechanics of the human body and who, forgetting the soul and all the worries which this figment of the imagination causes in fools and ignoramuses, concentrates solely on pure naturalism.

So let the so-called Mr Charp make fun of philosophers who have considered animals to be machines.[52] How different is my opinion! I believe that Descartes would have been an admirable man in all respects if he had been born in an age which he did not need to enlighten, and had consequently understood both the

[51] C. Huygens designed a mechanical model of the solar system; J. Leroy was a famous watchmaker, while J. de Vaucanson made ingenious mechanical animals and people.

[52] Another reference to the *Treatise on the Soul*; first published, as *The Natural History of the Soul*, under the pseudonym of Charp. La Mettrie's rejection of Cartesian animal-machines is in ch. VII, p. 52.

value of experiment and observation and the danger of straying from them. But it is just as fair for me to make true amends here to that great man for all those petty philosophers who make bad jokes and ape Locke and who, instead of laughing impudently in Descartes' face, would do better to realise that without him the field of philosophy would perhaps still be waste land, like the field of right thinking without Newton.

It is true that this famous philosopher made many mistakes, as nobody denies; but he understood animal nature and was the first to demonstrate perfectly that animals were mere machines. After such an important discovery which implies so much wisdom, how can we, without ingratitude, not pardon all his errors!

In my opinion they are all repaired by that great admission. For whatever he recounts about the distinction between the two substances, it is obvious that it was only a trick, a cunning device to make the theologians swallow the poison hidden behind an analogy that strikes everyone and that they alone cannot see. For it is precisely that strong analogy which forces all scholars and true judges to admit that, however much those haughty, vain beings – who are more distinguished by their pride than by the name of men – may wish to exalt themselves, they are basically only animals and vertically crawling machines. They all have that wonderful instinct, which education turns into intelligence and which is located in the brain or, failing that, when the brain is missing or ossified, in the medulla oblongata and never in the cerebellum; for I have seen it seriously injured and others[h] have found it tumefied without the soul ceasing to function.

To be a machine and to feel, to think and to be able to distinguish right from wrong, like blue from yellow – in a word to be born with intelligence and a sure instinct for morality and to be only an animal – are thus things which are no more contradictory than to be an ape or a parrot and to be able to give oneself pleasure. For since here we have an opportunity to say so, who would ever have guessed *a priori* that a drop of liquid ejaculated in mating would provoke such divine pleasure and that from it would be born a little creature that one day, given certain laws, would be able to enjoy the same delights? I believe thought to be so little incompatible with organised matter that it seems to be one of its properties, like electricity, motive power, impenetrability, extension, etc.

Do you want any more observations? Here are some which are unanswerable and which all prove that man is exactly like animals both in his origin and in all the points of comparison which we have already deemed to be essential.

I appeal to the good faith of observers. Let them say whether it is untrue that man is originally nothing more than a worm, which becomes a man just as

[h] Haller in the *Philosophical Transactions*.[53]

[53] 'Observatio de scirrho cerebelli', *Philosophical Transactions* (London, 1744).

a caterpillar becomes a butterfly. The most serious[i] authors have told us how to go about seeing this animalcule. All curious observers, like Hartsoeker, have seen it in the man's semen and not in the woman's; only fools have been hesitant.[54] As each drop of sperm contains an infinite number of these little worms, when they are launched towards the ovary, only the most skilful or the sturdiest has the strength to penetrate it and embed itself in the egg provided by the woman, which provides its first food. This egg, sometimes caught in the Fallopian tubes, is carried by these canals to the womb, where it takes root like a grain of wheat in the ground. But although it becomes monstrous during its nine-month growth, it is no different from the eggs of other females except for its skin (the amnion) which never hardens, and dilates enormously, as can be judged if one compares a foetus found in place and ready to hatch (which I had the pleasure of observing in a woman who died just before giving birth) with other little embryos which are very close to their beginnings. For it is always the egg in its shell, and the animal in the egg, which is hampered in its movements and tries automatically to see the light of day; to succeed, it begins by breaking this membrane with its head and then emerges like a chick, a bird, etc. from theirs. Here I shall add an observation that I have seen nowhere else: the fact that the amnion is enormously stretched does not make it any thinner. In this it is like the womb, whose very substance swells up with infiltrated fluids, independently of how far its vascular inflexions are filled up and spread out.

Let us look at man inside and outside his shell, and examine under a miroscope the youngest embryos, four, six, eight or fifteen days old; after this stage we can do it with the naked eye. What can we see? Only the head: a little round egg with two black dots which indicate the eyes. Before that, as everything is more formless, we can see only a medullary pulp, which is the brain, in which are formed first of all the origin of the nerves or the source of feeling and the heart which already, in this pulp, possesses by itself the capacity to beat: this is Malpighi's punctum saliens,[56] which perhaps already owes part of its liveliness to the influence of the nerves. Then we gradually see the head lengthening its neck, which dilates to form first the thorax, into which the heart has already dropped down and settled, and then the belly which is separated off by a dividing wall (the diaphragm). Dilatations create, here the arms, hands, fingers and hairs, there the thighs, legs, feet, etc., the only difference being their position which makes them act to support or balance the body. It constitutes a striking vegetative growth: the hair which covers the tops of our heads corresponds to leaves and flowers elsewhere. In all quarters nature is

i Boerhaave, *Institutions* and many others.[55]

54 N. Hartsoeker, a Dutch physicist, first described spermatozoa in letters to Huygens in 1678. La Mettrie is referring to the debate on reproduction and the roles of the egg and the sperm, to which he returns in *Man as Plant*.

55 Boerhaave, *Institutiones*, §651.

56 The chicken foetus's heart is described by Malpighi in *Dissertatio de formatione pulli in ovo* (London, 1673).

equally luxuriant. Finally the rector spirit [57] in plants is situated in the place where we have our soul, which is man's quintessence.

Such is nature's uniformity that we can begin to feel the analogy between the animal and vegetable kingdoms, between man and plant. Perhaps there are even animal plants; in other words plants that, while vegetating, either fight like polyps or perform other functions specific to animals.

That is more or less all that is known about reproduction. It is possible that those parts which attract each other, which are made to join together and to occupy such and such a place, all join together according to their natures and thus form the eyes, heart, stomach and finally the whole body, as certain great men have written.[58] But as experience abandons us in the middle of such subtleties, I refuse to hypothesise, considering whatever my senses do not perceive to be an impenetrable mystery. It is so rare for the two seminal fluids to meet in intercourse that I am tempted to consider the woman's to be useless for reproduction.

But how is one to explain the phenomena of reproduction without this convenient relationship of the parts, which accounts so well for the fact that children sometimes resemble their father and sometimes their mother? On the other hand, should problems with an explanation outweigh facts? It seems to me that the male does everything, whether the woman is asleep or is most lascivious. The organisation of the different parts of the body can thus be supposed to be fixed for eternity in the man's very seed or worm. But all this is far beyond the reach of even the most excellent observers. As they are not able to see any of this, they can no more judge the mechanism by which bodies are created and develop than a mole can judge the distance that can be covered by a deer.

We are veritable moles in the field of nature; we hardly cover more ground than that animal and it is only our pride that places limits on things that have none. We are like a watch saying (a storyteller would make it an important character in a frivolous work): 'What! Was I made by that stupid workman, I who can divide up time, who can indicate so precisely the sun's course, who can tell out loud the hours which I indicate! No, that is impossible.' In the same way, ungrateful wretches that we are, we despise the common mother of all the kingdoms, to use the language of the chemists. We imagine, or rather assume, a cause higher than the one to which we owe everything and which has truly created everything in an inconceivable way. No, there is nothing vile about matter, except for crude eyes which do not understand its most brilliant productions, and nature is not a worker of limited ability. The ease and pleasure with which she produces millions of men exceed the watchmaker's toil when he creates the most complicated of watches. Her power shines out as clearly in the creation of the meanest insect as in that of the

[57] A chemist's term, used by Boerhaave, to describe the essence or tenuous substance given off by plants in distillation, in *Elementa chymiae* (London, 1732), vol. I, Pt. II.

[58] A reference to the theory P L. M. de Maupertuis developed in his *Vénus physique*, (n.p., 1745); see the further discussion of the question in *Man as Plant*.

most splendid human; she does not expend greater effort on the animal than on the vegetable kingdom, or on the greatest genius than on an ear of corn. We should therefore judge what is hidden from our curious gaze and our research by what we can see, instead of imagining anything more. Observe the behaviour of the ape, the beaver, the elephant, etc. If it is clear that they could not act in that way without intelligence, why should we refuse it to those animals? And if you agree that they have a soul, you fanatics, you are doomed; however much you protest that you have said nothing about its nature and that you deny its immortality, anyone can see that that is an arbitrary statement. It is obvious to anyone that it must be either mortal or immortal, like ours, and must suffer the same fate, whatever that may be; thus you have fallen into Scylla while trying to avoid Charybdis.

Break the chains of your prejudices and take up the torch of experience, and you will honour nature in the way she deserves, instead of drawing derogatory conclusions from the ignorance in which she has left you. Simply open your eyes and ignore what you cannot understand, and you will see that a labourer whose mind and knowledge extend no further than the edges of his furrow is no different essentially from the greatest genius, as would have been proved by dissecting the brains of Descartes and Newton; you will be convinced that the imbecile or the idiot are animals in human form, in the same way as the clever ape is a little man in another form; and that, since everything depends absolutely on differences in organisation, a well-constructed animal who has learnt astronomy can predict an eclipse, as he can predict recovery or death when his genius and good eyesight have benefited from some time at the school of Hippocrates and at patients' bedsides. It is by means of this sequence of observation and truth that we can manage to link to matter the admirable property of thought, even if we cannot see how they are joined together because the subject of this attribute is essentially unknown to us.

We are not claiming that every machine, or every animal, perishes completely or takes on another form after death, for we know absolutely nothing on this subject. But to insist that an immortal machine is a paradox or a *being of reason* is as absurd a deduction as would be that of caterpillars if, on seeing the remains of their fellow caterpillars, they lamented bitterly the fate of their species which was apparently dying out. The souls of these insects (for each animal possesses its own) are too limited to understand nature's metamorphoses. Even the cleverest of them could never have imagined that it was destined to become a butterfly. We are the same. Do we know any more about our fate than about our origin? Let us therefore submit to invincible ignorance, on which our happiness depends.

Whosoever thinks in this way will be wise, just, untroubled about his fate and consequently happy. He will look forward to death without fearing it and without desiring it, cherishing life and scarcely comprehending how disgust can corrupt the heart in this delightful place; his respect for nature, thankfulness, attachment and tenderness will be in proportion to the feelings and the kindness he has received from her; he will be happy to experience her and to attend the enchanting spectacle of the universe, and will certainly never destroy her in himself or in others. What am I saying! He will be full of humanity and will love its imprint even in his enemies. Judge for yourself how he will treat others. He will pity the wicked without hating them; he will consider them as no more than misshapen men. But while pardoning defects in the construction of their minds and bodies, he will still admire just as much what beauty and virtue they possess. Those whom nature has favoured will seem to him more worthy of respect than those whom she has treated like a wicked stepmother. Thus we have seen that natural gifts, which are the root of everything that is acquired, will elicit from a materialist's mouth and heart a homage that is refused by everyone else without due reason. The materialist, convinced, whatever his vanity may object, that he is only a machine or an animal, will not ill-treat his fellows; he is too well informed as to the nature of that behaviour whose inhumanity is always proportionate to the degree of analogy that was demonstrated above. Following the law of nature given to all animals, he does not want to do to others what he would not like others to do to him.

Let us then conclude boldly that man is a machine and that there is in the whole universe only one diversely modified substance. This is not at all a hypothesis built up using questions and assumptions; it is not the work of prejudice or even of my reason alone. I would have disdained a guide that I consider to be so uncertain if my senses, carrying the torch, so to speak, had not encouraged me to follow reason by lighting its path. Experience thus spoke to me in reason's favour and so I applied them together.

But it must have been clear that I have only allowed myself the most rigorous and tightest reasoning, after a multitude of physical observations that no scholar can question. Scholars are also the only ones whom I allow to judge the consequences which I draw from these observations, for I reject here all prejudiced men who are neither anatomists nor versed in the only philosophy that is relevant here, that of the human body. What could the weak reeds of theology, metaphysics and the schools do against such a firm and solid oak, for they are childish weapons, like practice foils, which can give pleasure in fencing but can never wound an opponent. Do I need to explain that I am speaking of those empty, trivial ideas and that overused, pathetic reasoning concerning the so-called incompatibility of two substances that incessantly touch and move each other, which will be developed as long as there remains the shadow of a prejudice or superstition on earth? Here is my system, or rather the truth, unless I am very much mistaken. It is short and simple. Now if anyone wants to argue, let them!

Treatise on the Soul

Note on the text

The first printed version of this work was called the *Natural History of the Soul*, and indicated on the title page that it was translated from the English of 'Mr Charp' and that it was published by Jean Néaulme at the Hague. In fact it was printed clandestinely in Paris by David in June 1745, and most of the edition was seized. Another edition appeared, still as a translation from a work by 'Charp', in 1747, with the false address of Oxford. This edition was prefaced by a *Critical Letter by M. de La Mettrie* addressed to Madame du Châtelet. When La Mettrie revised the work extensively for publication in his *Philosophical Works* in 1750, where it was the second 'Mémoire' contributing to the natural history of man, he renamed the work the *Treatise on the Soul* (*Traité de l'âme*) which probably indicates his realisation that it was nearer to a philosophical treatise than any of his other essays; he attached to it an *Abrégé des systèmes pour faciliter l'intelligence du Traité de l'âme* (*Abstract of Philosophical Systems to Facilitate an Understanding of the Treatise on the Soul*). It is part of this *Treatise*, which is reproduced in all of the editions of La Mettrie's *Philosophical Works* and is the basis for Verbeek's critical edition, that is translated here.

Chapter I
Presentation of the work

Neither Aristotle, nor Plato, nor Descartes, nor Malebranche will teach you what your soul is. You will torture yourself in vain to learn its nature and, however much it affronts your vanity and insubordination, you will have to submit to ignorance and faith. The essence of the soul of man and animals is, and will always be, as mysterious as the essence of matter and bodies. I would go even further and say that the soul separated from the body by abstraction is like matter considered without any form. It cannot be conceived. The soul and the body were created together in the same instant and as if at a single brush stroke. They were thrown into the same mould, says a great theologian[a] who dared to think. He who would learn the properties of the soul must first seek those which clearly show themselves in the body, whose active principle the soul is.

This reflection leads naturally to the thought that there are no surer guides than the senses. They are my philosophers. However much one may criticise them, they alone can enlighten reason in the search for truth. Yes, it is to them alone that we must always return when we seriously wish to discover the truth.

So let us see, with both good faith and impartiality, what our senses can discover in matter and in the substance of bodies, especially organised bodies. But let us only see what is there and not imagine anything. Matter is in itself a passive principle; it has only a force of inertia. That is why each time that we see it move we can conclude that its movement comes from another principle, which a sound mind will never confuse with what contains it – I mean with the matter or substance of bodies – because the idea of the one and the idea of the other are two intellectual ideas that are as different as active and passive. Thus if there is a motive principle in bodies and if it is proved that the same principle which makes the heart beat also makes the nerves feel and the brain think, then surely it will clearly follow that this

[a] Tertullian, *On the Resurrection of the Flesh.*[1]

[1] *De resurrectio carnis*, §45.

is the principle to which we give the name of soul? It has been proved that the human body is at its origin only a worm, all of whose metamorphoses are no more surprising than those of any other insect. Why should one not be allowed to try to discover the nature or the properties of the unknown but obviously sensitive and active principle which makes this worm crawl conceitedly over the earth's surface? Surely truth was created for man more than the happiness to which he aspires. Or are we so avid and, as it were, so much in love with happiness only in order to embrace a cloud instead of a goddess, as the poets said about Ixion?[2]

Chapter II
On matter

All those philosophers who have attentively examined the nature of matter, considered in itself and independently of all the forms that constitute bodies, have discovered in this substance different properties which derive from an absolutely unknown essence. Such as: (1) the power of receiving different forms which are exhibited in matter itself and by means of which matter can acquire motive force and the faculty of feeling; (2) actual extension, which they have recognised as an attribute but not as the essence of matter.

There have however been some, including Descartes, who wished to reduce the essence of matter to simple extension and limit all the properties of matter to those of extension,[3] but this opinion was rejected by all the other Moderns, who paid more attention to all the properties of this substance; so that the power to acquire motive force and the faculty of feeling has in all ages been considered, like extension, as an essential property of matter.

All the different properties which can be observed in this unknown principle demonstrate an entity in which these same properties exist, an entity which consequently must exist of itself. But one cannot conceive, or rather it appears impossible, that an entity which exists by itself can either create itself or annihilate itself. It is obvious that it is only the forms to which its essential properties make it susceptible that can destroy and reproduce themselves in turn. Thus experience forces us to admit that nothing is made from nothing.

All those philosophers who did not know the light of faith thought that this substantial principle of bodies had always existed and would always exist, and that the elements of matter possessed an indestructible solidity which did not allow us to fear that the world might ever crumble. Most Christian philosophers also recognise that it necessarily exists of itself and that, by its nature, it is incapable of

2 See p. 22, note 28.
3 See the Fifth *Meditation* and *Principles of Philosophy*, I. 4.

having begun or of ending, as we can see in an author of the last century who taught[b] theology in Paris.

Chapter III
On the extension of matter[5]

Although we have no idea of the essence of matter, we cannot refuse our consent to the properties which our senses discover in it.

I open my eyes and I see about me only matter or extension. Extension is thus a property which is always appropriate to all matter, which is only appropriate to it alone and which is thus co-essential with its subject.

This property supposes three dimensions in the substance of bodies: length, breadth and depth. And indeed, if we consult our knowledge, which all comes from our senses, we cannot conceive of matter, or the substance of bodies, without the idea of an entity which is at once long, wide and deep, because the idea of these three dimensions is necessarily linked to the one we have of all size or quantity.

Those philosophers who have reflected most about matter do not understand by the extension of this substance a solid extension, formed of distinct parts and capable of resistance. Nothing is united and nothing is divided in this substance, for to divide one needs a force to disunite, and a force is also needed to unite the divided parts. But according to these physicists, matter has no actually active force, because all force can only come from movement or from some effort or attempt at movement, and they only recognise in matter deprived by abstraction of all forms a potential motive force.[6]

This theory is difficult to conceive but, once the principles have been laid down, it is rigorously true in its consequences. These truths are like algebraic truths, which we know to be certain but which our minds cannot grasp.

The extension of matter is thus only a metaphysical extension which has nothing perceptible about it, according to the idea of the same philosophers. They rightly think that only solid extension can strike our senses.

It thus seems to us that extension is an essential attribute of matter, and one

[b] Goudin, *Philosophy according to the Teaching of Saint Thomas.*[4]

[4] Antoine Goudin's *Philosophia juxta inconcussa tutissimaque Divi Thomæ Dogmata* (Leiden, 1678) seems to be La Mettrie's main source for Scholastic philosophy. In this discussion, La Mettrie mixes elements from Spinozism, Scholastic philosophy and Lucretian principles, to show the eternity of matter.

[5] A large part of this chapter and the following one is taken or adapted from Madame du Châtelet's *Institutions physiques* (Paris, 1740), but with the addition of elements taken from the Scholastic or Gassendist traditions.

[6] La Mettrie here seems to be referring to the Leibnizians, but using the explanations provided by Mme du Châtelet.

which is part of its metaphysical form; but we are far from believing that solid extension constitutes its essence.

Yet before Descartes some ancient philosophers made the essence of matter consist in solid extension. But this opinion, which the Cartesians have so much emphasised, has been victoriously combated in all ages by means of obvious reasons that we shall expound below. For to follow an orderly plan, we must first examine to what the properties of extension can be reduced.

Chapter IV
On the passive mechanical properties of matter which depend on extension

What is called form in general consists in the different states or the different modifications of which matter is capable. These modifications receive being, or their existence, from matter itself, in the same way as the imprint of a seal receives it from the wax which it modifies. They all constitute different states of this substance, and it is by means of them that it assumes all the different forms of bodies and that it constitutes these bodies themselves.

We shall not examine here what the nature of this principle can be, considered separately from its extension and from any other form. It is enough to admit that it is unknown; thus it is pointless to try to discover whether matter can exist deprived of all these forms, without which we cannot conceive of it. Those who like frivolous disputes can, following in the footsteps of the Scholastics, continue with the questions that can be posed on this subject; as for us, we shall only teach what must be precisely known concerning the doctrine of forms.

There are two types of form, active and passive. In this chapter, I shall discuss only the latter. They number four, that is to say size, shape, rest and position. These forms are simple states, passive dependencies on matter, modes which can never abandon it nor destroy its simplicity.

The Ancients believed, not without reason, that these passive mechanical forms of matter had no source other than extension; they were convinced that matter contained potentially all these forms within itself, by the very fact that what is extended – a being endowed with the dimensions we have mentioned – can obviously receive such and such a size, shape, position, etc.

These are then the passive mechanical forms potentially contained in matter and absolutely dependent on the three dimensions of matter and on their different combinations. And it is in this sense that we can say that matter, considered simply in its extension, is itself only a passive principle. But this simple extension, which makes it capable of receiving an infinite number of forms, does not allow it to receive any without its own motive force. For it is matter already possessing forms, by means of which it has received motive power or actual movement, which procures for itself successively all the different forms which it receives. Following the same idea, if matter is the mother of forms, as Aristotle says,[7] it is only thanks to its marriage or its union with motive power itself.

That given, if matter is sometimes forced to take on one particular form and not another, it cannot come from its too inert nature or from its passive mechanical forms which depend on extension, but from a new form which deserves here a pre-eminent rank because it plays the greatest role in nature. This is the active form, or motive power, the form, I repeat, by means of which matter displays those forms it receives.

But before mentioning this motive principle, may I be allowed to indicate in passing that matter considered solely as a passive entity seems to deserve nothing more than the mere name of matter, to which it was formerly restricted, and that matter seen as absolutely inseparable from extension, impenetrability, divisibility and the other passive mechanical forms was not considered by the Ancients to be the same thing as what we today call substance. Far from confusing the two terms as the Moderns do, they took matter simply as an attribute or part of that substance, so constituted or raised to the dignity of body by the motive power which I am now going to discuss.

Chapter V
On the motive power of matter

The Ancients, who were persuaded that no bodies could exist without a motive force, considered the substance of bodies to be made up of two primitive attributes: by one, this substance had the power to move, and by the other, the power to be moved. Indeed, in any moving body it is impossible not to conceive of these two attributes, namely the thing which moves and the same thing which is moved.

We have just said that the name 'matter' used to be given to the substance of bodies inasmuch as it was susceptible of movement; when this same matter had become capable of moving, it was considered under the name of 'active principle', which was then given to the same substance. But these two attributes seem so essentially dependent on one another that, in order to express better this essential, primitive union of matter with its motive principle, Cicero[c] said that they both exist in each other, which very well expresses the idea of the Ancients.

From which we can understand that the Moderns have only given us an inexact

[c] *Academic Philosophy*, Book I.[8]

[7] La Mettrie could have found this idea in P. Barbay's commentary on Aristotle's *Physics*, *Commentarius in Aristotelis Physicam* (Paris, 1675), which refers the reader to *De coelo*.

[8] La Mettrie provides in his note the Latin quotation: 'In utroque tandem utrumque' (*Academicarum quaestionum*, I, vi.24).

idea of matter when they wanted, due to a misunderstood confusion, to give this name to the substance of bodies; for, once again, matter or the passive principle of the substance of bodies, is only part of this substance. Thus it is not surprising that they did not discover motive force and the faculty of feeling.

We should now, I believe, be able to see at a glance that if an active principle exists, it must have a source in the unknown essence of matter other than extension; which confirms that simple extension does not give a complete idea of the whole essence, or metaphysical form, of the substance of bodies, for the simple reason that it excludes the idea of any activity in matter. That is why, if we demonstrate the existence of this motive principle and if we show that matter, far from being as indifferent to movement and rest as is commonly believed, must be regarded as an active as well as a passive substance, then what argument will be left to those for whom its essence is extension?

The two principles about which we have just spoken – extension and motive force – are only powers of the substance of bodies. For in the same way as this substance is susceptible of movement without actually having any, so it always has, even when it is not moving, the faculty to move.

The Ancients really noticed that this motive force only acted in the substance of bodies when this substance possessed certain forms. They also observed that the different movements which it produced were all subject to, or controlled by, these different forms. That is why the forms by means of which the substance of bodies could not only move but did move in different ways were called 'material forms'.[9]

It was enough for these first masters to glance at all the phenomena of nature to discover in the substance of bodies the force to move itself. For either this substance moves by itself or, when it is in movement, this movement is given by another substance. But can we see in this substance anything other than itself in action? And if it sometimes seems to receive a movement which it does not possess, does it receive it from any cause other than this same type of substance whose parts are acting one upon another?

Thus if we suppose the existence of another agent, I would like to know what it is and to be given proofs of its existence; but since we have not the slightest idea of it, it is not even a 'being of reason'.[10]

Hence it is clear that the Ancients must have easily recognised an intrinsic force of movement within the substance of bodies, since one can neither prove nor conceive of any other substance acting on it.

But these same authors admitted, or rather proved, at the same time that it was impossible to understand how this mystery of nature could work, because we know nothing about the essence of bodies. If we do not know the agent, how could we ever know the way it acts? And surely the difficulty would remain the same if we

[9] La Mettrie is not in fact using this expression in its Scholastic sense, but in the sense of Mme du Châtelet, to denote extension and the force of inertia.

[10] On this expression, see p. 24, note 33.

admitted another substance, mainly a being of which we have no idea and whose existence we could not even reasonably recognise.

It is also not without justification that they thought that the substance of bodies considered without any form had no existence but that it was 'all in potentiality'.[11] Could the human body, for example, deprived of its specific form, execute the movements which depend on it? In the same way, could the matter which makes up all the parts of the universe produce all the different phenomena which strike our senses without the order and arrangement of these parts?

But the parts of this substance which receive forms cannot give them to themselves; it is always other parts of this same substance, already possessing forms, which provide them. Thus the forms by which the motive force of bodies becomes actually active arise from the action of these parts when pressed against one another.

In my opinion we should reduce to heat and cold, as did the Ancients, the forms which produce other forms; because it is in fact by means of these two active general qualities that all sublunary bodies are, in all likelihood, produced.

Descartes, that genius made to open up new paths and to lose his way, claimed, together with some other philosophers, that God was the sole efficient cause of movement and that he impressed it on all bodies at every moment. But this opinion was only a hypothesis which he tried to accommodate to the light of faith, in which case one is no longer speaking as a philosopher or to philosophers, in particular to those who can be convinced only by the force of evidence.

Christian Scholastics in recent centuries realised very well the importance of this simple reflection, which is why they wisely limited themselves to purely philosophical knowledge concerning the movement of matter, although they could have shown that God himself said that he had 'impressed an active principle on the elements of matter' (Genesis I, Isaiah 66).[12]

It would be possible to develop here a long chain of authorities and take from the most famous professors the essence of the doctrine of all the others. But without a jumble of quotations, it is clear enough that matter contains the motive force which animates it and which is the immediate cause of all the laws of movement.

Chapter VI
On the sensitive faculty of matter

We have spoken of two essential attributes of matter, on which most of its properties depend, namely extension and motive force. Now we only have to prove

11 La Mettrie here gives, in a note, the expression 'totum in fieri', whose source I, like Verbeek, have been unable to locate.

12 This reference is obscure as it does not, despite the quotation marks, reproduce the biblical text. La Mettrie has taken the references from Barbay and Goudin while omitting their quotations.

a third attribute, by which I mean the faculty of feeling, which philosophers[d] of all ages have recognised in the same substance. I say all philosophers, although I am aware of all the efforts vainly made by the Cartesians to take it away from matter. But in order to remove insuperable difficulties they plunged into a labyrinth from which they thought they could extricate themselves with the absurd system 'that animals are mere machines'.

Such a ridiculous opinion has never been accepted by philosophers except as a joke or a philosophical amusement,[13] which is why we shall not stop to refute it. Experience proves that the faculty of feeling exists in animals just as much as it does in men. Besides myself, who am perfectly sure that I feel, I have no proof of feeling in other men beyond the signs of it that they give me. Conventional language, by which I mean speech, is not the sign which best expresses it.[14] There is another, common to men and animals, which shows it more certainly; I am speaking of the language of feeling, such as moans, cries, caresses, flight, sighs, song, in a word all the expressions of pain, sadness, aversion, fear, daring, submission, anger, pleasure, joy, tenderness, etc. Such energetic language has much greater power to convince us than all of Descartes' sophistry has to persuade us.

Perhaps the Cartesians, as they cannot ignore their own intimate feelings, believe that they are more justified in recognising the same faculty of feeling in all men than in the other animals because the latter do not indeed have an exactly human appearance. But those philosophers, satisfying themselves thus with the surface of things, seem to have paid very little attention to the perfect resemblance, which strikes the well-informed, between man and beast; for here it is only a question of the similarities between sense organs which, a few modifications apart, are completely the same and obviously indicate the same uses.

While this parallel was not seized by Descartes or his followers, it did not escape the attention of other philosophers and, above all, of those who applied themselves with curiosity to comparative anatomy.[16]

Here there is another difficulty, which concerns more our self-esteem; it is our incapacity to conceive of this property as a dependency or attribute of matter. But we should pay attention to the fact that this substance only gives us glimpses of inexpressible things. Do we understand any better how extension derives from its essence, how it can be moved by a primitive force whose action works without any contact, and a thousand other marvels which hide so well from the investigations of

d See the thesis which Mr Leibniz defended for Prince Eugene and *The Ancient Origins of Modern Physics*, by Father Regnault.[15]

13 Probably a reference to Bougeant's *Amusement philosophique sur le langage des bêtes* (Paris, 1739).

14 This refers to Descartes' argument in the *Discourse on Method*, Pt. v.

15 See Leibniz, *Principes de la nature et de la grâce* (1718), §4 and N. Regnault, *L'Origine ancienne de la physique nouvelle* (Paris, 1734).

16 Particularly the school of Boerhaave.

the most piercing gaze that they only reveal the screen which hides them, to adopt the idea of a distinguished Modern.[e17]

But could we not suppose, as some have done, that the feeling which we observe in animate bodies belongs to an entity distinct from the matter of those bodies, a substance of a different nature, which happens to be united with them? Does the light of reason allow us to admit in good faith such conjectures? In bodies, we have knowledge only of matter and we observe the faculty of feeling only in these bodies; on what basis should we then set up an ideal being, disproved by all our knowledge?

We must nevertheless admit equally frankly that we do not know whether matter has in itself the immediate faculty of feeling or only the power of acquiring it through the modification or forms of which it is susceptible. For it is true that this faculty only appears in organised bodies.[18]

Here then is yet another faculty which likewise seems to inhere in matter only potentially, like all the others we have mentioned; and this was again the opinion of the Ancients whose philosophy, full of insight and penetration, deserves to be raised on the ruins of that of the Moderns. However much the latter scorn sources which are too distant from them, ancient philosophy[f] will always prevail for those who are worthy of judging it, because it constitutes (at least in relation to the subject I am treating) a solid, well co-ordinated system and a sort of body which all the disparate limbs of modern physics lack.[19]

Chapter VII
On substantial forms

We have seen that matter is mobile, that it has the power to move by itself and that it is susceptible of sensation and feeling. But it does not seem, at least if we judge from experience, the great master of philosophers, that these properties can be exercised until the substance is, so to speak, clothed in certain forms which give it the faculty of moving and feeling. That is why the Ancients considered forms to be part of the reality of bodies and that is the reason why they called them 'substantial forms'.[g] Indeed, matter considered in the abstract, or separately from any form, is

e Leibniz.

f Metaphysics.

g Goudin, II, pp. 94, 98.

17 La Mettrie has taken the expression concerning Leibniz from A. F. Boureau-Deslandes, *Histoire critique de la philosophie* (3 vols., Amsterdam, 1737), vol. 2, pp. 246–7.

18 This remained a problem for La Mettrie, as for Diderot; in *Machine Man* (pp. 26ff.) he prudently only talks of feeling in organised bodies.

19 La Mettrie comes down firmly on the side of the Ancients in the current dispute between the Ancients and Moderns, discussed at much greater length when La Mettrie comes, later in the *Treatise*, to literary questions.

an incomplete entity, according to the language of the Schools, a being which does not exist in that state and with which at least the senses and reason have no contact. It is thus truly the forms which make it perceptible and, so to speak, make it real. Hence although, rigorously speaking, they are not substances but mere modifications, it was right to call them substantial forms because they perfect the substance of bodies and are in a way part of them.

In any case, provided that the ideas are clearly exposed, we shall not bother to reform words which are hallowed by use and cannot mislead when they are defined and clearly understood.

The Ancients[20] gave the name of substantial forms only to those modifications which essentially constituted bodies and gave to each those decisive characteristics which distinguished them from one another. Those modifications which came about by accident and whose destruction did not necessarily lead to the destruction of the forms which constituted the nature of the bodies were called only 'accidental' forms; such is the local movement of the human body, which can cease without altering the integrity of its organisation.

Substantial forms are divided into simple and compound. Simple forms are those which modify parts of matter, such as size, shape, movement, rest and position; and the parts of matter possessing these forms are what are called 'simple bodies' or 'elements'. Compound forms consist in an assemblage of simple bodies, united and arranged in the order and quantity necessary to construct or form the different mixtures.

The same philosophers of antiquity also distinguished in a way two sorts of substantial forms in living bodies, namely those which constitute the organic parts of these bodies and those which are considered to be their principle of life. The name 'soul' was given to the latter. They distinguished three types: the vegetative soul, which belongs to plants; the sensitive soul, common to man and beast; but since man's seems to have more power, more extensive functions and grander perceptions, they called it the 'rational soul'. We shall say a word about the vegetative soul, but first may I be permitted to reply to an objection which was made to me by a clever man. 'You do not admit', he said, 'as the principle of feeling in animals any substance other than matter; why then treat Cartesianism as absurd for supposing that animals are pure machines, and what such great difference is there between these two opinions?' I reply in a single word: Descartes refused all feeling, all faculty of sensation, to his machines or to the matter which, he supposed, alone composed animals, while I prove clearly, unless I am very much mistaken, that if there is a being, so to speak, steeped in feeling, it is the animal. Animals seem to have been paid completely in this coin, which (in another sense) so many men lack. That is the difference between the famous Modern I have just mentioned and the author of this work.

[20] In what follows, La Mettrie appears to be relying on Barbay's commentary of Aristotle.

Chapter VIII
On the vegetative soul

We have said that those forms which produce all bodies' forms must be equated to cold and heat. An excellent commentary on this doctrine of the Ancients has been published by Mr Quesnay; that clever man demonstrates it by all the research and all the experiments of modern physics, ingeniously gathered together in a *Treatise on Fire*, in which ether, subtly revived, plays the main role in the formation of bodies.[21] Doctor Lamy did not think he had to limit thus the influence of ether; he explains the formation of the souls of all bodies by this same cause. Ether is an infinitely subtle spirit, a very fine matter which is always in motion, known by the name of pure celestial flame because the Ancients placed its source in the sun, from which, according to them, it is projected into all bodies to a greater or lesser extent according to their nature and consistency. And

> although of itself it does not burn, it burns and gives out heat thanks to the different movements which it communicates to the parts of the bodies in which it is enclosed. All parts of the world have some portion of this elementary flame, which several Ancients considered to be the soul of the world. Visible fire has a lot of this spirit and so does air; water has much less and earth has very little. Of the mixtures, the minerals have less of it, the plants more and the animals much more. This fire or spirit is their soul, which increases with the body by means of the food which contains it and from which it is separated with the chyle so that it becomes capable of feeling, thanks to a certain mixture of humours and that particular structure of organs which form animate bodies. For animals, minerals and even plants, as well as the bones which are the basis of our bodies, have no feeling although they each have a portion of that ether, because they do not possess the same organisation.[22]

By vegetative soul, the Ancients meant the cause which directs all the operations of generation, nutrition and growth, in all living bodies.

The Moderns, who paid little attention to the idea that these first masters had of this type of soul, confused it with the very organisation of vegetables and animals, whereas it is the cause which guides and directs this organisation.

Indeed, one cannot conceive of the formation of living bodies without a cause presiding over them, without a principle regulating and leading everything to a fixed end, whether this principle consists in general laws by which all the

[21] See the second edition of F. Quesnay's *Essai physique sur l'économie animale* (Paris, 1747), in which a commentary on theories of fire has been added.

[22] An adapted extract from Guillaume Lamy's *Discours anatomiques* (Paris, 1679), Sixth Discourse, pp. 227–9, included in the *Traité des trois imposteurs*. See Introduction, p. xii.

mechanism and actions of these bodies work,[h] or is limited to particular laws, originally residing or included in the seed of these very bodies, by which all its functions are executed during their growth and existence.

The philosophers I am discussing did not look beyond the properties of matter in order to establish these principles. This substance, to which they attributed the faculty of moving by itself, also had the power to guide itself in its movements, the one being unable to subsist without the other; since we conceive clearly that the same force must be both the principle of these movements and the principle of this determination, which constitute two absolutely individual and inseparable things. This is why they considered the vegetative soul to be a purely material substantial form, despite the sort of intelligence of which they imagined it was not bereft.

Chapter IX
On the sensitive soul of animals

The material principle or substantial form which feels, discerns and knows in animals was generally called the 'sensitive soul' by the Ancients. This principle must be carefully distinguished from the organic bodies of animals and from the operations of these bodies, which they attributed to the vegetative soul, as we have just observed. Yet it is the very organs of these animate bodies which provide this sensitive being with the sensations which affect it.

The name 'senses' has been given to the organs which are particularly destined to arouse these feelings in the soul. Physicians divide them into external and internal senses, but here we are only concerned with the former which, as everyone knows, number five: sight, hearing, smell, taste and touch, whose realm covers a large number of sensations, which are all forms of touching.

These organs work by means of the nerves and of a matter which flows within their imperceptible cavity, so tenuous that it has been called the animal spirit; its existence has been so well demonstrated elsewhere by a host of experiments and solid reasoning that I shall not waste time here in proving it.[24]

When the sense organs are struck by some object, the nerves which enter into the structure of these organs are agitated and the modified movement of the spirits is transmitted to the brain as far as the sensorium, i.e. as far as the very spot where

h Boerhaave, *Elements of Chemistry*, pp. 35, 36; *Abstract of his Chemical Theory*, pp. 6, 7.[23]

23 Incorrect references; it could be Boerhaave, *Elementa chymiae* (Leiden, 1732), probably vol. 1, pp. 3 or 70–1; La Mettrie, *Abrégé de la théorie chimique de la terre, tirée des propres écrits de M. Hermann Boerhaave* (Paris, 1741), probably p. 13.

24 See in particular Boerhaave's *Institutiones rei medicae* and Haller's edition of them, the *Praelectiones academicae* (7 vols., Göttingen, 1739–44), from which much of what follows in this and the next chapter is taken.

the sensitive soul receives the sensations thanks to this flow of spirits, which act on it by their movement.

If the impression of a body on a sensitive nerve is strong and profound, if it stretches, tears, burns or breaks it, the result on the soul is a sensation which is no longer simple but painful; and likewise if the organ is too feebly affected, there is no sensation. Thus, in order for the senses to fulfil their functions, the objects must impress a movement in proportion to the weak or strong nature of the sensitive organ.

Thus there is no sensation without some change in the organ which is destined for it, or rather only in the surface of that organ's nerve. Can this change come about by the intromission of the body which is felt? No; the hard envelopes of the nerves obviously make this impossible. The change is only produced by the different properties of sensitive bodies, and this is where the different types of feeling come from.

Many experiments have taught us that it is actually in the brain that the soul is affected by the sensations specific to animals. For when this part is seriously wounded, the animal no longer possesses feeling, discernment or knowledge. All the parts which are above the wounds and ligatures conserve, between themselves and the brain, movement and feeling, which are lost lower down, between the ligature and the extremity. Section or corruption of the nerves and the brain, even the compression of this part, etc., taught Galen the same truth. Thus that scholar knew perfectly well the seat of the soul and the absolute need for nerves for sensation; he knew (1) that the soul feels and is really only affected in the brain by those feelings specific to animals; (2) that the soul only possesses feeling and knowledge as long as it is receiving the impression of the animal spirits.[25]

We shall not give here the opinions of Aristotle, Chrysippus, Plato, Descartes, Vieussens, Rosettus, Willis, Lancisi, etc.[26] One should always go back to Galen, as to truth itself. Hippocrates also seems to have been aware of the place in which the soul resides.

Yet most ancient philosophers, led by the Stoics, and Perrault, Stuart and Tabor[27] among the Moderns, thought that the soul felt in all parts of the body because they all have nerves. But we have no proof of such universally disseminated sensibility. Experience even teaches us that when a part of the body is cut off, the soul still has sensations, which seem to be given to it by that part of the body which no longer exists. Thus the soul does not feel in the precise place where it believes it

[25] See Galen, *De Hippocratis et Platonis decretis*, quoted in Haller's *Praelectiones*, §568, as are most of the other authors mentioned in the next paragraph.

[26] J. T. Rosettus, *Systema novum mechanico-hippocraticum de morbis fluidorum et solidorum* (Venice, 1734). R. Vieussens wrote *Neurographie universalis* (The Hague, 1684). On Willis and Lancisi, see p. 10, notes 11 and 12.

[27] Perrault, *De la mécanique des animaux* (see what La Mettrie says about him in *Machine Man*, p. 32); A. Stuart, *Dissertatio de structura et motu musculari* (The Hague, 1738); J. Tabor, *Exercitationes medicae* (1724).

does. Its mistake consists in the way in which it feels, which makes it attribute its own feeling to the organs which occasion it and warn it, as it were, of the impression which they themselves receive from external causes. Yet we cannot affirm that the substance of these organs is not itself susceptible of feeling and does not actually feel. But these modifications could only be known by that substance itself and not by the whole, i.e. by the animal, to which they do not belong and are not at all useful.

As the doubts we can have on this subject are based only on conjecture, we shall pay attention only to what experience, which alone should guide us, teaches us about the sensations which the soul receives in animate bodies.

Many authors place the seat of the soul almost in a single point in the brain, and in a single point in the corpus callosum, from which, as from a throne, it governs all the parts of the body.

Having thus limited the sensitive being and restricted it within such narrow limits, they distinguish it: (1) from all animate bodies, whose different organs only contribute to providing it with sensations; (2) from the spirits themselves, which touch, move and penetrate it by the differing force of their contact with it, and make it feel in such different ways.

To make their idea clearer, they compare the soul to the mainspring in a watch, because indeed in a way the soul is in the body what the mainspring is in a watch. The whole body of that machine, its springs and cogs are only instruments which, by their movements, all contribute together to the regularity of the hammer's action on the mainspring, which is, as it were, waiting for that action and only receives it. For when the hammer does not strike the mainspring, it is as if isolated from the whole body of the watch and in no way participates in any of its movements.

Such is the soul during a deep sleep. Deprived of all feeling, with absolutely no knowledge of whatever is happening outside and inside the body it inhabits, it seems to be waiting for its awakening in order to receive, as it were, the hammer stroke of the spirits on its mainspring. For indeed it is only when it is awake that it is affected by different sensations, which inform it of the nature of the impressions which external bodies communicate to its organs.

It does not matter for our system whether the soul occupies only a point in the brain or whether its seat is more extended. It is certain that to judge from heat, damp, astringency, pain, etc., which all the nerves feel equally, one would think that they must all be intimately joined together in order to form this sort of meeting-place of all the feelings. Yet we shall see that the nerves do not come together in any one place in the brain, the cerebellum or the medulla oblongata.

However that may be, once we have properly established the principles which we have laid down, it should be clear that all knowledge, even the most usual and familiar to the soul, resides in it only at the very instant when it is affected by it. The habitual character of this knowledge consists only in the permanent modifications of the movement of the spirits, which present the modifications to the soul or rather provide them very frequently. From which it follows that the frequent repetition of the same movements is what constitutes memory, imagination, inclinations, passions and all the other faculties which put order into our ideas and sustain it, and render sensations more or less strong and widespread. It is also the source of penetration, conception, accuracy and the association of knowledge, all according to the degree of excellence or perfection of different animals' organs.

Chapter X
On the faculties of the body which can be attributed to the sensitive soul

Philosophers have attributed to the sensitive soul all those faculties which are used to incite sensation in it. Yet we must carefully distinguish those faculties which are purely mechanical from those which truly belong to the sensitive being. That is why we shall reduce them to two classes.

The faculties of the body which provide sensations are those which depend on the sense organs and solely on the movement of the spirits contained in the nerves of these organs, and on the modifications of these movements. Such are the diverse movements of the spirits excited in the nerves of different organs, which give rise to the diverse sensations which depend on each of them, in the very instant when they are struck or affected by external objects. Here we can include the habitual modifications of these same movements, which necessarily recall those same sensations which the soul has already received from the impression of the objects on the senses. These often-repeated modifications form the memory, the imagination and the passions.

But there are others, just as ordinary and habitual, which do not come from the same source but originally depend on the diverse organic dispositions of animate bodies, forming the inclinations, appetites, penetration, instinct and conception.

The second class includes the faculties which properly belong to the sensitive being, like sensations, perceptions, discernment, knowledge, etc.[28]

§I. On the senses

The diversity of sensations varies according to the nature of the organs which transmit them to the soul. Hearing carries to the soul the sensation of noise or sound; sight impresses on it the feelings of light and colours, which represent the image of the objects which come before one's eyes; the soul receives from the sense of smell all the sensations known as odours, while savours come to it thanks to the taste. Finally touch, a sense which is universally spread over the whole of the body's constitution, gives rise to feelings of all the qualities called 'tactile', such as

[28] Discussed in ch. XI.

heat, cold, hardness, softness, smoothness, roughness, pain and pleasure, which depend on the different organs of touch, among which we include the reproductive organs, whose vivid feeling penetrates and transports the soul into the sweetest and happiest moments of our existence.

Since the optic and the auditory nerves are the only ones which, respectively, see colours and hear sounds, since the motor nerves alone carry the idea of movements to the soul and we only perceive odours thanks to the sense of smell, etc., it follows that each nerve is apt to give rise to different sensations; thus the sensorium has, so to speak, different territories, each of which has its own nerve and receives and houses the ideas brought by this tube. Yet one must not place the cause of the diversity of sensations in the nerves themselves, for the enlargement of the auditory nerve resembles the retina, and yet completely opposed sensations result. This variety seems clearly to depend on that of the organs placed before the nerves, so that a dioptric organ, for example, must naturally be used for vision.

Not only do the different senses excite different sensations, but in addition each one also introduces an infinite variety into the sensations which it carries to the soul, according to the different ways in which they are affected by external bodies. That is why the sensation of noise can be modified by a multitude of different tones and can make the soul perceive the distance and location of the cause producing this sensation. In the same way, the eyes, by modifying the light, can provide more or less bright sensations of light and colours and, by these different modifications, form the ideas of extension, shape, distance, etc. Everything we have just said is exactly true of the other senses.

§II. Mechanism of the sensations

Let us try, with the help of the eye, to penetrate inside the subtlest mechanism of the sensations. As the eye is the only one of all the sensitive organs in which the actions of exterior objects is visibly painted and represented, it alone can help us to conceive what sort of change these objects work on the nerves which are struck by them. Take an ox's eye, carefully remove its sclerotic and choroid and, in the place of the first of these membranes, put a piece of paper whose concavity fits exactly the eye's convexity. Then put any object at all in front of the hole of the pupil and you will see very clearly the image of this object at the back of the eye. From which I infer, by the way, that the seat of vision is not in the choroid but in the retina.

What does the depiction of objects consist in? In a proportionally reduced trace of the light rays given off by these objects. This trace creates an impression of the greatest delicacy, as can easily be judged from all the rays of the full moon which, when concentrated in the focus of a burning mirror and reflected onto the most sensitive of thermometers, do not make the instrument's mercury rise at all. If, in addition, one considers that there are as many fibres in this enlargement of the optic nerve as there are points in the image of the object, and that these fibres are infinitely soft and tender and form little more than a veritable pulp or nerve substance, one will understand not only that each little fibre carries only a tiny portion of the rays but, in addition, that due to its extreme delicacy it will undergo only a simple, light, weak or very superficial change. As a result the animal spirits will hardly be agitated and will flow back extremely slowly; as they return towards the beginning of the optic nerve, their movement will become slower and slower, and consequently the impression of the image will not be able to extend and be propagated along the optic cord without becoming weaker. Now, what do you think of this impression being carried as far as the soul itself? Surely the soul must be affected so weakly that it hardly feels it?

Further experiments give additional support to this theory. Apply your ear to one end of a long straight tree while someone scratches the other end lightly with his nail. Such a weak cause must produce so little noise that it would seem that it must be smothered or vanish in all the length of the wood. Indeed, it vanishes for everyone else, and you alone hear a muffled, almost inaudible sound. The same thing happens on a smaller scale in the optic nerve because it is infinitely less solid. Once the impression is received by the end of a cylindrical conduit full of a non-elastic fluid, it must necessarily be carried to the other end, as in the wood I have just mentioned, and in the well-known experiment with billiard balls.[29] And nerves are cylindrical tubes, or at least each sensitive nerve fibre clearly appears to have this shape.

But little cylinders with such a narrow diameter can probably contain no more than one single globule abreast, or one line or row of animal spirits. This follows from the extreme ease with which these fluids move at the slightest shock, or from the regularity of their movements and from the precision and the faithfulness of the traces or ideas which result in the brain. All these effects prove that nerve fluid is composed of globular elements, perhaps swimming in an ethereal matter; they would be inexplicable if we supposed different sorts of globules in the nerves, as in the other vessels, whose vortices would change the most attentive and prudent man into what we call a complete scatter-brain.

Whether the nerve fluid is elastic or not and whatever form the elements have, if we wish to explain the phenomena of sensations, we must admit, (1) the existence and circulation of animal spirits; (2) that when these spirits are set in motion by the action of external bodies, they go back as far as the soul; (3) in each cylindrical fibre a single row of spherical globules, which run at the slightest touch and gallop at the slightest signal from the will. That said, how fast must the first globule, when pushed, push the last one and, so to speak, throw it at the soul, which wakes up at this hammer blow and receives more or less vivid ideas, according to the movement impressed on it. This naturally leads us to the laws of sensations, as follows.

[29] This experiment on the transmission of movement in a row of billiard balls was carried out by C. Huygens; see his 'Règles du mouvement dans la rencontre des corps', *Journal des sçavans* (1669).

§III. Laws of sensations

LAW I. The more distinctly an object acts on the sensorium, the more the idea resulting from it is clear and distinct.

LAW II. The more vividly it acts on the same material part of the brain, the clearer the idea is.

LAW III. The same clarity results from the frequently repeated impression of objects.

LAW IV. The more vivid the object's effect is, the more different it is from any other or the more extraordinary it is, and the more vivid and striking the idea is. It is not often easily chased away by other ideas, as Spinoza says he experienced when he saw one of those tall men from Brazil.[30] Thus a black man and a white man seeing each other for the first time will never forget each other because the soul looks at an extraordinary object for a long time and thinks about it and is preoccupied by it all the time. One's mind and one's eyes run lightly over things which can be seen every day. A new plant strikes only a botanist. We can see from this that it is dangerous to give children frightening ideas, such as the fear of the Devil, of wolves, etc.

We only grasp complicated ideas by reflecting on simple notions; simple notions must all be clearly represented to the soul and be distinctly conceived one after the other. In other words one must choose a single simple subject acting entirely on the sensorium and undisturbed by any other object, like mathematicians who, through habit, possess the talent melancholics acquire through illness, of not losing sight of their object. This is the first conclusion which we should draw from our first Law. The second is that it is better to meditate than to study out loud like schoolchildren, for one then only retains sounds which are continually carried away by a new torrent of ideas. In addition, according to the third Law, those traces which are more often made are more difficult to eradicate, and people who are not in a state to meditate can hardly learn, except by the bad practice I have mentioned.

Finally, just as an object which one wants to see clearly through a microscope must be well-lit while all the surrounding parts are in the dark, in the same way, in order to hear clearly a sound which seemed confused at first it is enough to listen carefully; as the sound then reaches an ear well-prepared for it and harmonically attentive, it strikes the brain more vividly. By the same means, a chain of reasoning which at first seemed obscure finally turns out to be clear. That follows from the second Law.

§IV. That sensations do not inform us about the nature of bodies and they change with the organs

However luminous our sensations may be, they never enlighten us about the nature of either the active object or the passive organ. Figure, movement, mass and

[30] Letter XVII from Spinoza to Peter Balling, 20 July 1664 (*Opera*, ed. J. Van Vloten and J. P. N. Land, The Hague, 1914, vol. 3, p. 56).

hardness are certainly attributes of bodies with which our senses come into contact. But how many other properties reside in the body's smallest elements and are not grasped by our organs, which only have a confused contact with them, which represents them badly or not at all? Colours, heat, pain, taste, touch, etc. vary so much that the same object can appear sometimes warm and sometimes cold to the same person, whose sensitive organ consequently does not represent to the soul the true state of bodies. And surely colours change also, according to modifications in the light? Thus they cannot be considered as properties of bodies. The soul judges tastes in a confused way, and they do not even show it the shape of salts.

I would go even further and say that we do not have any better conception of the primary qualities of objects. The ideas of size, hardness, etc. are determined only by our organs. If we had other senses, we would have other ideas of the same attributes, and if we had other ideas, we would think differently from the way we think about whatever is called a work of genius or feeling. But I shall keep a discussion of this subject for elsewhere.[31]

If all bodies possessed the same movement, the same shape, the same density, however different they were otherwise from each other, it follows that we would believe there was only one body in nature, because they would all affect the sensitive organ in the same way.

Hence our ideas come neither from a knowledge of the properties of bodies, nor from what the change experienced by our organs consists in. They are produced by this change alone. According to its nature and its degree, ideas arise in our soul which have no connection with their occasional or efficient causes, nor probably with the will, despite which they find a place for themselves in the cerebral matter. Pain, heat, the colour red or white, have nothing in common with fire or flame; the idea of this element is so remote from these sensations that a man with no awareness of physics would never imagine it.

In addition, feelings change with the organs. In some jaundices, everything appears yellow. Change your axis of vision with your finger and you will multiply objects and vary their place and attitude at will. Chilblains, etc. remove the sense of touch. The slightest blockage in the Eustachian tube is enough to make one deaf. Leucorrhoea removes all feeling from the vagina. A leucoma on the cornea, according to whether it corresponds more or less to the centre of the pupil, makes one see objects differently. Cataracts, amaurosis, etc. plunge one into blindness.

Thus sensations do not at all represent things as they really are in themselves, since they depend entirely on the parts of the body which open the path for them.

But do they therefore deceive us? No, of course, whatever one may say,[32] as they were given to us more to conserve our machine than to acquire knowledge. The reflection of light produces a yellow colour in an eye filled with bile; consequently

[31] In ch. XII there is a long discussion of taste and genius.

[32] A reference to the long discussion of the errors of the senses in Malebranche's *De la recherche de la vérité*, Bk. I.

the soul must see yellow. Salt and sugar inspire opposing movements in the taste-buds; as a result, we will have contrary ideas which will make the one seem salty and the other sweet. In fact, our senses never deceive us, except when we make too hasty judgements on their reports; for otherwise they are faithful ministers. The soul can count on being securely warned by them of the traps laid for it; the senses are always on the look out and are always ready to correct each others' errors. But, as the soul depends in turn on the organs which serve it, if all the senses are themselves deceived, how can one prevent the sensorium from joining in such a general mistake?

§ V. Anatomical reasons for the differences in sensations

Even if all the nerves came together, the sensations would still be different; but apart from the fact that it is far from being true, except for the optic and auditory nerves, it is a fact that the nerves are really separated in the brain. (1) The origin of each nerve cannot be very far from the place where the scalpel shows them to be and can no longer follow them, as can be seen in the auditory and pathetic nerves. (2) It can clearly be seen without a microscope that the nerve principles are quite far apart (this can be particularly seen in the olfactory, optic and auditory nerves, which are a great distance from one another) and that the nerve fibres do not go in the same direction, as is again proved by the nerves I have just mentioned. (3) The extreme softness of all these fibres means that they are easily confused with the medulla; the fourth and eighth pairs are good examples of this. (4) Such is the impenetrability alone of bodies that the primary filaments of so many different nerves cannot all come together in a single point. (5) The diversity of sensations such as heat, pain, colour or smell, which are felt at the same time, and the two distinct feelings when one touches something with one finger of the right hand and one finger of the left hand, or even when one rolls a single little round object under one finger over which the neighbouring finger is bent – all this proves that each sense has its own little department in the cerebral matter and that the seat of the soul is therefore made up of as many parts as there are different corresponding sensations. Who could enumerate them? And how many reasons there are to multiply and modify feeling to an infinite degree: the material of the nerve cases, which can be more or less solid, their softer or harder pulp, their more or less lax position, the difference in construction at one end and the other, etc.

It follows from what we have said up to now that each nerve differs from the others at its origin, and it therefore appears to carry only one sort of feeling or idea to the soul. Indeed, the physiological history of all the senses proves that each nerve has feeling in relation to its nature and, even more, to the nature of the organ through which the external impressions are modified. If the organ is dioptric, it gives the idea of light and colours; if it is acoustic, we hear, as has already been said, and so on.

§ VI. On the smallness of ideas

These impressions of outside bodies constitute therefore the true physical cause of all our ideas, but how extraordinarily small this cause is! When we look at the sky through the smallest hole, all this vast hemisphere is painted on the back of the eye, and its image is much smaller than the hole through which it passes. What then would be a star of the sixth size or a sixth of a globule of blood? Yet the soul sees it perfectly clearly with a good microscope. What an infinitely tiny cause, and hence how slight must our sensations and ideas be! And how necessary this slightness of sensations and ideas seems in relation to the immensity of memory! Where indeed could so much knowledge be housed without the small space it needs and without the extent of the brain's substance and the different places knowledge inhabits?

§ VII. Different seats of the soul

In order to fix or indicate precisely which are the different territories of our ideas, we must again have recourse to anatomy, without which we can know nothing about the body, and which alone helps us to lift most of the veils which hide the soul from our curious gaze and research.

Each nerve originates in the spot where the last tiny artery of the brain's cortical substance ends; its origin is thus at the visible beginning of the medullary filament, running from this fine tube, which can be seen, without a microscope, starting and coming out of it. This is really the place from which most of the nerves seem to originate, where they meet together, and where the sensitive being seems to be hiding. Can the sensations and animal movements be reasonably placed in the artery? This tube is of itself devoid of feeling and cannot be changed by any effort of the will. Likewise, sensations are not in the nerve below its continuity with the medulla, as wounds and other observations convince us. In their turn, movements are not situated below the continuity of the nerve with the artery, because every nerve moves at the will's bidding. Here we can see that the sensorium is certainly established as being in the medulla, up to the very arterial origin of this medullary substance. From which, once again, it follows that the seat of the soul is more extended than one imagines, and even then its limits would be too narrow, in particular in a very learned man, without the immense smallness or slightness of ideas that we have mentioned.

§ VIII. On the extent of the soul

If the seat of the soul possesses a certain extent, if the soul feels in different places in the brain or, which comes to the same thing, if it really has different seats in the brain, it must necessarily not be unextended itself, as Descartes claims. For in his system the soul could not act on the body and it would be impossible to explain the union and the reciprocal action of the two substances, just as it can easily be explained by those who think that a being without extent cannot be conceived. Indeed, the body and the soul are, according to Descartes, two entirely opposed natures: the body is capable only of movement and the soul only of knowledge.[33] It is thus impossible for the soul to act on the body and the body to act on the soul. If the body moves, the soul, which is not subject to movements, will not feel any effect. If the soul thinks, the body will feel nothing, since it only obeys movements.

Surely this is to say, with Lucretius, that if the soul is not material it cannot act on the body, or that it is in fact material because it touches and moves it in so many ways, which can only be appropriate to a body?[i]

However small and imperceptible we suppose the extent of the soul to be, despite the phenomena which seem to prove the opposite and to demonstrate the existence of several souls rather than one unextended soul,[j] it must always have an extent, whatever it may be, since it immediately touches that other huge extent of the body, as we imagine the earth's globe to be touched by the whole surface of the tiniest grain of sand placed on its summit. The soul's extent constitutes thus, as it were, the body of this sensitive active being, and because of the closeness of the connection, which is such that one would think the two substances to be individually attached and joined together and to form a single whole, Aristotle says, 'that there is no soul without body and that the soul is not a body'.[k] In truth, although the soul acts on the body and is doubtless determined by its own specific activity, yet I do not know if it is ever active before having been passive. For it seems that, in order to act, the soul needs to receive the impressions of the spirits modified by the bodily faculties. This is perhaps what made several people say that the soul depends so much on the temperament and the disposition of the organs that it is perfected and embellished with them.

You can see that, in order to explain the union of the soul with the body, there is no need to torture one's mind as much as those great geniuses Aristotle, Plato, Descartes, Malebranche, Leibniz and Stahl did, and that it is enough to keep going in a straight line and not look behind or to the side when the truth is in front of one. But there are people who have so many prejudices that they would not even bend down to pick up the truth if they found it where they did not want it to be.

You can imagine, after all that has been said on the diverse origins of the nerves and the different seats of the soul, that there may well be some truth in all the different opinions of authors on this subject, however contradictory they may seem. And since diseases of the brain, according to the place they attack, destroy sometimes one sense and sometimes another, are those who place the seat of the

i Nothing can touch and be touched if it is not body.[34]

j Some ancient philosophers admitted their existence in order to explain the different contradictions which surprise the soul itself, such as for example the tears of a wife who would be very angry to see her husband resuscitate, and vice versa.

k *On the Soul*, 26.c.2.[35]

33 See Descartes, Sixth *Meditation*.

34 A slightly altered quotation from *De rerum natura*, Bk. I, 304: 'Tangere nec tangi, nisi corpus, nulla potest res.'

35 In fact *De anima*, Bk. II, ch. 2.

soul in one of the pairs of optic lobes any more wrong than those who would like to limit it to the oval centre, the corpus callosum or even the pineal gland?[36] We can therefore apply to the whole of the brain's matter what Virgil says of the whole body,[1] throughout which he claims, with the Stoics, that the soul is spread.

For indeed where is your soul when your sense of smell sends it odours which please it or upset it, if it is not in the layers in which the olfactory nerves originate? Where is it when it takes pleasure in observing a beautiful sky or a beautiful view, if it is not in the optic layers? In order to hear, it must be placed at the root of the auditory nerve, etc. Hence everything proves that the mainspring, to which we have compared the soul in order to give a tangible idea of it, is found in several places in the brain, since it is really struck through several of its gates. But I do not mean to say that there are therefore several souls; one is no doubt enough, given the extent of the medullary seat which experience has forced us to accord it. I repeat, it is enough, to act, feel and think as much as the organs allow.

§ IX. That the sensitive being is consequently material

But what doubts arise in my soul, and how weak and restricted our understanding is! My soul manifests constantly, not thought, which is accidental to it whatever the Cartesians may say, but activity and sensibility. Here are two undeniable properties, recognised by all those philosophers who have not allowed themselves to be blinded by systematic thinking, the most dangerous type of thinking. All properties, they say, suppose as their basis a subject which exists by itself and to which these same properties belong as of right. Thus, they conclude, the soul is a being separated from the body, a sort of spiritual monad or substantial form, as the clever, prudent Scholastics say; that is to say a substance whose life does not depend on that of the body. This is no doubt perfect reasoning, but why should I imagine the subject of these properties as being of an absolutely distinct nature from the body, when I can see clearly that it is the very organisation of the medulla right at the beginning of its emergence (that is, at the end of the cortex) which in a healthy state exercises so freely all these properties? For there exists a host of sound observations and experiments which prove what I claim, while those who say the opposite can display a lot of metaphysics without giving us a single idea. But could it therefore be the medullary fibres which form the soul? And how can we conceive that matter can feel and think? I admit that I cannot conceive it; but in addition to the fact that it is irreligious to limit the Creator's supreme power by claiming that he cannot have made matter think – he who with a single word created light – should I deprive a being of properties which strike my senses because the essence of that

1 'Immanent mind, flowing through all its parts and leavening its mass', Virgil, *Æneid*, Bk. VI.[37]

36 References to the opinions of Willis and Descartes, amongst others.

37 Lines 726–7: 'Totus diffusa per artus/ Mens agitat molem, & magno se corpore miscet', (trans. C. Day Lewis, London, 1952).

being is unknown to me? I can see only matter in the brain and only extension, as we have proved, in its sensitive part; when alive, healthy, and well-organised, this organ contains at the source of the nerves an active principle spread throughout the medullary substance. I can see this principle, which feels and thinks, being disturbed, falling asleep and dying with the body. What am I saying! The soul is the first to sleep; its fire goes out as the fibres which seem to constitute it weaken and collapse onto each other. If everything can be explained by what anatomy and physiology reveal to me in the medulla, what need have I to forge an ideal being? If I confuse the soul with the bodily organs, it is because all phenomena force me to do so, and in any case God has given my soul no idea of itself, but only enough discernment and good faith to recognise itself in any mirror and not to be embarrassed at being born in filth. If it is virtuous and embellished by a great amount of splendid knowledge, it is noble and respectable enough.

We shall go back to expounding the phenomena which I have just mentioned when we show how little influence the soul has over the body and how much the will is subordinate to it.[38] But the order of the subjects with which I am dealing demands that memory comes after feelings, which have led me much further than I expected.

§ X. On memory

All judgement is the comparison of two ideas which the soul is able to distinguish from each other. But as it can only contemplate a single idea at a time, if I have no memory, when I go to compare the second idea I have lost the first. Thus (and this is a way of making amends to memory which is too often denigrated) to have no memory means to have no judgement. Neither speech, nor the knowledge of objects, nor the internal awareness of our own existence are certain to remain in us without memory. If we have forgotten what we used to know, it is as if we are only just emerging from oblivion; we have no idea that we have ever existed and that we will continue to exist for some time still. Wepfer speaks of a patient who had lost the very ideas of things and no longer had any exact perceptions; he mistook the handle of a spoon for its bowl. He cites another who could never finish a sentence because he had forgotten the beginning before he finished it, and recounts the story of a third who could neither spell nor read for want of memory. La Motte mentions someone who had lost the use of sound formation and speech. In certain brain disorders it is not rare to see patients with no awareness of hunger and thirst; Bonet cites numerous examples of this.[39] Consequently a man who had lost all memory

[38] La Mettrie comes back to the will in ch. XII, §2.

[39] J. J. Wepfer, *Observationes medico-practicae de affectibus capitis internis et externis* (Schaffhausen, 1727); G. M. de La Motte, *Traité complet de chirurgie* (Paris, 1722), obs. 163; T. Bonet, *Prodromus anatomiae pract., Liber I, cap.1* (Geneva, 1675), All these examples are taken from Boerhaave, *Praelectiones academicae*, §681.

would be a thinking atom, if one can think without it: he would not know himself or what happened to him, and he would recall nothing.

The cause of memory is completely mechanical, like memory itself; it seems to depend on the fact that the physical impressions in the brain, which are the traces of successive ideas, are close together and on the fact that the soul is unable to discover one trace or one idea without recalling the others which habitually went with them. This is very true of what we learnt in our youth. If we cannot at first remember what we are seeking, a line of poetry or a single word brings it back. This phenomenon demonstrates that ideas have separate territories, but in some order. Because for a new movement, for example the beginning of a line of poetry or a sound which strikes the ears, to communicate its impression immediately to that part of the brain which corresponds to the one where the first trace of what we are seeking is to be found – in other words that other part of the medulla in which the memory or the trace of the following lines is hidden – and to represent to the soul what follows the first idea or the first words, the new ideas need to be carried, thanks to a constant law, to the same place in which the other similar ideas were engraved in the past. For if it happened differently, the tree beneath which we had been robbed would not infallibly summon up the idea of a robber, any more than any other object. What confirms the same truth is the fact that certain brain disorders destroy a particular sense without affecting the others. The surgeon I have quoted saw a man who lost his sense of touch from a blow on the head; Hildanus speaks of a man made blind by concussion.[40] I have seen a lady who, after being cured of apoplexy, took more than a year to recover her memory; she had to go back to the A.B.C. of elementary knowledge, which increased and rose up, as it were, with the brain's flaccid fibres, whose collapse had simply stopped and intercepted her ideas. Father Mabillon was very limited; an illness developed his mind and gave rise to great penetration and aptitude for learning.[41] This is one of those lucky illnesses for which many people would barter their health, and they would do a golden deal. Blind people usually have good memories. All the objects around them have lost the means of distracting them, and attention and reflection do not cost them a great effort; thus one can concentrate for a long time on all sides of an object, and the presence of ideas is more stable and less fleeting. Mr de la Motte of the *Académie française* dictated all at once his tragedy *Inès de Castro*.[42] What a copious memory, to hold two thousand lines of poetry which file past the soul in order at the beck of the will! How is it that there is no confusion in that sort of chaos! Even more is recounted of Pascal; it is said that he never forgot what he had learned. It is thought in addition, with some justification, since it is a fact, that

[40] The surgeon is La Motte, *Traité complet de chirurgie*, obs. 168; Hildanus, *Observationem et curationem chirurgicarum centuriae* (Oppenhaim, 1619), III, obs. 9 (from Boerhaave, *Praelectiones academicae*, §580).

[41] J. Mabillon, a prolific Benedictine scholar, historian and writer on diplomacy.

[42] This is Antoine Houdar de La Motte (1672–1731), not the surgeon just mentioned.

those who have a good memory are not usually suspected of good judgement, any more than physicians are suspected of religion, because the brain substance is so full of old ideas that the new ones have difficulty finding a separate place. I mean those parent ideas, if I may be allowed to use this expression, which can judge others by comparing them and deducing correctly a third idea from the combination of the first two. But who had more judgement, intelligence and memory than the two famous men I have just mentioned?

We can conclude, from all that has been said on the subject of the memory, that it is a faculty of the soul which consists in the permanent modifications of the movements of the animal spirits, stirred up by the impressions of objects which have acted vigorously or very frequently on the senses; so that these modifications remind the soul of the same sensations, with the same circumstances of place, time, etc., which accompanied them at the moment when they received them through the feeling organs.

When we feel that we have previously had an idea similar to the one which is now passing through our head, this sensation is called 'memory' and, whether the will agrees or not, this same idea is necessarily awoken on the occasion of a disposition in the brain, or an internal cause, similar to the one which gave rise to it before, or of another idea which has some affinity with it.

§ XI. On the imagination

The imagination merges the different incomplete sensations which the memory recalls to the brain and makes images or pictures out of them, representing objects which are different either in circumstance, or in what accompanies them, or in the variety of their combinations; I mean objects which are different from the precise sensations previously received through the senses.

But in order to speak more clearly about imagination, we shall define it as the perception of an idea produced by internal causes, similar to one of the ideas to which external causes usually gave rise. Thus when material causes, hidden in any part of the body whatsoever, affect the nerves, spirits or brain in the same way as external bodily causes and as a result excite the same ideas, we have what is called 'imagination'. For, when a physical disposition perfectly similar to the one produced by some external cause is born in the brain, the same idea must be formed, even though there is no cause present outside. That is why the objects of imagination are called phantoms or spectres, φαντασματα.

Thus internal senses, like external ones, occasion changes of thought; they differ from each other neither in the way one thinks, which is always the same for everybody, nor in the change taking place in the sensorium, but simply in the absence of external objects. It is hardly surprising that internal causes can imitate external causes, as we can see by pressing our eye (which changes vision so remarkably), in dreams, in vivid imaginings, in delirium and so on.

Imagination in a sane man is weaker than the perception of external sensations and, to tell the truth, gives no real perceptions at all. I may well imagine, when crossing the Pont Neuf at night, the magnificent sight of the lanterns all lit up, but I will only have a perception of it when my eyes are struck by it. When I think of the opera, the theatre or love, how far I am from experiencing the feelings of those who are enchanted by Mlle le Maure, those who are weeping with Mérope or those who are in their mistress's arms![43] But in those who are dreaming or in delirium, imagination provides true perceptions; which proves clearly that it is no different in nature and in its effect on the sensorium, even though the multiplication of ideas and the rapidity with which they follow one another weaken the former ideas the brain has retained. That is true of all new impressions of other bodies on ours.

Imagination is true or false, strong or weak. True imagination represents objects in their natural state, while in false imagination the soul sees them as other than they are. Sometimes it recognises this illusion and then it is only vertigo, like Pascal's; he had so exhausted his brain's spirits by study that he imagined he saw on his left-hand side a precipice of flame, from which he always shielded himself with chairs or any other sort of rampart which could prevent him from seeing that terrifying fantastic chasm, which that great man knew for what it was. Sometimes the soul participates in the general error of all the internal and external senses, and believes that objects really resemble the phantoms produced in the imagination, and then it is true delirium.

The weak imagination is one which is as lightly affected by the state of the internal senses as by impressions from the external ones, while those who have a strong imagination are vividly affected and upset by the slightest causes. One can say that they have been favoured by nature since, in order to produce good works of genius and feeling, one needs a certain strength in one's spirits, able to engrave vividly and deeply on the brain the ideas produced by the imagination and the passions which it wishes to depict. Corneille doubtless had organs endowed with a very superior force of this type; his theatre teaches us grandeur of the soul, as Mr de Voltaire remarks.[44] This force is also seen in Lucretius himself, a great poet although usually lacking harmony. In order to be a great poet one needs great passions.

When some idea is awoken in the brain, by the effect of memory and a vivid imagination, with as much force as when it was engraved there for the first time, we think we can see externally the known object of this thought. A strong present internal cause, linked to a vivid memory, can plunge the wisest into this error, which is frequent in the delirium without fever of the melancholic. But if the will intervenes and if the resulting feelings in the soul irritate it, then one is truly in a state of fury.

Maniacs, always preoccupied by the same object, have fixed its idea so well in

[43] Catherine Nicole le Maure (1704–83) was a famous opera singer in Paris. *Mérope* is a tragedy by Voltaire, first staged in 1743.

[44] Voltaire, *Lettre à un premier commis* (1733), published in *Oeuvres* ('Londres' [Trévoux], 1746), vol. 4.

their minds that the soul becomes accustomed to it and gives its consent. Many of them are similar in that, apart from their mad fixation, their judgement is right and sane; if they are seduced by the very object of their error, it is only as a result of a false hypothesis, and the more coherent they usually are, the further it leads them from reason. Michel Montaigne has a chapter on the imagination which is extremely curious;[45] he shows that the wisest man has an object of delirium and, as they say, his eccentricity. It is a very singular and humiliating thing for man, to see that any sublime genius, whose works are admired throughout Europe, only has to concentrate too long on an idea, however extravagant and unworthy of him it might be, for him to adopt it even to the extent of never wanting to abandon it. The more he sees and touches, for example, his thigh and his nose, the more he is convinced that one is made of straw and the other of glass, however clearly convinced he is of the contrary as soon as the soul loses sight of the object and reason has re-established itself. That is what we see in mania.

This disease of the mind is controlled by known bodily causes and if it is so difficult to cure, it is because the patients do not think that they are ill and refuse to hear it said that they are; so that if a physician has no more wit than he has gravity or Galenism, his gauche and clumsy reasoning irritates and increases their mania. The soul is only the prey of a strong dominant impression which alone absorbs it entirely, as in the most violent love, which is a sort of mania. What is the use, then, of trying obstinately to talk reason to a man who no longer has any? 'What value have vows and shrines?'[46] The whole aim and mystery of the art of medicine is to try to arouse in the brain a stronger idea which will abolish the ridiculous idea preoccupying the soul; for by this means one brings back judgement and reason with the equitable distribution of the blood and the spirits.

§ XII. On the passions

The passions are the habitual modifications of the animal spirits, which almost continually supply the soul with pleasant or unpleasant sensations, and which inspire in it desire or aversion for the objects which gave rise to the usual modifications in the movement of these spirits. Hence arise love, hatred, fear, audacity, pity, ferocity, anger, gentleness and a tendency to particular sensual pleasures. Thus it is obvious that the passions should not be confused with the other recording faculties such as the memory and the imagination, from which they are distinguished by the pleasant or unpleasant impression of the soul's sensations, whereas the other agents of our remembrance are only esteemed to the extent that they merely recall feelings as they were received, without paying attention to the pain or pleasure accompanying them.

Such is the association of ideas in the latter case that external ideas are not represented at all as they are outside but are joined to certain movements which

45 *Essays*, Bk. I, ch. 21, 'On the power of the imagination'.

46 *Æneid*, IV, 65: 'Quid vota furentem, quid delubra juvant'.

disturb the sensorium; and in the former, the imagination is strongly impressed and instead of retaining all the notions, hardly receives a single simple notion of a complex idea, or rather only sees the object of its internal fixation.[47]

But let us go into more detail concerning the passions. When the soul perceives the ideas which come to it by means of the senses, either they produce, with this representation of the object, feelings of joy or sadness, or they arouse neither one nor the other. These passions are called 'indifferent', while the former make one love or hate the object whose action gave rise to them.

If the will, which is the result of an idea traced in the brain, enjoys contemplating and retaining this idea – as when we think of a pretty woman, of a particular success, etc. – it is what we call 'joy', 'sensuality' or 'pleasure'. When the will is disagreeably affected, suffers at having an idea and wants it taken away, the result is sadness. Love and hatred are two passions on which all the others depend. Love for a present object delights me, love for a past object is a pleasant memory and love for a future object is what is called 'desire' or 'hope', when we desire or hope to enjoy it. A present evil arouses sadness or hatred, a past evil gives an unpleasant memory and fear comes from a future evil. The other affections of the soul are different degrees of love or hatred. But if these affections are strong and imprint such deep traces in the brain that all our economy is upset and no longer knows the laws of reason, then this violent state is called 'passion', which draws us towards its object in spite of our soul. The ideas which arouse neither joy nor sadness are called indifferent, as we have just said; such is the idea of the air, a stone, a circle, a house and so on. But except for those ideas, all the others partake of either love or hatred, and everything in man is steeped in passion. Every age has its own; we naturally wish for what suits the present state of our body. Strong, vigorous youth loves war, the pleasures of love and all types of sensuality. Impotent old age is timid instead of being warlike and miserly instead of enjoying expense; in its eyes audacity is temerity and gratification is a crime, as old age is no longer made for it. We can see the same appetites and the same behaviour in beasts which, like us, are carefree, playful and in love when they are young and afterwards gradually become numb to all pleasures. On the occasion of that state of the soul which makes one love or hate, there are muscular movements in the body, by means of which we can unite bodily or in thought with the object of our pleasure and remove the object whose presence revolts us.

Of the disorders of the soul, some happen consciously or with an internal awareness and others without this awareness. The first type of affection comes from the law according to which the body obeys the will; there is no need trying to find out how it happens. To explain these consequences or effects of the passions, it is enough to look to some acceleration or slowing down in the movement of the nervous fluid, which seems to take place at the origin of the nerve. Those of the

47 The two cases mentioned here are not clear at all and seem to refer rather to the preceding section, on the imagination.

second type are more hidden and the movements they arouse have not yet been well described. In very violent joy, there is a great dilation in the heart, the pulse quickens, the heart palpitates so much that its palpitations can sometimes be heard and there is sometimes so much transpiration that fainting often follows, and even sudden death. Anger increases all the blood's movements and consequently its circulation, which means that the body becomes hot, red and trembling, suddenly ready to evacuate certain secretions that irritate it, and subject to bleeding. Hence frequently apoplexy, diarrhoea, scars which reopen, inflammation, icterus and an increase in transpiration. Terror, that passion which disturbs the whole machine and, so to speak, puts it on guard to defend itself, produces more or less the same effects as anger; it opens up the arteries, sometimes suddenly cures paralysis, lethargy and gout, saves a patient from the jaws of death, leads to apoplexy or sudden death and, in a word, causes the most terrible effects. A slight fear reduces all movements, produces cold, stops transpiration, prepares the body to receive contagious miasma, produces paleness, horror, weakness, relaxation in the sphincters and so on. Sorrow produces the same phenomena but less strongly, and mainly slows down all the vital and animal movements. Yet a great sorrow has sometimes made people die suddenly. If you link all these effects to their causes you will find that the nerves must necessarily act on the blood, so that its movement, regulated by that of the spirits, is quickened or slowed down with the movement of the spirits. The nerves, which hold the arteries as if in nets, thus seem, in anger and joy, to excite the circulation of arterial blood by reviving the elasticity of the arteries; in fear and sorrow, a passion which seems to be a lesser version of fear (at least in its effects), the arteries are restricted, even strangled, and the blood flows through them with difficulty. Where are these nerve nets not found? They are in the internal carotid, in the temporal artery, in the great meningeal, in the vertebral, in the subclavian, at the root of the right subclavian and of the carotid, at the trunk of the aorta, in the brachial arteries, in the coeliac, the mesenteric and those which come out of the pelvis, and they are everywhere quite capable of producing these effects. Shame, which is a sort of fear, constricts the temporal vein where it is surrounded by branches of the portio durum and retains the blood in the face. Surely an erection, an effect which so obviously depends on the stopping of the blood, also comes about by the action of the nerves? Is it not certain that the imagination alone brings about this state even in eunuchs, and that the same single cause produces ejaculation, not only at night but even sometimes during the day; and that impotence is often dictated by a defect in imagination, as well as a too vivid or extremely calm imagination, or by different diseases of the imagination, examples of which can be found in Venette or Montaigne?[48] Even an excess of modesty or a certain restraint or timidity, of which one is quickly cured at the school of the ladies of the town, often reduces the most amorous man to being incapable of satisfying

[48] N. Venette, *De la génération de l'homme ou tableau de l'amour conjugal* (Amsterdam, 1687), ch. 3; Montaigne, *Essays*, Bk. I, ch. 21.

them. Here we have the theory of both love and all the other passions; the one comes wonderfully to the help of the others. It is obvious that the nerves play the greatest role here and that they are the principal spring of the passions. Although we do not know passions by their causes, the enlightenment brought today by the mechanism of the body's movements allows us at least to explain them all clearly enough by their effects. When, for example, we know that sorrow restricts the tubes' diameters, even though we do not know the original cause which makes the nerves contract around them as if to strangle them, it is easy to conceive of all the ensuing effects: melancholia, black bile and mania. The imagination, affected by a strong idea or a violent passion, has an influence on the body and the temperament, and vice versa, the body's illnesses attack the imagination and the mind. Once melancholy, in the physician's sense, is formed in the bodies of the most carefree persons and has become atrabilious, it will necesarily make them sadder, and instead of the pleasures which they used to love so much, they will have a taste only for solitude.

Man as Plant

Note on the text

L'Homme-plante first appeared in 1748, published by C. F. Voss in Potsdam. It contained a large number of notes, consisting mainly of references, which were all removed when the text was reworked in 1750 for inclusion in La Mettrie's *Philosophical Works*. Otherwise the changes were only slight. F. L. Rougier published an edition of the work (New York, Columbia University, 1936) giving the text of 1748, which is very rare. The present translation is based on the 1750 version.

Preface

Man is here metamorphosed into a plant, but do not think this is a fiction in the style of those of Ovid. A simple analogy between the vegetable kingdom and the animal kingdom has shown me that the main parts of the one are found in the other. If my imagination sometimes plays here, it is, so to speak, on the sounding board of truth; my field of battle is that of nature, whose variations I could have hidden from view, if I had not wanted to single myself out.

Chapter I

We are beginning to glimpse the uniformity of nature; these as yet still weak rays of light are due to the study of natural history. But how far does this uniformity go?

We should be careful not to push nature too far; it is not so uniform that it does not often stray from even its most favourite laws. We should try to see only what exists, without flattering ourselves that we can see everything. Everything contains a trap or a pitfall for a vain and unwary mind.

In order to judge the analogy existing between the two main kingdoms, we must compare the parts of plants with those of man, and apply what I say about man to animals.

In our species, as in plants, there is a main root and capillary roots. One is formed by the reservoir of the lumbar region and the thoracic canal, and the other by the lacteal veins. Everywhere we see the same uses and the same functions. Food is carried by these roots throughout the whole of the organised body.

Thus man is not an upturned tree whose brain is its root, since this root is the result of the activity of abdominal vessels alone; they are the ones which are formed first, or at least they are formed before the teguments which cover them and constitute man's bark. In the plant's seed, one of the first things that one sees is its little root and then its stem; one goes downwards and the other upwards.

The lungs are our leaves, which replace this organ in vegetals, as in us the organ replaces the leaves which we lack. If the plant's lungs have branches, it is in order to multiply their extent so that as a result more air enters them; which means that vegetals, and trees in particular, breathe more comfortably. Why should we need leaves and boughs? The quantity of our vessels and pulmonary vesicles is so well proportioned to the mass of our body and its small circumference that it is enough for us. It is very enjoyable to observe these vessels and the circulation in them, particularly in amphibians!

But what could be more similar than those which have been discovered and described by the Harveys of botany! Ruysch, Boerhaave, etc. have found in man the same numerous series of vessels that Malpighi, Leeuwenhoek and van Royen discovered in plants.[1] The heart beats in animals and swells their veins with those torrents of blood which carry feeling and life into the whole machine. Heat, that other heart of nature, that fire from the earth and the sun, which seems to have passed into the imagination of the poets who have depicted it, likewise makes the fluids circulate in the tubes of the plants, which transpire like us.[2] Indeed, what other cause could make everything in the universe germinate, grow, flower and multiply?

The air seems to produce in vegetals the same effects which are, with reason, attributed in man to that subtle nerve fluid whose existence has been proved by a thousand experiments.

It is this element whose excitation and elasticity sometimes make plants rise up above the water's surface and open and close, as one opens and closes one's hand. It was perhaps a consideration of this phenomenon which gave rise to the opinion of those who considered ether to be part of the animal spirits and to be mixed with them in the nerves.[3]

If flowers have leaves or petals, we can consider our arms and legs as similar parts. The nectarium, which is the reservoir of honey in some flowers such as the tulip, the rose, etc., is the reservoir of milk in the female plant of our species, when the male brings it on. It is double and its seat is at the lateral base of each petal, immediately on an important muscle, the greater pectoral.

We can consider the virgin, or rather non-pregnant, womb or, if one prefers, the ovary, to be like a seed which is not yet fertilised. The woman's stylus is her vagina; her vulva and her mons veneris, with the odour given off by the glands in these parts, correspond to the stigma; and these things – the womb, the vagina and the vulva – form the pistil, which is the name that modern botanists give to all the female parts of plants.

I compare the pericarp to the womb in a state of pregnancy because its function is to cover the foetus. We have our seed, like the plants, and it is sometimes very abundant.

The nectarium serves to distinguish between the sexes of our species when we are satisfied with a single glance, but the easiest research is not always the most certain. In order to have the essence of woman, we must combine the pistil and the nectarium; for the first can be found without the second, but the second is never

[1] W. Harvey discovered the circulation of the blood. F. Ruysch studied human vessels; see in particular *Curae renovatae seu Thesauraus anatomicus* (Amsterdam, 1728). On Boerhaave see Introduction, p. xiii. Malpighi turned to botany after his anatomical work, and was considered to be the founder of the microscopic study of plant anatomy, especially with his *Anatome plantarum* (London, 1675). A. van Leeuwenhoek, particularly studied micro-organisms and reproduction in plants and animals; in a note to the 1748 edition, La Mettrie refers the reader to *Arcana Natura detecta* (Delft, 1695). A. van Royen was director of the Leiden Botanical Gardens after Boerhaave; in 1748, La Mettrie referred the reader to his *Flore de Leyde*, or *Florae Leydensis prodromus* (Leiden, 1740), which put forward a new method of plant classification.

[2] In the 1748 edition, La Mettrie here referred to S. Hales's *Vegetable Staticks* (London, 1727).

[3] In the 1748 edition, La Mettrie here referred to Quesnay's *Essai physique sur l'économie animale*.

without the first, except in very portly men whose breasts in fact imitate those of women, even to the extent of producing milk, as Morgagni[4] and many others recount they have observed. No unperforated woman – if one can call 'woman' a being without a sex, like the one I have mentioned several times[5] – has breasts. Breasts are like the buds on a vine, particularly when it is cultivated.

I shall not discuss the calix, or rather the corolla, because it is alien to us, as I shall explain.

This is enough, as I do not wish to follow in the tracks of Cornelius Agrippa.[6] I have described botanically the most beautiful plant of our species, by which I mean woman. If she is virtuous, although metamorphosed into a flower, she will not be any the easier to gather.

As for us men, for whom a glance is enough, sons of Priapus, spermatic animals, our stamen is, as it were, rolled up in a cylindrical tube, which is our penis, and sperm is our fertilising powder. Like those plants which have only one male, we are *monandria* and women are *monogynia*, as they have only one vagina. And the human race, in which the male is separated from the female, goes to increase the class of *dieciae*: I use the words derived from Greek and imagined by Linnaeus.[7]

I thought it was necessary to expound first of all the analogy between plants and fully formed men because it is the more evident and easier to grasp. Now here is a more subtle one which I shall draw from procreation in the two kingdoms.

Plants are male and female, and shake like man does in copulation. But in what does this important action, which renews the whole of nature, consist? Infinitely tiny globules, which come out of the grains of that dust with which the stamens of flowers are covered, are wrapped up in the shells of these grains, more or less like some eggs, according to Needham and to the truth.[8] It seems to me that the drops of our semen correspond quite well to these grains and our little worms to their globules. Man's animalcules are truly enclosed in two liquids, the most common of which, the prostate fluid, contains the most precious, which is the veritable semen, and on the model of each globule of vegetable powder, they probably contain a miniature version of the human plant.[9] I do not know why Needham tried to deny what is so easy to see. How could a scrupulous physicist, one of those so-called followers of experiment alone, dare to conclude, from observations made on a single species, that the same phenomena must be found in another, which he had nevertheless not studied at all, according to his own admission? Such conclusions,

4 G. B. Morgagni, *Adversaria anatomica* (Pavia, 1717–19).

5 See *Machine Man*, p. 16 and *The System of Epicurus*, §XIV.

6 H. C. Agrippa von Nettesheim, *De nobilitate et praecellentia feminei sexus* (Antwerp, 1529), a work in praise of women, translated into French as *Traité de la prééminence des femmes* (Paris, 1578).

7 C. Linnaeus developed the system of classification of living beings, starting with plants; see *Systema naturae* (Leiden, 1735).

8 Needham, *An Account of Some New Microscopical Discoveries*, ch. 7, 'The Farina Fœcundans of Vegetables'.

9 Here La Mettrie seems to favour the preformationist theory, although in *Machine Man* was more circumspect.

drawn to honour a hypothesis – for people hate only the word 'hypothesis' and regret the absence of the thing – do little honour to their author. A man of Needham's merit had even less need of diminishing the merit of Mr Geoffroy who, as far as I can judge from his work on the structure and the principal uses of flowers, did more than speculate that plants were fertilised by the powder in their stamens.[10] This is by the way.

The plant's liquid dissolves, better than any other, the matter which is to fertilise it, so that only the most subtle part of this matter reaches its goal.

Does not the most subtle part of man's semen likewise carry its worm or little fish into the woman's ovary?

Needham compares the action of the fertilising globules to that of a violently heated aeolipile. It also resembles a sort of little windbag, both in nature or when it is observed, and in the image that this illustrious young English naturalist has given us of plants' ejaculation.

If the fluid specific to each vegetal produces this action in an incomprehensible manner by acting on the grain of dust, as common water also does, do we understand any better how a sleeping man's imagination produces wet dreams by acting on the erector and ejaculatory muscles which, even alone and without the aid of the imagination, sometimes cause the same accidents? Unless the phenomena which can be seen in both cases come from the same cause, by which I mean a principle of arousal which, after having tensed the springs, makes them relax. Thus pure water, and mainly the plant's liquid, would act no differently on the grains of dust than the blood and spirits would on the muscles and the reserves of semen.

The ejaculation of plants lasts only a second or two, but does ours last much longer? I do not think so, although abstinence provides variations which depend on the greater or lesser amount of sperm accumulated in the seminal vesicles. As it happens while breathing out, it had to be short, otherwise prolonged pleasure would have been our grave. For lack of air or inhalation, each animal would only have given life at the expense of its own and would truly have died of pleasure.

The same ovaries, the same eggs and the same fertilising capacity; the tiniest drop of sperm containing a great number of little worms can, as we have seen, bring life into a large number of eggs.

Again, the same sterility and the same impotence on both sides; just as there are few grains which reach their goal and are truly fertile, few animalcules penetrate the female egg. But once it is implanted, it is immediately nourished like the powder globule, and both of them, in time, form a being of their own species, a man or a plant.

Eggs or plant grains, improperly called germs, never become foetuses if they are not fertilised by the dust I am discussing. Similarly, a woman will not produce any children unless the man projects, as it were, a smaller version of himself into her entrails.

[10] Claude Joseph Geoffroy, 'Sur la structure et sur l'usage des principales parties des fleurs', a paper read to the Académie des Sciences in 1711.

Must this powder have acquired a certain degree of maturity in order to be fertile? Man's seed is no apter for procreation in his youth, perhaps because our little worm is then in the state of a nymph, as Needham's translator has speculated.[11] The same thing happens when one is extremely exhausted, no doubt because the undernourished animalcules die, or are at least too weak. Such seeds, whether animal or vegetable, are sown in vain; they are sterile and produce nothing. Wisdom is the mother of fecundity.

The amnios, the chorion, the umbilical cord, the womb, etc. are found in both kingdoms. The human foetus finally comes out of the maternal prison by its own efforts, and the plant's foetus – or to say it neologically, the embryonic plant – falls at the slightest movement as soon as it is ripe. That is vegetable birth.

If man is not a vegetal production, like the tree of Diana[12] and others, he is at least an insect whose roots grow into the womb, as the fertilised plant germs do in theirs. However there would be nothing surprising about the idea, since Needham observes that polyps, barnacles and other animals multiply themselves by vegetation. Again, do we not, so to speak, prune a man like a tree? A universally learned author said so before me: the forest of splendid men covering Prussia is due to the care and research of the late King.[13] Generosity has even more effect on the mind; it spurs it on and it alone can prune it, so to speak, into trees worthy of the gardens at Marly and, what is more, into trees which although previously sterile, will bear the finest fruit. Is it therefore surprising that the arts have today chosen Prussia for their native land? And surely intelligence was justified in expecting the most enticing advantages from a Prince who has so many himself?

Among plants there are also blacks and mulattos, and marks in which the imagination plays no part, unless it is Mr Colonna's imagination.[14] There are strange head-feathers, monsters, wens, goitres and monkeys' and birds' tails. And finally, what provides the greatest and most amazing analogy is the fact that the plant's foetus is fed, as Mr Monro has proved,[15] by means of a mixture of the mechanisms of oviparous and viviparous animals. I have said enough on the analogy of the two kingdoms.[16]

11 J. N. S. Allamand's translation of Needham's work was published in 1747, together with Trembley's paper on polyps, under the title of *Nouvelles découvertes faites avec le microscope* (Leiden). This remark appears in the translator's preface, as La Mettrie could have read in the *Bibliothèque raisonnée* in 1747 (vol. 39).

12 A crystal formation made by mixing several substances together in a test-tube.

13 Frederick William I. See Maupertuis, *Vénus physique*, Pt. II, 'Variétés dans l'espèce humaine', ch. 3, concerning the improvement of species by selective breeding.

14 F. M. P. Colonna, *Principes de la nature ou de la génération des choses* (Paris, 1731), a work attributing to animals, vegetables and minerals a soul which was part of the universal soul. La Mettrie is also referring to the theory that the mother's imagination affects the human foetus, referred to in *Machine Man*. See p. 29 note 43.

15 A. Monro the Elder, *Essay on Comparative Anatomy* (London, 1744).

16 The first edition of 1748 included here a botanical description of the human being in Latin according to the Linnaean categories of classification.

Chapter II

I now come to the second part of this work, or to the difference between the two kingdoms.

The plant is rooted in the earth which nourishes it, it has no needs, it fertilises itself, it does not have the faculty of moving and it has been regarded as an immobile animal which however lacks intelligence and even feeling.

Although the animal is a mobile plant, it can be considered as a being of a very different species, for not only has it the power to move – and movement costs it so little that it has an influence on the healthiness of the organs on which it depends – but it can also feel, think, and satisfy the host of needs which assail it.

The reasons for these variations are to be found in the variations themselves, together with the laws I am about to describe.

The more an organised body has needs, the more means nature has given it to satisfy them; these means are the different degrees of wisdom, called instinct in animals and the soul in man.

The fewer necessities an organised body has, the less difficult it is to nourish and bring it up and the smaller is its share of intelligence.

Beings without needs are also without a mind. This is the last law, which follows from the two others.

An infant attached to its wet-nurse's nipple, which it never stops sucking, provides an accurate idea of a plant. It is the earth's suckling and it leaves its breast only when it dies. As long as life lasts, the plant is identified with the earth, their organs are one and can only be separated by force. Hence no worry, no anxiety about having enough to eat and consequently no needs in that direction.

And again, plants make love without difficulty; for either they contain within themselves the twofold instrument of procreation and are the only hermaphrodites that can impregnate themselves, or if each flower is of a single sex, it is enough for the flowers not to be too far apart from each other for them to be able to mingle. Sometimes copulation even takes place although at a distance, and even a great distance. Pontanus's palm tree is not the only example of trees being fertilised from a great distance.[17] We have known for a long time that the winds, true messengers of vegetable love, carry the male sperm to female plants. It is not exposure to the wind that generally makes ours run the same risks!

The earth is not only the plants' nurse; it is also in a way their dressmaker. It is not satisfied with suckling them, but also clothes them. With the same juices that nourish them, it can spin garments to cover them. Such is the corolla I have mentioned, which is decorated with the most beautiful colours. The corolla of man, and above all woman, consists in garments and different

17 J. Pontanus, minister to the King of Naples, described a palm tree fertilised by the pollen brought on the wind by the only male, several miles away.

ornaments, during the daytime, for at night they are flowers almost without any covering.

What a difference there is between the plants of our species and those which cover the earth's surface! They rival the stars and form the bright patchwork of the meadows, but they experience neither pain nor pleasure. How evenly balanced everything is! They die as they have lived, without feeling it. It would not have been fair for those who live without pleasure to die in pain.

Not only do plants have no soul, but in addition, this substance would have been no use to them. As they have none of the necessities of animal life, no sort of anxiety, no cares, no steps to take and no desires, any trace of intelligence would have been as superfluous for them as light for a blind man. In the absence of philosophical proofs, this reason, combined with our senses, is evidence against the souls of vegetals.

Instinct has even more legitimately been denied to all bodies permanently fixed to rocks or ships, or formed in the bowels of the earth.

Perhaps minerals are formed according to the laws of attraction, so that iron never attracts gold nor gold iron, all heterogeneous parts repel each other and only homogeneous parts unite or form a single body together. But without deciding anything in the obscurity which covers all sorts of reproduction, should I, because I do not know how fossils are formed, call on, or rather suppose, a soul to explain the formation of these bodies? That would be rich (particularly after having deprived organised beings in which there are as many vessels as in man); it would, I repeat, be rich to want to give one to bodies with a simple, crude, compact structure!

They are nothing but imaginings and ancient fancies, all those souls generously distributed to all the kingdoms! And follies of the Moderns who have tried to revive them with a subtle breath! Let us leave their names and their shades in peace; Sennert, the Germans' Galen, would be too ill-treated.[18]

I consider everything they have said as philosophical games and trifles, whose only merit is their difficulty: 'difficult frivolities'.[19] Do we need to resort to a soul to explain plants' growth, which is infinitely faster that that of stones? And in the vegetation of all bodies, from the softest to the hardest, surely everything is determined by nourishing fluids, which are more or less terrestrial and applied with differing degrees of force to more or less hard masses? From which I can indeed see that a stone must grow less in a hundred years than a plant does in a week.

But we must forgive the Ancients for their general and particular souls; for lack of experimental physics and anatomy, they were not at all versed in the structure and organisation of bodies. Everything must have been as incomprehensible to them as to children or savages seeing a watch for the first time; knowing nothing of its springs, they think it to be animate or endowed with a soul like them, while it is

[18] D. Sennert, *Hypomnemata physica* (Frankfurt, 1636), attributes the formation of bodies to the soul and explains that minerals are created by spirits.

[19] La Mettrie uses the expression, 'difficiles nugae', an unidentifiable quotation.

enough to glance at the artifice of this machine; it is a simple artifice which really implies, not the possession of its own soul, but the soul of an intelligent workman without whom chance would never have been able to indicate the time and the sun's passage.

As we are much more enlightened by physics, which shows us that there is no other soul of the world than God and movement, and no other soul of plants than heat; as we are more enlightened by anatomy, whose scalpel is exercised as happily on them as on us and the animals; as we are more informed by microscopic observations which have revealed to us the reproduction of plants, our eyes cannot open to the broad daylight of so many discoveries without seeing, despite the great analogy described above, that the differences between man and plant are perhaps even greater than the similarities. Man is, of all the beings hitherto known, the one which has the most soul, as if it were necessary for that to be so; and the plant is likewise the one which has, and was destined to have, the least of all, if we exclude minerals. What a splendid soul it would be, after all, paying no attention to any objects or any desires, without passions, without vices, without virtues and above all without needs, and not even entrusted with the care of providing food for its body!

After the vegetables and the minerals – bodies without a soul – come beings which begin to be animate, such as the polyp and all the animal-plants still unknown today, which other favoured Trembleys will discover in time.[20]

The more the nature of those bodies I have mentioned is vegetable, the less instinct they will have and the less discernment will be seen in their workings.

The more animality they have, or the more their functions are like ours, the more generously they will be provided with that precious gift. These intermediate or compound beings – which I call thus because they are children of both kingdoms – will have, in short, intelligence in proportion to the quantity of movement they will have to make in order to find their subsistence.

Here, the most intelligent of animal-plants follows the lowest or meanest of animals, by which I mean the one which, of all the true beings of this species, makes the least movement or effort in order to find its food and its female, but always a little more than the highest animal-plant. This animal will have more instinct than the animal-plant, even if this surplus movement is only a hair's-breadth. It is the same for all the rest, in relation to the anxieties which torment them. For without this intelligence relative to their needs, one would not be able to stretch out its neck, another to crawl or a third to lower or lift up its head, swim, fly or walk, and all this clearly on purpose to find food. Thus, for lack of an aptitude to replace the loss incurred by even the animals which transpire the least, each individual would be unable to go on living. It would die as it was produced and, as a result, bodies would be produced in vain if God had not given them all,

[20] On Trembley's discovery of the freshwater polyp in 1739, see p. 12 note 19.

so to speak, that portion of himself which Virgil extols so magnificently in the Bees.[21]

Chapter III

Nothing could be more charming than this contemplation; its object is that ladder which is so imperceptibly graduated that we can see nature passing exactly through all its levels without ever missing out, so to speak, a single rung in all its different productions! What a picture is provided by the spectacle of the universe! Everything is perfectly matched, nothing is out of place; if it moves from white to black, it does so through an infinite number of tones or levels, which make the transition infinitely pleasant.

Man and plant are white and black, and the quadrupeds, birds, fish, insects and amphibians correspond to the intermediate colours which soften the striking contrast. Without these colours – without the workings of animals, all different from one another, which I refer to with this word – man, that arrogant animal, made of clay like the others, would have thought he was God on earth and would have worshipped only himself.

There is no animal, however feeble and mean in appearance, the sight of which does not diminish a philosopher's self-esteem. If chance has placed us at the top of the scale, do not forget that a trifle more or less in the brain, in which is found the soul of all men (except the Leibnizians), can immediately plunge us to the bottom, and let us not despise beings whose origin is the same as ours. They are, in truth, only on the second rung, but their position is more solid and stable.

If we look down from the cleverest man to the meanest of vegetals and even the fossils, and then back up from the lowest of these bodies to the greatest genius, thus taking in the whole circle of natural kingdoms, we admire everywhere the uniform variety of nature. Mind seems to finish here, and there we see it about to be extinguished, like a flame lacking fuel. Elsewhere it revives; it shines in us and it guides animals.

One could insert here a curious chapter of natural history to show that intelligence has been given to all animals according to their needs, but what is the point of so many examples and facts? They would overburden us without enlightening us any more and, in any case, these facts can be found in the books of those indefatigable observers whom I dare to call philosophers' labourers.

Let whoever wishes, bore us with all the wonders of nature; let one spend his life observing insects and another counting the little bones in certain fishes' hearing membranes, or even, if you want, measuring how far a flea can jump, to say nothing of so many other pathetic objects. I, who am interested only in philosophy and am troubled only at not being able to extend its bounds, will always consider active

[21] Virgil, *Georgics*, IV., esp. ll. 49–50.

nature to be my sole viewpoint. I like seeing far, on a large scale and in general, and not the particulars or little details which, although they are necessary to a certain extent in all science, are usually the sign of a lack of genius in those who concern themselves with them. It is only thanks to this way of looking at things that we can be certain, not only that man is not entirely a plant, but also that he is not even an animal like any other. Do I need to repeat the reason why? It is because, having infinitely more needs, he had to have infinitely more mind.

Who would have believed that such a sad cause would produce such great effects? Who would have believed that such a troublesome subordination to all of life's unwelcome necessities, which remind as at every instant of the misery of our origin and condition, who would have believed, I repeat, that such a principle could be the source of our happiness and our dignity? We could go so far as to say that it is the source of our mind's sensual pleasure, which is so superior to that of our body. Certainly, if our needs are, as we cannot doubt, a necessary consequence of the structure of our organs, it is equally obvious that our soul is determined directly by our needs, which it is so vigilant in satisfying and in foreseeing that nothing takes precedence over them. Even our will must obey them. We can therefore say that our soul takes on strength and wisdom in relation to their number, like a general whose expertise and courage increases with the number of enemies he has to fight.

I know that the ape resembles man in many ways, and not only by its teeth, as comparative anatomy shows, although the teeth were enough for Linnaeus to put man in the category of quadrupeds (at its head, in fact). But however docile that animal may be, man, the most intelligent of the quadrupeds, shows a much greater aptitude for education. We are right to praise the excellence of animals' workings, and they are worthy of being compared to man's. Descartes did them an injustice and he had reasons for doing so; but whatever one may say about them and whatever prodigies are recounted, it does not diminish our soul's pre-eminence. Our soul is certainly made of the same material and in the same way, but it is not of the same quality, far from it. It is this superior quality of the human soul and this excess of enlightenment, obviously the result of our organisation, which make man the king of the animals and the only one apt for society, whose languages were invented by his work and whose laws and customs were invented by his wisdom.

All that is left for me to do is to answer in advance a possible objection. If, people will say, your principle were generally true and if the needs of bodies were the yardstick of their intelligence, why up to a certain age, when man has more needs than ever – because, the nearer he is to his origin, the more he grows – does he have so little instinct that without great permanent care he would infallibly perish? Animals, on the contrary, when they are hardly born, already show so much wisdom, they who, in your hypothesis and even in truth, have so few needs.

This argument will be disregarded if it is considered that, when animals come into the world, they have already spent a long part of their short life in the womb and hence they are so well formed that a day-old lamb, for example, runs in the meadow and eats grass like its father and mother.

The state of man-foetus is proportionately shorter; he spends in the womb only a possible hundred and twenty-fifth of his long life; as he is not formed enough, he cannot think and his organs must have time to harden, to acquire that strength which is to produce the light of instinct, for the same reasons that a stone will not produce sparks if it is not hard. Man, born of more naked parents and himself more naked and delicate than an animal, cannot receive his intelligence as quickly; intelligence comes late in man, and it is only fair that it should be precocious in the animal. Man is all the better for his wait, as nature repays him with interest by giving him more mobile and freer organs.

To fashion discernment like ours needs more time than nature takes to construct the discernment of animals. One must go through childhood to reach reason, and one must experience the disadvantages and suffering of animality in order to acquire the advantages which characterise man.

If the instinct of animals had been given to man at birth, it would not have been enough for all the handicaps which assail him in his cradle. All the cunning of animals would be defeated in such a state. Likewise, give a child only the instinct of those animals which have the most, and he will not even be able to tie his umbilical cord, even less to find his nurse's nipple. Give animals our original disadvantages and they will all die.

I have considered the soul as forming part of the natural history of animate bodies, but I have been careful not to present the gradations from one to the next as being as new as the reasons for this gradual transition. For how many philosophers, and even theologians, have given animals a soul, so that man's soul, according to one of the latter,[22] is to an animal's soul what an angel's soul is to man's and, apparently rising ever higher, what God's soul is to that of an angel.

[22] D. Boullier, a Protestant theologian, *Essai philosophique sur l'âme des bêtes* (Amsterdam, 1727).

The System of Epicurus

How miserable is the origin of the proudest of animals!

Pliny[1]

1 'Quam misera animalium superbissimi origo', Pliny the Elder, *Natural History*, Bk. VII, §43; the original quotation reads: 'quam sit frivola animalium superbissimi origo'.

Note on the text

The first version of the *Système d'Epicure*, entitled *Réflexions philosophiques sur l'origine des animaux* (*Philosophical Reflections on the Origin of Animals*), consisting of only thirty-one paragraphs, was published anonymously 'A Londres, chez Jean Nourse, 1750', in fact in Berlin and possibly in the previous year. It became, mainly by the addition of further paragraphs and with only minor changes to the existing paragraphs, the *Système d'Epicure* in La Mettrie's *Philosophical Works* in 1750, which is the text that is translated here. It is possible, as Falvey surmises in his edition of *Anti-Seneca* (pp. 65–6), that the additions were made in part because La Mettrie had finally to drop his *Anti-Seneca* from that volume, as some of the added paragraphs deal with the same themes. This work has only ever been republished in its entirety in the various editions of the *Philosophical Works*; the *Philosophical Reflections* were published in *Corpus*, no. 5/6, 1987.

I

When I read in Virgil, *Georgics*, Bk. II:

'Happy was the man who was able to know the causes of things!'[2]

I ask, 'who was?' No, the wings of our genius cannot lift us up to the knowledge of causes. The most ignorant of men is as enlightened in this respect as the greatest philosopher. We see all objects and everything that happens in the universe as a beautiful opera set, whose pulleys and counterweights we do not notice. The primary springs of all bodies, as well as of our own, are hidden from us and will probably always be. It is easy to console ourselves for being deprived of knowledge which would not make us any better or happier.

II

I cannot see children enjoying themselves with a pipe and soapy water, making pretty coloured bubbles which their breath expands so amazingly, without comparing them to nature. It seems to me that, like them, without realising, nature uses the simplest means to operate. It is true that she does not expend more effort in giving the earth a prince who is to make it tremble with fear, than in bringing forth the grass we trample underfoot. A little clay and a drop of mucus fashion both man and insect, and the tiniest portion of movement was enough to make the machine of the world function.

III

The wonders of all the kingdoms, as the chemists say, and all those things we admire, which so amaze us, were produced, so to speak, from more or less the same mixture of water and soap, and as if from our children's pipes.

2 'Felix qui potuit rerum cognoscere causas.' (Virgil, *Georgics*, II.490). This quotation is also used as the epigraph of *Anti-Seneca*.

IV

How can we 'catch nature in the act'? She has never caught herself in the act. She is deprived of knowledge and feeling, and makes silk like the *Bourgeois gentilhomme*[3] makes prose, without knowing that she is doing so. She is as blind when she gives life as she is innocent when she destroys it.

V

Physicists consider the air to be the universal chaos of all objects. We can say that it is almost nothing but a sort of fine water in which they all swim as long as they are lighter than it. When the support of this water, that unknown spring by which we all live and which constitutes, or is itself, the true air, when, I repeat, that spring no longer has enough strength to carry the seeds scattered throughout the atmosphere, either they fall onto the earth under their own weight, or they are thrown here and there by the winds on its surface. Hence all those vegetable growths which suddenly cover ditches, walls, marshes and stagnant water, which were not long ago devoid of grass and greenery.

VI

How many caterpillars and other insects sometimes also come to eat trees in bloom and attack our gardens! Where do they come from if not from the air?

VII

Thus there are both animal and vegetable grains or seeds in the air; they exist and have always existed. Each individual attracts those of its own species or those which are specific to it, unless one prefers to say that these seeds go looking for the bodies in which they can ripen, germinate and develop.

VIII

Thus their first womb was the air, whose warmth began to prepare them; they then take on more life in their second womb – by which I mean the sperm ducts, the testicles and the seminal vesicles – by means of heat, chafing and stagnation for a great number of years. For we know that it is only in puberty, and thus after a long period of digestion in the male's body, that virile seeds become apt for

3 M. Jourdain, in *Le Bourgeois gentilhomme*, by Molière.

reproduction. Their third and last womb is the female's, where the fertilised egg, having come down from the ovary through the Fallopian tubes, is as it were incubated internally and easily takes root.

IX

Do the same seeds, which produce so many sorts of animalcules in the fluids exposed to the air, and which move into the male, by way of the organs of respiration and deglutition, as easily as they do from the male into the female, in a form which is finally visible – do these seeds, I repeat, which are implanted and germinate with such great facility in the uterus, imply that humans, fully formed humans, of both sexes, have always existed?

X

If humans have not always existed as we see them today (and how can we believe they came into the world grown up, as mother and father, and perfectly capable of procreating beings like themselves!), the earth must have acted as the uterus of mankind. It must have opened up its bosom to human seeds, already prepared so that, given certain laws, this proud animal could come forth. Why, I ask you, modern Anti-Epicureans, why should the earth, that mother and nurse of all objects, have refused to animal seeds what she allowed to the meanest, most useless and most harmful vegetables? They still find her bowels fertile, and this womb after all is no more surprising than that of woman.

XI

But the earth is no longer the cradle of humanity! We no longer see it producing men! Do not reproach it for its present sterility. It has produced its brood in that respect. An old hen no longer lays and an old woman no longer has children; this is more or less Lucretius's reply to that objection.[4]

XII

I appreciate all the difficulties created by such a provenance, and how difficult it is to avoid them. But as one can find one's way out of such a daring supposition only by producing others, here is one which I submit to the judgement of philosophers.

[4] See *De rerum natura*, Bk. V, 821–36.

XIII

The first generations must have been very imperfect. One must have lacked an oesophagus, another a stomach, vulva or intestines, and so on. It is obvious that the only animals which were able to live, survive and propagate their species were those which happened to be provided with all the elements necessary for reproduction and which, in a word, lacked no essential part. Likewise, those which were deprived of some absolutely necessary part died, either shortly after their birth, or at least without reproducing themselves. Perfection was no more achieved in a day in nature than in art.

XIV

I have seen that woman without sexual organs,[a] an indefinable animal, completely castrated in her mother's womb; she had neither mound nor clitoris, nor nipples, nor vulva, nor labia majora, nor vagina, nor womb, nor periods, and here is the proof: a tube put into the ureter could be touched through the anus, and a lancet pushed well into the place where the large opening always is in women found only fat and flesh with few vessels, which bled very little. A plan to fashion a vulva for her had to be abandoned, and her marriage had to be annulled after ten years with a peasant who was as stupid as she was and who, being ignorant, was far from informing his wife of what she lacked. He quite simply believed that the channel of excretion was also for reproduction, and he acted accordingly, loving his wife, who loved him also very much, and he was very upset when his secret was discovered. The Lieutenant-General, the Count of Erouville, and all the doctors and surgeons in Ghent saw this incomplete woman and drew up a report. She was completely deprived of any feeling of sexual pleasure and, however much one stimulated the seat of her absent clitoris, she experienced no pleasant feeling. Her breasts never swelled.

XV

If even today nature relaxes her vigilance to such an extent, if she is capable of such a surprising mistake, how much more frequent must similar games have been in the past! Such far-reaching distraction, so to say, such exceptional, extraordinary absent-mindedness, explains all those to which nature must have been subject in the distant past when reproduction was uncertain, difficult, ill-established and equivalent to trials rather than masterstrokes.

[a] She has already been mentioned in *Man a Machine*.[5]

[5] See p. 16 above.

XVI

Through what an infinite number of combinations must matter have passed before reaching the only combination which could result in a perfect animal, and through how many others before reproduction reached the degree of perfection it enjoys today!

XVII

The natural consequence is that only those to whom lucky combinations finally gave eyes and ears, formed and placed exactly like ours, had the faculty of seeing, hearing and so on.

XVIII

Once the elements of matter, by dint of moving about and mixing together, had managed to create eyes, it was as impossible not to see as it is impossible not to see oneself in a natural or artificial mirror. The eye happened to be the mirror of objects, which in turn often act as a mirror for it. Nature no more thought of making the eye to see, than she thought of making water to act as a mirror for the simple shepherdess. Water happened to be appropriate for sending back images; the shepherdess saw her pretty little face with pleasure. This is how the author of *Machine Man* thinks.

XIX

Was there not once a painter who, unable to reproduce a foaming horse as he wished, succeeded admirably and created the most beautiful foam by throwing his brush onto his canvas?

Chance often goes further than prudence.

XX

Everything written by physicians and naturalists on the use of the parts of animate bodies has always seemed totally unfounded to me. All their reasoning on final causes is so superficial that if Lucretius refuted them so badly, he must have been as poor a physician as he was a great poet.

XXI

The eyes were made in the same way as sight or hearing is lost and recovered, and as a particular body reflects sound or light. No more artifice was needed to construct the eye or the ear than to fabricate an echo.

XXII

If there is a grain of dust in the Eustachian tube we cannot hear; if Ridley's arteries in the retina are swollen with blood and take over part of the area which receives rays of light, we see floating specks. If the optic nerve is obstructed, the eyes are blank and see nothing. A trifle upsets nature's optics, which it therefore did not invent all at once.

XXIII

Art's fumblings to imitate nature give us an idea of what nature's were like.

XXIV

People say that all eyes are made optically and all ears mathematically! How do they know that? Because they have observed nature; they were astonished to see that its productions were so equal, and even superior, to art. They could not do otherwise than suppose that it had some aim or enlightened purposes. Nature thus existed before art, which was created following in her steps and came from her as the son comes from his mother. And a chance arrangement, providing the same privileges as an arrangement made on purpose by all possible hard work, earned our common mother an honour which is due only to the laws of movement.

XXV

Man, that animal which is curious about everything, prefers making the knot he wishes to untie more indissoluble, rather than not piling up question upon question, the last of which always makes the problem more difficult. If all bodies are moved by fire, what gives fire its movement? Ether. What gives it to ether? D*** is right: our philosophy is no better than that of the Indians.[6]

6 Diderot, in the *Lettre sur les aveugles* ('Londres' [Paris], 1749), refers to an Indian who explains that the world is carried on the back of an elephant and, when asked what carries the elephant, replies that it is a tortoise, and so on; Diderot claims that our explanations are no better.

XXVI

Let us take things for what they seem to be. Let us look all around us: this circumspection is not devoid of pleasure and the sight is enchanting. Let us watch it admiringly, but without that useless itch to understand everything and without being tortured by curiosity, which is always superfluous when our senses do not share it with our minds.

XXVII

As, given certain physical laws, it was not possible for the sea not to ebb and flow, in the same way, once certain laws of movement existed, they fashioned eyes which could see, ears which could hear, nerves which could feel and a tongue sometimes capable and sometimes incapable of speaking, according to its organisation; and they constructed the organ of thought. Nature made, inside man's machine, another machine which turned out to be good at retaining ideas and making new ones, as in woman the womb makes a child from a drop of liquid. Having made eyes which can see without itself being able to see, nature made a machine which can think without itself being able to think. When we see a bit of mucus producing a living creature full of wit and beauty and capable of rising to the sublime in style, morals and sensuality, should we be surprised that a little bit more or less cerebellum constitutes genius or idiocy?

XXVIII

As the faculty of thought has no different a source from that of sight, hearing, speech and reproduction, I do not see why it should be absurd to make an intelligent being come from a blind cause. How many extremely intelligent children there are, whose father and mother are perfectly stupid and imbecile!

XXIX

But, good God, how many mean insects have more or less as much wit as those who spend their whole learnedly puerile lives watching them! In what animal – even the most useless, the most poisonous and the most ferocious, of which the earth cannot be too soon rid – does some ray of intelligence not shine? Must we suppose an enlightened cause, which gives some a being so easily destroyed by others, and which has so intertwined everything that it is only by means of chance experiments that we can distinguish poison from its antidote and what is to be sought from what is to be avoided? It seems to me that, given the extreme disorder of all things, if we do not attribute everything to nature's blindness we commit a sort of impiety. For nature alone can do harm and good innocently.

XXX

By making our vainglorious sight extend further, nature plays with our reason, even more than people played with the reason of that pauper in Paris who used his skull as a begging bowl, when they amused themselves by pressing his brain.

XXXI

Let us forget

> That proud reason, of which we boast so much.

In order to destroy it, we do not need to resort to delirium, fever, rabies or any poisoned miasma inserted into the veins by the tiniest type of innoculation;

> A little wine upsets it, a child seduces it.[7]

Thanks to reason, we can manage to accord reason little importance. It is a mechanism which can go wrong like any other and even more easily.

XXXII

Can all animals, and thus man, whom no wise man even thought of removing from that category, be truly the sons of the earth, as the fable says of the giants? As the sea perhaps originally covered the whole surface of our world, could it not have been itself the floating cradle of all the beings eternally enclosed in its breast? That is the theory of the author of *Telliamed*,[8] which comes down more or less to that of Lucretius; for it still needs the sea, absorbed by the earth's pores and consumed little by little by the sun's heat over an infinite period of time, to have been forced on withdrawing to leave the human egg beached on the shore, as it sometimes leaves fish. As a result of which, without any other incubation than the sun, man or any other animal could come out of its shell, as some still hatch out today in hot countries, and as chickens do in warm dung thanks to the naturalist's art.

7 The two lines are taken from a poem by the seventeenth-century Libertin poet Mme A. Deshoulières, 'Les Moutons', published in *Nouveau mercure galant* (Paris, 1677): 'Cette fière raison, dont on fait tant de bruit/Un peu de vin la trouble, un enfant la séduit.'

8 See Introduction, p. xx.

XXXIII

However that may be, it is likely that animals, being less perfect than man, could have been fashioned the first. As they imitated each other, so man probably imitated them; for their whole kingdom is in truth only made up of different, more or less skilful apes, at the head of which Pope placed Newton.[9] The posterity of the birth, or of the development of the structure contained in the human germ, would not then be so surprising. For the same reason that it takes more time to make a man, or an animal endowed with all his limbs and faculties, than to make an imperfect or truncated man, it likewise takes more time to bring man into being than to hatch out an animal. If we accord anteriority to the production of beasts, it is not in order to explain their precocious instinct, but to account for the imperfection of their species.

XXXIV

We should not believe that it would have been impossible for a human foetus, coming out of an egg rooted in the earth, to find the means of survival. In any part of this globe and however the earth gave birth to men, the first ones must have fed on what the earth produced itself without cultivation, as can be proved from reading the most ancient historians and naturalists. Do you believe that the first newborn baby found a nipple or a river of milk ready for its subsistence?

XXXV

When man was nourished by the earth's vigorous sap throughout his embryonic state, he may have been stronger and more robust than he is now that he has been enervated by an infinite series of soft and delicate generations; as a result, he may have enjoyed precocious animal instinct, which only seems to come from the fact that the bodies of animals, which have less time to live, are formed earlier. In addition, animals – which, far from being pitiless, have often shown more pity in barbaric exhibitions than have their organisers – may, in order to add outside help to those resources which belong to man, have provided him with better shelter than that in which he chanced to be born; they may have carried him, together with their little ones, to places where he would suffer less from exposure. Perhaps even, moved to compassion at the sight of so much difficulty and feebleness, they may have been willing to suckle him, as several apparently trustworthy writers affirm sometimes happens in Poland; I am referring to those charitable bears which, after having, they say, kidnapped almost newborn babies left on doorsteps by unwary

[9] See Pope's *Essay on Man*, Epistle II, ll. 31–4.

nurses, fed them and treated them with as much love and kindness as their own pups.[10] All this paternal care given to man by animals probably lasted until he was older and stronger and was able to crawl like them, hide in woods and hollow tree trunks and live off grass like them. I could add that if men ever lived longer than they do today, such a surprising longevity could only be reasonably attributed to such behaviour and food.

XXXVI

This, it is true, creates new difficulties for the means and the ease of perpetuating our species; for if so many men and so many animals had a short life because they were deprived in some cases of a part of the body and in others of a pair of organs, how many would have died without the help which, as I have just indicated, they may have received! But if perhaps two in a thousand survived and were able to procreate their fellow beings, that is all I require, both for the hypothesis of generations which are so difficult to perfect, and for the hypothesis of children of the earth who are difficult to bring up, or even so impossible to bring up, when we consider that, if those of today were abandoned as soon as they were brought into the world, they would all, or almost all, perish.

XXXVII

There are however some certain facts which teach us that there are many things we can do of necessity, which our habits alone, more than reason itself, make us believe absolutely impossible. The author of the *Treatise on the Soul* has provided a curious collection of them.[11] We can see that children left in a desert young enough to have lost all memory and to believe that they have neither beginning nor end, or lost for years in uninhabited forests after a shipwreck, live off the same food as animals, crawl like them instead of walking upright and only pronounce more or less horrible inarticulate sounds instead of having a distinct pronunciation, according to the animals which they have mechanically imitated. Man does not bring his reason with him at birth; he is more stupid than any animal, but more favourably organised in having memory and the ability to learn. If his instinct comes later, it does so only in order to change quickly into a little reason which, like a well-nourished body, is gradually strengthened by being cultivated. If this instinct is left untended, the caterpillar will not have the honour of becoming a butterfly and man will be nothing but an animal like any other.

10 La Mettrie recounts several such stories from Poland in *Treatise on the Soul*, ch. XV, story V.

11 Likewise in ch. XV, 'Stories which confirm that all our ideas come from our senses'.

XXXVIII

The person who considered man as a plant and hardly accorded him more esteem essentially than a cabbage did not do this splendid species more harm than the one who made him a pure machine.[12] Man grows in the womb by vegetation and his body is disturbed and recovers like a watch, either thanks to his own springs, whose working is often beneficent, or thanks to the skill of those who understand them, not as watchmakers (the anatomists) but as physico-chemists.

XXXIX

The first animals which came into the world – hatched from an eternal germ, whatever it was – produced, by dint of mixing with each other, according to certain philosophers, that splendid monster called man. And man in turn, by mixing with animals, is said to have given birth to the different peoples of the universe. An author who thought of everything but did not say everything says that the first kings of Denmark were supposed to have come from intercourse between a bitch and a man; the people of Pegu boast of being descended from a dog and a Chinese woman brought to their country in a shipwreck, and the origin of the first Chinese is said to be the same.

XL

The striking difference between the physiognomies and characters of different peoples must have made them imagine these strange unions and these bizarre amalgams; and, seeing an intelligent man brought into the world thanks to the activities and whim of a fool, people must have believed that there was nothing more impossible or more surprising about man being engendered by animals.

XLI

So many philosophers have supported Epicurus's opinion, that I have dared to add my feeble voice to theirs; and like them I have only produced a system. Which shows us what an abyss we venture into when, desiring to penetrate the depths of time, we want to extend our presumptuous gaze to what is not open to it. For whether you accept the Creation or deny it, the same mystery is everywhere and the same incomprehensibility is everywhere. How was the earth I inhabit formed? Is it the only inhabited planet? Where have I come from? Where am I? What is the

[12] La Mettrie is referring to his own *Man as Plant* and *Machine Man*.

nature of what I can see or of all those bright phantoms whose illusion I love? Did I exist before not existing at all? Shall I exist when I no longer exist? What state preceded the awareness of my existence? What state will follow the loss of that awareness? That is what the greatest geniuses will never know. They will beat philosophically about the bush,[b] as I did, they will make religious believers raise the alarm and they will teach us nothing.

XLII

In the same way as medicine is usually only a science of remedies with admirable names, so philosophy is only a science of fine words. It is a two-fold stroke of luck when the remedies cure people and the fine words mean something. After such a confession, how could such a work be dangerous? It can only humiliate philosophers' vanity and invite them to submit to faith.

XLIII

Oh, how charming in the eyes of a philosopher is such a varied picture as that of the universe and its inhabitants, and such a changing stage with such beautiful scenery! Although the philosopher does not understand its first causes (and glories in this ignorance), from the corner of the stalls in which he is hidden, seeing without being seen and far from the populace and the noise, he watches a spectacle in which everything delights him and nothing surprises him, not even the fact that he is there.

XLIV

He finds it amusing to be alive, amusing to make fun of himself, to play such a comic role and to believe that he is an important character.

XLV

The reason why nothing surprises a philosopher is that he knows that madness and wisdom, instinct and reason, grandeur and pettiness, childishness and good sense, vice and virtue are as close to each other in man as adolescence and childhood, and as the rector spirit[13] and oil in vegetals or the pure and the impure in fossils. The

[b] See Mr de Buffon's ingenious new hypothesis.[14]

[13] See p. 37 note 57.

[14] The first three volumes of Buffon's *Natural History* had been published in Paris in 1749.

philosopher compares the hard but true man to a carriage lined with precious material but badly hung; in his eyes the fop is only a peacock admiring its tail, the weak vacillating man is only a weathercock turning at every change of wind, the violent man is only a rocket taking off as soon as it is lit or milk which boils over the edge of its dish, and so on.

XLVI

A man who examines everything as a physicist is less difficult in friendship, in love, etc. and easier to satisfy and to live with; for him, lack of confidence in a friend and lack of faithfulness in a wife or a mistress are only slight defects in humanity, and even theft, seen with the same eyes, is a bad habit rather than a crime. Do you know why I still have some respect for men? Because I seriously believe them to be machines. If I believed the opposite hypothesis, I know few of them with whom I would wish to associate. Materialism is the antidote to misanthropy.

XLVII

One cannot make such wise reflections without benefiting from them oneself. That is why the philosopher, holding up the same aegis against his own vices as against adversity, feels no greater interior pain at the unhappy necessity for his own bad qualities than he feels vanity and pride at his good qualities. If by chance he has as good an organisation as society can, and every reasonable man should, hope for, the philosopher will welcome it and will even be glad, but without smugness or presumption. For the opposite reason, as he did not create himself, if the springs of his machine work badly he is angry and bemoans it as a good citizen, but as a philosopher, he does not consider himself to be responsible. He is too enlightened to consider himself guilty of thoughts and actions which originate and happen despite him. He sighs at man's ill-fated condition and does not allow himself to be tortured by remorse, the bitter fruit of education which was never borne by the tree of nature.

XLVIII

We are in nature's hands like a pendulum in the hands of a watchmaker; she kneads us as she wishes, or rather as she can. So when we follow the imprint of the original movements which govern us, we are no more criminal than the Nile is because of its floods or the sea because of the ravages it causes.

XLIX

Having spoken about the origin of animals, I shall now add some reflections on death, followed by others on life and sensuality. Both are in fact a *Project for Life and Death* worthy of crowning an Epicurean system.

L

To change the subject from life to death is no more abrupt than to make the actual transition. The gap separating them is only a dot, both in relation to the nature of life, hanging by a thread which can be broken by so many causes, and in the immense duration of beings. Alas, as man worries, thrashes about and ceaselessly torments himself in this dot, one can truly say that reason has only made him mad.

LI

How fleeting is life! The shapes of bodies sparkle for as long as topical songs are sung. Men and roses appear in the morning and have vanished by nightfall. Everything is replaced, everything disappears and nothing is destroyed.

LII

To tremble at death's approach is to be like children who are afraid of ghosts and spirits. The pale spectre can knock on my door when it wants; I shall not be terrified of it. The philosopher alone is brave where most brave men are not brave at all.

LIII

When a leaf falls from a tree, what harm does it do itself? The earth receives it benignly into its bosom; and when the sun's heat has increased the activity of its constituent parts, they float in the air and are the plaything of the winds.

LIV

What difference is there between a man and a plant once they are reduced to powder? Surely animal ashes resemble vegetable ashes?

LV

Those who defined cold as a 'privation of fire'[c] said what cold was not and not what it was. Death is not the same; to say what it is not, to say that it is a privation of air which makes all movement, all heat and all feeling stop, is to declare well enough what it is. Nothing positive. Nothing. Less than nothing, if that could be imagined. No, nothing real, nothing that concerns us, nothing that belongs to us, as Lucretius said very well.[15] Death in the nature of things is only what zero is in arithmetic.

LVI

And yet (who would have believed it?) it is this zero, this number which does not count and which is not itself a number, this number for which there is nothing to pay, that causes so much alarm and anxiety, suspends some people in cruel uncertainty and makes others quake so much that they cannot think of it without horror. The very name of death makes them shudder. Is the passage from something to nothing, from life to death and from being to nothingness therefore more unimaginable than the passage from nothing to something, from nothingness to being or to life? No, it is no less natural and while it is more violent, it is also more necessary.

LVII

Let us accustom ourselves to this thought, and we shall not be distressed at seeing ourselves die, any more than at seeing a knife finally wearing out a sheath, and we shall not shed childish tears at what must indispensably happen. Do we really need such force of mind to sacrifice ourselves, and to be always ready to do so? What other force holds us to what is leaving us?

LVIII

To be truly wise, it is not enough to be able to live contentedly in obscurity; we must be able to leave everything behind impassively when the time comes. The more we leave behind, the greater is our heroism. Our last moment constitutes the main touchstone of our wisdom; it is, so to speak, in the crucible of death that wisdom must be tested.

[c] Boerhaave, *Elements of Chemistry*, vol. I, 'Fire'.

[15] *De rerum natura*, Bk. III, 830–1.

LIX

If you fear death, if you are too attached to life, your last breath will be terrible; death will act as your cruellest torturer. It is torture to fear it.

LX

Why is the warrior who has acquired such glory in the field of Mars, and who has so often shown himself formidable in single combat, unable to face a duel with death, so to speak, when he is ill in bed?

LXI

On our death-bed it is no longer a question of that ostentation or that noisy panoply of war, which arouses the mind and calls automatically to arms. Honour, the Frenchman's great stimulus, no longer exists. We no longer have before our eyes the example of so many fellow soldiers who, no doubt made brave by the others rather than by themselves, incite each other to a thirst for carnage. There are no more onlookers and no more booty or prominence to expect. When we see that the void is the only reward for our courage, what reason can there be to keep up our self-respect?

LXII

I am not at all surprised to see people dying like cowards in their beds and like brave men in action. The Duke of ***[16] met cannons intrepidly in the rear of the trenches, and wept on his toilet. There a hero and here a faint-heart, sometimes Achilles and at others Thersites – such is man![17] What could be more appropriate to the inconsistency of such a bizarre mind?

LXIII

Thank God, I have come through so many ordeals without quaking that I am justified in believing I shall die in the same way, like a philosopher. In those violent crises in which I thought I was about to pass from life to death, in those moments of weakness in which the soul is extinguished together with the body – moments

[16] Is La Mettrie perhaps referring to the Duke of Grammont, whose personal physician he had been?
[17] Both Achilles and Thersites appear in Homer's *Iliad*.

which are terrible for so many great men – how have I, weak and delicate machine that I am, the strength to joke, jest and laugh?

LXIV

I have neither fears nor hopes and no imprint of my early education; luckily that mass of prejudices, sucked in, so to speak, with my milk, disappeared early on in the divine brilliance of philosophy. That soft tender substance, on which the seal of error had been so deeply imprinted, is today blank and has retained no trace either of my colleges or of my pedants. I have been courageous enough to forget what I had been weak enough to learn; it is all crossed out (what luck!), all erased and all pulled up by the roots. And this is the great work of reflection and philosophy; they alone could remove the chaff and sow the good seed in the furrows which used to be filled with weeds.

LXV

That is enough of that fatal sword which is suspended over our heads. If we cannot think of it with equanimity, let us at least forget that it is only hanging by a thread. Let us live calmly, in order to die in the same way.

LXVI

Epictetus, Antoninus, Seneca, Petronius, Anacreon, Chaulieu, etc.,[18] be my evangelists and my directors in the last moments of my life – But no, you will be of no use to me. I shall have no need to steel myself, or to amuse or distract myself. My eyes veiled, I shall plunge into that river of eternal forgetfulness which swallows up everything with no way back. Fate's sickle will no sooner be raised than, unbuttoning my collar myself, I shall be ready to receive its blow.

LXVII

The sickle! A poetic illusion! Death is not armed with a sharp instrument. One could say (as far as I have been able to judge from its closest approach) that it only puts around the neck of dying people a noose which acts with narcotic softness rather than tightening. It is death's opium; all the blood is inebriated by it, and the

[18] Epictetus, Marcus Aurelius Antoninus and Seneca were all Stoics, while Petronius was the author of the *Satyricon*, and Anacreon and the seventeenth-century French poet Abbé G. A. de Chaulieu wrote love poetry.

senses are dulled. We feel ourselves dying as we feel ourselves falling asleep or fainting, not without a certain voluptuousness.

LXVIII

Indeed, how calm and sweet is a death that creeps up, as it were, and that neither surprises nor wounds! A death foreseen, in which one has only enough awareness to be able to enjoy it! I am not at all surprised that the pleasant illusion held out by that sort of death is seductive. It is accompanied by nothing painful or violent, and as the vessels are blocked only one by one, life ebbs away little by little with a certain soft nonchalance. One feels oneself pulled so gently in one direction that one scarcely even deigns to turn to the other. It costs a lot, it does violence to nature, not to give in to the temptation to die, when disgust with life makes death a pleasure.

LXIX

Death and love are consummated in the same way, by expiration. We reproduce ourselves when we die from love, and we are annihilated when we die from Atropos's scissors. Let us thank nature which, having devoted the most vivid pleasures to the propagation of our species, usually reserves other quite sweet pleasures for those moments when she can no longer keep us alive.

LXX

I saw thousands of soldiers die – a sorry sight! – in those great military hospitals of which I was in charge in Flanders during the last war. Pleasant deaths such as those I have just depicted seemed to me much rarer than painful deaths. The most frequent ones happen unawares. We leave the world as we come into it, without realising it.

LXXI

What do we risk by dying? And do we not risk by living?

LXXII

Death is the end of everything; after it, I repeat, there is a void, an eternal nothingness. Everything has been said, and everything has been done. The sum of good is equal to the sum of evil. There are no more cares, no more problems, no more characters to play: 'the comedy is over'.[d]

LXXIII

'Why did I not take advantage of my illnesses, or rather of one of them, to end this comedy of the world? The cost of my death had already been paid. Here is an unfinished work, to which I shall always have to come back. Like a watch whose movements, even when slow, always describe the same circle although less quickly, and bring the hand back to the place where it was when it started to turn, we all come back likewise to the point from which we are running away. The most enlightened or luckiest medicine can only slow down the movements of the hand. What is the point of so much suffering and effort! After having courageously mounted the scaffold, he who comes down again to run once more the gauntlet of life's beatings and lashings is both deluded and cowardly.' Here is language worthy of a man devoured by ambition, gnawed by envy, a prey to an unhappy love or pursued by other furies!

LXXIV

No, I shall not be the corrupter of that innate taste for life which we have; I shall not spread Stoicism's dangerous poison on the fine days and even on the prosperity of our Luciliuses.[20] On the contrary, I shall try to blunt life's thorns if I cannot reduce their number, in order to increase the pleasure of gathering its roses. And I pray those who, due to a deplorably unfavourable organisation, are dissatisfied with the world's splendid spectacle, to stay here, for religion's sake if they have no humanity or, which is grander, for humanity's sake if they have no religion. I shall show simple minds the great good that religion promises to those who have the patience to endure what a great man called 'weariness with life',[21] and the eternal torments with which it threatens those who do not wish to remain a prey to pain or dissatisfaction. As for the others, those for whom religion is only what it is, a fable, as I cannot restrain them with ties which have been broken, I shall try to seduce them with generous feelings and inspire in them that greatness of soul which defeats everything; and putting forward the claims of humanity, which precede everything, I shall show those cherished, sacred relations which are more touching than the most eloquent speech. I shall show a wife or a mistress in tears, and

[d] Rabelais.[19]

[19] His dying words according to Boureau-Deslandes, *Réflexions sur les grands hommes qui sont morts en plaisantant*, (Amsterdam, 1712), ch. 9.

[20] A reference to Seneca, whose *De vita beata* La Mettrie translated; see *Anti-Seneca*.

[21] Maupertuis, *Essai de philosophie morale* (Berlin, 1749), ch. 2.

heartbroken children who will be left by their father's death without education on the face of the earth. Who would not listen to such touching cries from the graveside? Who would not reopen his dying eyes? What coward refuses to carry a burden that is useful to several people? What monster sees his only aim as freeing himself, thanks to a momentary pain, from the most sacred of duties, by tearing himself from his family, his friends and his country!

LXXV

What can be done, against such arguments, by all those members of a sect which, whatever one may say,[e] has only produced great men at the expense of humanity!

LXXVI

It does not matter how we spur men on to virtue. Religion is only necessary for those who are incapable of feeling humanity. It is certain (who does not observe or experience it every day?) that it is useless to the intercourse of honest people. But only superior souls can feel this great truth. For whom then is the wonderful construction of politics made? For minds who would perhaps have found other checks insufficient, a species which unfortunately constitutes the greatest number; an imbecile, low, crawling species, which society thought it could exploit only by seizing hold of it by the motive of all minds – interest. Interest in an illusory happiness.

LXXVII

I have undertaken to paint myself in my writings as Montaigne did in his *Essays*. Why should one not write about oneself? It is a subject which is as good as any other into which we have less insight. And once one has said that one means oneself, one has made one's excuse, or rather one does not need to make any.

LXXVIII

I am not one of those misanthropes, like Le Vayer, who would not like to begin their lives again; hypochondriac dissatisfaction is too alien to me.[22] But I would not

[e] *Spirit of the Laws*, vol. I.[23]

[22] This is F. de La Mothe le Vayer, author of *The Virtue of the Pagans* (*De la vertu des payens*, Paris, 1642), a frequent source for clandestine irreligious works, also mentioned frequently in *Anti-Seneca*, where La Mettrie quotes Bayle's discussion of La Mothe le Vayer's dissatisfaction with life.

[23] C. L. de Montesquieu's discussion of the Stoics is in Bk. XXIV, ch. 10.

like to go a second time through the stupid childhood which begins and ends our career. I already willingly attach, as Montaigne says, 'a philosopher's tail'[24] to the prime of my life, but in order to fill up as much as possible with my mind the gaps left in my heart, and not to repent of having filled them in the past with love. I would only like to live again as I have lived, in the midst of good food, good company, joyfulness, study and seduction, dividing my time between women – that charming school of the Graces – Hippocrates and the Muses, always both hostile to debauchery and favourable to sensuality, and entirely given over to that charming mixture of wisdom and folly which together, by sharpening each other, make life more enjoyable and, in a way, more spicy.

LXXIX

Lament, poor mortals! Who is stopping you? But lament on the brevity of your moments of wildness; their delirium is worth far more than cold reason, which disconcerts, freezes the imagination and makes pleasures flee.

LXXX

Instead of being tormented by remorse, that torturer, let us regret that charming time, irreparably past, only in the same way as we shall be entitled one day to regret (moderately) ourselves, when we shall, so to speak, have to leave ourselves. Oh reasonable regret, I shall calm you even more by strewing flowers on my final steps and almost on my own grave! These flowers are cheerfulness, the memory of my pleasures and those of young people which remind me of my own, the conversation of charming people, the sight of pretty women, by whom I would like to be surrounded when I am dying, in order to leave the world as I would leave an enchanting show, and sweet friendship, which cannot make one totally forget tender love. Delicious reminiscence, enjoyable books, delightful philosophical poetry, artistic taste, charming friends, you who make reason itself speak the language of the Graces, never leave me.

LXXXI

Let us enjoy the present; we are only what it is. We die from each year that we have lived; the future which has not yet arrived is no more in our power than is the past which has vanished. If we do not take advantage of the pleasures we come across, if

[24] Montaigne, *Essays*, Bk. III, ch. 2, 'On repenting', from which part of the next sentence is taken as well. See *The Complete Essays*, trans. M. A. Screech (Harmondsworth, 1991), p. 920.

we flee those which seem to seek us out today, the day will come when we shall seek them out in vain and they will flee us even more in their turn.

LXXXII

To put off enjoyment until the winter of our years is like waiting to eat in a feast until the dishes have been taken away. There is no other season to follow winter. The cold north winds blow until the end, and even joy will then be more frozen in our hearts than our liquids in their tubes.

LXXXIII

I shall not prefer the sunset of my days to high noon; if I can compare the last part, in which we vegetate, to anything, it is to the time when we used to vegetate. Far from cursing the past, I shall pay it my tribute of well-deserved praise and bless it in the prime of my children who, reassured by my gentleness, contrasting with my apparent severity, will love and seek the company of a good father instead of fearing and fleeing it.

LXXXIV

See the earth covered with snow and frost! Crystals of ice are the only decoration of the unclothed trees; thick mists so eclipse the daystar that hesitant mortals can hardly see to guide themselves. All is languishing, all is numb; the rivers are changed to marble, the fire in bodies is extinguished and cold seems to have nature in chains. A terrible image of old age! Man's sap no longer waters the places it used to. Do you recognise that pitilessly blemished beauty, whom your loving heart used to worship? Sad, seeing the blood frozen in her veins, as poets paint naiads in the halted current of their waters, how many other reasons to lament has he for whom beauty is the greatest gift of the gods! Her mouth is deprived of its finest ornament, a bald head has replaced her blonde naturally curling hair, which used to float playfully on a beautiful breast which has vanished. She has been transformed into a sort of tomb, and the most seductive charms of the fair sex seem to have collapsed and to be as if buried. That skin, so soft, so perfect, so white, is nothing but a mass of scales with hideously crooked furrows and folds; stupid idiocy inhabits those yellow jagged wrinkles instead of the expected wisdom. The crumpled brain, collapsing every day a little more, hardly gives out a ray of intelligence, and the dulled soul wakes as it falls asleep, with no ideas. Such is man's last childhood; could it be any more like the first, and come from a more different cause?

LXXXV

How could that age, although so vaunted, be preferred to that of Hebe? Could it be under the specious pretext of long experience, which a tottering, unsteady reason can usually hardly grasp? It is ingratitude on our part to put the most disgusting part of our being, not above, but on a level with, the most beautiful, flourishing one. While advanced age merits respect, youth, beauty, genius and strength merit homage and worship. Oh happy time when, living without any worries, I knew no duty other than that of pleasure; oh season of love and the heart, charming age, golden age, what has become of you!

LXXXVI

To prefer old age to youth is like putting winter first when deciding the advantages of the seasons. It is like valuing the gifts of Flora, Ceres and Pomona less than snow, ice and black frost; valuing wheat, grapes, fruit and all the sweet-smelling flowers with which the air is so deliciously perfumed, less than sterile fields where not a single rose grows amidst an infinite number of prickles; it is like valuing a beautiful smiling countryside less than sad deserted heaths, from which the birds have fled, where their song is no longer heard and where, instead of the jollity and songs of the reapers and harvesters, only desolation and silence reign.

LXXXVII

As the frozen heart of the earth opens to the soft breath of the zephyr, the seeds which are sown germinate and the earth is covered with flowers and greenery. Oh pleasant livery of spring, everything has a different face when we see you; all of nature is renewed, everything in the universe is happier and more cheerful! Man alone, alas, is not renewed; for him there is no fountain of eternal youth, no Jupiter wanting to bring youth back to our Titons, perhaps no Aurora deigning to implore Jupiter generously for hers.

LXXXVIII

The longest life should not alarm charming people. The Graces do not age; they sometimes exist among wrinkles and white hair; they make reason jest at all times and at all times they prevent the mind from stagnating. Thus thanks to them we can please at any age; at any age we can even arouse love, as happened to Abbé

Gédoin with the charming octogenarian Ninon de Lenclos,[25] who had predicted that it would.

LXXXIX

When I am only able to take one meal a day with Comus, I shall still take one a week, if I can, with Venus, in order to preserve that sweet sociable temper which is, if not more pleasant, at least more necessary for society than wit. Those who associate with that goddess can be recognised by their urbanity and polish and the pleasure of their company. When I have said, alas, an eternal farewell to her worship, I shall still celebrate it in those pretty songs and those joyful words which smooth out wrinkles and still make bright youth gather around rejuvenated old men.

XC

When we can no longer enjoy pleasures, we criticise them. Why upset youth? Surely it is its turn to frolic and to feel love? We should forbid pleasures only as they did in Sparta, in order to increase their charm and fertility. Thus we shall be reasonable old men, despite being old before old age, and we shall be bearable and perhaps still charming afterwards.

XCI

I shall perhaps abandon love sooner than I think but I shall never abandon Themira. I shall not sacrifice her to the gods. I want her pretty hands, which have amused me so often on waking, to close my eyes. I want it to be difficult to say which contributed most to my end, Fate or voluptuousness. Could I but truly die in her arms, where I have so often known sweet oblivion! And (to employ language which smiles at the imagination and paints nature so well), could but my soul, wandering in the Elysian Fields and as if trying to pick out its other half, ask all the shades for her, as astonished to see no longer the tender object which held it only a moment before in such sweet embrace as Themira is to feel deathly cold in a heart which promised, by the strength with which it was beating, to beat for her a long time still. Such are my *Projects for Life and Death*: a voluptuous Epicurean in the course of life until my last breath, and a steady Stoic at the approach of death.

[25] Ninon de Lenclos (1616–1706) was a famous beauty who held a salon which attracted free-thinkers.

XCII

Here are two very different sorts of reflections, which I wanted to include in this Epicurean system. Do you want to know what I think about them myself? The second have left in my soul a feeling of voluptuousness which does not prevent me from laughing at the first. What folly to put into perhaps mediocre prose what is scarcely bearable when it is in beautiful poetry! And how deceived we are to waste our time in vain research; it is, alas, so short and much better spent in enjoyment than in a search for knowledge.

XCIII

I salute you, favourable climate where any man who lives like others can think differently from others; where theologians do not act as judges of philosophers, a role of which they are incapable; where the freedom of the mind, humanity's finest attribute, is not chained by prejudices; where one is not ashamed to say what one does not blush to think; and where there is no risk of becoming a martyr to the doctrine whose apostle one is. I salute you, country already celebrated by philosophers, where all those persecuted by tyranny find (if they are deserving and reputable), not a safe asylum but a glorious harbour; where one feels how far the victories of the mind are above all others; where the philosopher, finally crowned with honours and kindness, is only a monster to the minds of the mindless. May you, oh fortunate land, bloom more and more! May you appreciate your good fortune and make yourself worthy in everything, if possible, of the great man who is your King! Muses, Graces, Cupids and you, wise Minerva, when crowning with the most splendid laurels the august brow of this modern Julian[26] – as worthy of governing, as learned, as clever and as philosophical as the classical one – you are only crowning your own handiwork.

[26] The Emperor Julian 'the Apostate' (361–3) was a hero for all heterodox thinkers, and La Mothe le Vayer devoted a chapter to him in *The Virtue of the Pagans*. La Mettrie is of course referring to Frederick II of Prussia, at whose court he was.

Anti-Seneca or the Sovereign Good

Happy was the man who was able to know the causes of things![1]

1 Virgil, *Georgics*, II. 490; see §1 of *The System of Epicurus* and note.

Note on the text

Of all La Mettrie's works, this is the one that he seems to have rewritten the most. It first took the form of an introduction to his translation of Seneca, on which La Mettrie began to work during 1748, published under the title of *Traité de la vie heureuse, par Senèque. Avec un Discours du traducteur sur le même sujet* (*Treatise on the Happy Life, by Seneca, with a Discourse by the Translator on the same Subject*), by Voss in Potsdam in late 1748. La Mettrie reworked it extensively in 1750, probably for inclusion in his philosophical works; in doing this, he was perhaps following the advice contained in a remark which appeared in the *Bibliothèque raisonnée* in 1748. However, the work was not finally included in the volume of philosophical works, perhaps due to opposition from Maupertuis and fear of an unfavourable reaction from the King, and it was published separately, in an edition of only twelve copies, under the title of *Anti-Senèque ou le souverain bien* (*Anti-Seneca, or the Sovereign Good*), Potsdam, 1750. La Mettrie then decided to alter it again, and published another edition with the same title, giving the publisher as J. Wetstein in Amsterdam, in 1751. This edition included a polemical preface (not given here), defending the work against attacks, in which he develops some of the points already made in the *Preliminary Discourse*. It is this last version of the text that is the basis for Falvey's edition of the work, and also for the extract translated here. The posthumous editions of La Mettrie's *Philosophical Works* all included the work, usually under the title of *Discours sur le bonheur* (*On Happiness*), but not necessarily the same version of it. Because of the name given to it in these posthumous editions, the work has become known as *Discours sur le bonheur*, but this was not the title the author himself gave.

Philosophers agree on happiness as they do on everything else. For some it resides in what is dirtiest and most shameless; they can be recognised by their cynical air and they never blush. For others it consists in sensual pleasure, understood in different ways: sometimes it is pleasure given by the most refined sexuality, and sometimes it is the same pleasure, but moderate and reasonable, and subject not to the debauched whims of an inflamed imagination but to the needs of nature alone; for some, it is the sensuality of the mind concerned with the search for the truth, or delighted with its possession, while for others, it is the satisfaction of the mind, the aim and purpose of all our actions, which Epicurus again dubbed sensual pleasure. This word is dangerously ambiguous and is the reason why his disciples have taken from his teaching a very different fruit from that which this great man was entitled to expect. Some have placed the sovereign good in all the perfections of the mind and the body. For Zeno it consisted in honour and virtue.[2] Seneca, the most illustrious of the Stoics, or rather of the Eclectics (for he was Epicurean and Stoic at the same time, and he chose and took what he found best in each sect), added the knowledge of truth, without defining explicitly which truth.

In the midst of so many other superficial opinions, about which I shall say nothing, few philosophers have had enough taste to place happiness in the continuation of those sweet habits which constitute pure friendship or tender love. But how can one be happy, even on the throne, when one does not live with those one loves! And what misery when one is forced to live with those one detests!

To live peacefully, without ambition and without desire; to make use of riches instead of enjoying them; to keep them without anxiety and to lose them without regret; to be master of them instead of their slave; not to be upset or moved by any passion, or rather not to experience any, and to be contented in both pain and pleasure; to possess a strong, healthy soul in a weak, sick body; to experience neither fear nor fright; to rid oneself of all anxiety; to disdain pleasures and sensuality; to agree to experience pleasure and to be rich without seeking these sources of happiness; to despise life itself; and to achieve virtue by a knowledge of the truth – all these things constitute the Sovereign Good of Seneca and the Stoics in general, and the perfect bliss which follows from it.

But we shall be Anti-Stoics! Those philosophers are sad, strict and unyielding; we shall be cheerful, sweet-natured and indulgent. They are all soul and ignore their bodies; we shall be all body and ignore our souls. They appear impervious to pleasure or pain; we shall glory in feeling both. They aspire to the sublime and rise above all events, considering themselves to be truly men only to the extent that they cease to be men. As for us, we shall not try to control what rules us; we shall not give orders to our sensations. We shall recognise their dominion and our slavery and try to make it pleasant for us, convinced as we are that happiness in life lies there; we shall consider ourselves happier when we are more truly men, or

2 Zeno was the founder of Stoicism.

more worthy of being men, and when we experience humanity, nature and all the social virtues. We shall accept no others and no other life but this one. Thus we can see that the chain of truths necessary for happiness will be shorter than those of Hegesias,[3] Descartes and so many other philosophers. To explain the mechanism of happiness we shall consult only nature and reason, the only stars capable of enlightening and guiding us, if we open up our souls so widely to their rays that we are absolutely impervious to all the poisonous miasma that makes up the atmosphere of fanaticism and prejudice. Now let us come to the point.

Our organs are capable of feeling or being modified in a way that pleases us and makes us enjoy life. If the impression created by this feeling is short, it constitutes pleasure; if longer, sensuality and if permanent, happiness. It is always the same feeling; only its duration and intensity differ. I have added the latter word because there is no Sovereign Good as exquisite as the great pleasure of love, in which it perhaps consists.

The more long-lasting, delicious, enticing, uninterrupted and untroubled this feeling is, the happier one is.

The briefer and more intense it is, the closer it is to the nature of pleasure.

The longer-lasting and calmer it is, the further from pleasure and the closer to happiness it comes.

The more worried, agitated and tormented the soul is, the more bliss eludes it.

To experience neither fear nor desire, as Seneca says, is negative happiness inasmuch as the soul is exempt from all that affects its tranquillity. Descartes wants us to know why we should desire and fear nothing.[4] Those reasons implied by our Stoic no doubt make the spirit firmer and steadier; but as long as one fears nothing, does it matter whether it comes from a mechanical or a philosophical virtue?

To have everything one wants – a favourable organisation, beauty, science, wit, grace, talents, honours, wealth, health, pleasure and glory – is true, perfect happiness.

It follows from all these aphorisms that everything that creates, maintains, nourishes or incites the innate feeling of well-being therefore becomes a cause of happiness. For this reason, in order to lead the way to happiness, it is enough, in my opinion, to show all the causes of a pleasant circulation, and so of pleasing perceptions. These causes are internal and external, or intrinsic and accessory.

Internal or intrinsic causes, which are thought to depend on ourselves, do not do so at all; they arise from our organisation. The others are (1) education, which, so to speak, bends our soul and modifies our organs; (2) pleasures of the senses; (3) wealth; (4) honours, reputation, etc.

[3] Cyrenian philosopher who founded a school around 416 AD. He was said to have so vaunted the future life that his followers committed suicide.

[4] All the references to Descartes in this work are to his letters to Princess Elisabeth of Bohemia concerning Seneca's philosophy, published in a volume of his letters in 1724 (*Lettres ... qui traitent de plusieurs belles questions*).

Happiness which depends on the organisation is the steadiest and most difficult to upset. It needs little nourishment and is nature's finest gift. Unhappiness which comes from the same source has no remedy, apart from a few very uncertain palliatives.

Happiness caused by education consists in following the feelings that it instils in us, which are difficult to erase. The soul is willingly carried away; the slope is gentle and the path well-trod, so that to resist is to do itself violence. Yet its supreme achievement is to defeat this inclination, to dissipate childhood prejudices and to purify the soul by the torch of reason. Such happiness is reserved for philosophers.

I agree that we can be happy by doing nothing that leads to remorse. But in that way we abstain from what makes nature suffer, if we are deaf to her voice; we abstain from a thousand things that we cannot help desiring and loving. This is only a childish happiness, the fruit of a misconceived education and a preoccupied imagination; instead of which, by refusing to deprive oneself of a thousand sources of pleasure and a thousand sweet things which, while harming no-one, do much good to those who enjoy them, and by knowing that it is sheer childishness to repent of the pleasure that we have experienced, we shall experience true, positive happiness, or reasoned felicity, uncorrupted by any feelings of remorse.

In order to ban those disturbers of the human race, we only need to explain them. We shall see that it is both advantageous and easy to relieve society of an oppressive burden, and that the virtues instituted by society are enough for its maintenance, safety and happiness. We shall see that there is only one truth that men need to know, a truth in relation to which all the others are only frivolities, or more or less difficult fantasies. In the system based on nature and reason, happiness is open to the ignorant and poor as much as to the learned and rich; there is a happiness for all classes – and this will revolt prejudiced minds – for the wicked as well as the good.

The internal causes of happiness are inherent and specific to man. That is why they must take precedence over external causes which are alien to him, and which for that reason will take up the shortest and last part of this work. It is natural for man to feel because he is an animate body, but it is no more natural for him to be learned and virtuous than to be richly dressed. As truth, virtue, science and all that can be learnt and that comes from outside thus presuppose feeling already developed in the man who is being taught, I should therefore only speak of these brilliant advantages after I have examined whether this naked, unadorned feeling cannot make man's happiness. Afterwards will come reputation, good fortune and sensuality, at the end.

What convinces me of the truth of what I have just raised is the fact that I see so many ignorant people who are happy due to their very ignorance and their prejudices. While they experience none of that pleasure which self-esteem derives from the discovery of the most sterile of truths, there is a compensation for everything; they experience none of that suffering and sorrow caused by the most important discoveries. They do not care at all whether it is the earth or the sun that revolves, and whether the earth is flattened or rounded.[5] Instead of worrying about the course of nature, they let it follow chance and they themselves bustle gaily on their way, led by their white stick. They take pleasure in eating, drinking, sleeping and vegetating.

To develop this subject, I hope I may be allowed to indulge in some reflections. All things being equal, some people are more subject to joy, vanity, anger, melancholy and even remorse than are others. What is the cause of this if not that particular organic disposition which produces mania, idiocy, vivacity, slowness, calm, perspicacity, etc.? Well, I dare to include organic happiness among those effects of the human bodily structure. It is given to those happy mortals who only need to feel in order to be happy, to those happy temperaments, those blissful people about whom we hear every day. Their constitution is such that sorrow, misfortune, illness, minor pains, the loss of what is held dearest – everything that affects others in fact – slide over their souls, hardly touching them. That chance combination, that circulation, that mixture of solids and fluids which creates the favoured genius and the limited mind also produces that feeling which makes us happy or unhappy. There is no other source of happiness, as nature's uniformity teaches us. What remarkable partiality is shown here! He whom nature has favoured to that extent is content with the necessary minimum and no longer remembers that he used to float, or rather drown, in superfluity. And if his luck returns, as he is prodigal by temperament, when temperament is enough for happiness, he will again consider money like the leaves that the wind blows away; sand would not flow more easily through his hands. The miser, meanwhile, believes that those who want to rob him have more than two hands, and he groans when his safe is only half full.

How fortunate is he who carries happiness in his veins! Like another Bias,[6] he carries everything with him and needs almost nothing. For such a well-organised man, a whole day will never be sad and cloudy; every day will break clear and calm. He is amused by what worries others and hardly affected by what saddens or angers them, and he is glad to see that he is as carefree (despite having just as much income) as the bird that flits from branch to branch and lives on grain thrown here and there. Nothing can upset a man who is so happily formed. He is as patient and calm as one can be in pain; it hardly disturbs his normal state. One can judge how steady he is in adversity. He laughs to see how chance was misled in thinking it could make him sad; he sets little store by chance, as a Pyrrhonian sets little store by the truth. I have seen some of these fortunate characters, who were even sometimes in a better mood when they were ill than when they were well, or when they were poor than when they were rich. And these changes in feeling should again be put down to changes in their organs, on which they clearly depend. Every

[5] There was an important scientific debate on the shape of the earth in the first half of the eighteenth century, in which Maupertuis was involved. To resolve the issue, expeditions were sent to take measurements at the Equator and the Arctic circle, the latter expedition being led by Maupertuis in 1736–7.

[6] Bias was one of the seven wise men of Greece; this remark refers to a story that when forced to flee, he took no belongings, saying that he carried everything with him.

day physicians see illness producing even more surprising metamorphoses. Sometimes it changes an intelligent man into a fool who never recovers, and sometimes it raises a fool to the level of an immortal genius. Nothing is bizarre for nature; we are the ones who are bizarre when we accuse her of being so.

There is no better proof of the existence of a temperamental happiness than all those happy ignoramuses or all those idiots whom everyone knows, while so many intelligent people are unhappy. It seems that thought tortures feeling. In addition, animals can be cited in support of this system. When they are in good health and their appetites are satisfied, they enjoy the pleasant feelings associated with this satisfaction, and consequently this species is happy in its own fashion. Seneca denies this in vain.[a] His opinion is based on the fact that they have no intellectual idea of happiness, as if metaphysical ideas had an influence on well-being and as if it required reflection. If happiness consists in living and dying in tranquillity, then, alas, how much happier than we are animals! How many stupid men there are, who can be suspected of reflecting less than an animal does, and who are perfectly happy! Reflection increases feeling but it does not create it, any more than sensuality[b] gives rise to pleasure. Alas, should we be glad of this faculty? It appears every day and is exercised, so to speak, in such a wrong way that it crushes feeling and ruins everything. I know that when one is happy thanks to reflection, and when reflection seems like a continuation of feeling, then we are all the happier for it; feeling is as if spurred on by it. But in case of unhappiness, taken in its usual sense, what gift could be more cruel and ill-fated! It poisons life. Reflection is often almost remorse. On the contrary, a man who is instinctively contented, is always so without knowing how or why and at little cost. It did not cost more to create this machine than that of an animal, while there are an infinite number of others, for whose contentment fortune, reputation, love and nature exhausted themselves in vain. They are unhappy at a great cost, because they are anxious, impatient, miserly, jealous, proud, and slaves of a thousand passions. It is as if feeling were only given them in order to annoy them, or as if genius came to them only in order to torment them and deprave their feeling. We shall now confirm this idea with further proofs.

Surely certain remedies are another proof of that happiness which I call organic, automatic or natural, because the soul is not involved at all and can claim no credit for it, as it is independent of its will. I am referring to that pleasant, calm state caused by opium, in which one would like to remain for eternity; it would be the true paradise of the soul if it were permanent. This happy state is only the result of the gentle regularity of the circulation and a pleasant, half-paralytic relaxation of the solid fibres. What wonders are performed by a single grain of narcotic juice added to the blood and flowing with it in the vessels! What magic makes it transmit more happiness to us than the treatises of all the philosophers! And what would be

a *On the Happy Life.*

b See *The School of Sensuality.*[7]

7 A reference to La Mettrie's own work, *La Volupté* (see p. xxi n. 16).

the fate of someone whose organisation was all his life as it is when under the influence of that divine remedy! How happy he would be!

Dreams, which do not need opium in order to be often very pleasant, confirm the same point. As a loved one is pictured better absent than present, because reality sets limits on the imagination which are not there when it is left to its own devices, in the same way depictions are more vivid when one is asleep than waking. The soul, which is not then distracted by anything, is completely given over to the internal tumult of the senses and enjoys better and at greater length the pleasures which pervade it. Conversely, it is also more alarmed and frightened by the phantoms, formed in the brain at night, which are never as horrible when one is awake because they are rapidly driven away by outside objects. Such black dreams principally affect those whose imaginations are always as if in mourning and in the daytime indulge in sad, dreary or sinister ideas instead of chasing them away as much as possible. Descartes says in his *Letters* that he is glad not to have more unpleasant ideas at night than during the day.

You can see that even the illusions produced by medicines or dreams are the true causes of our mechanical happiness or unhappiness. So that if I had to choose to be unhappy during the night and happy during the day, I would perhaps have difficulty choosing, for what do I care what state my body is in when I am discontented, worried, sad or afflicted? Even if in the incubus there is not really a weight on my chest, surely my soul has a nightmare nevertheless? And though the charming objects which give me a delicious dream are not really with me, I am nevertheless with them and I nevertheless feel the same pleasures as I would if they were present.

There are the same advantages in delirium and in madness, which is itself a delirium. To cure these illnesses is often to do a disservice; it means disturbing a pleasant dream and providing the sad perspective of poverty to a man who, like the famous madman of Athens, saw only wealth and ships belonging to himself. The imagination can thus provide contentment in illness or health, and while awake or asleep.

A feeling which affects us pleasantly or unpleasantly does not therefore need the action of the external senses in order to make life pleasurable or disagreeable. It is enough for my internal senses to be more or less open or awake, to deliver up my sensitive faculty to the chaos of their ideas without suffocating it, and to give my soul the sensation of pleasure or pain and, so to speak, of comedy or tragedy.[c]

But are we sure that even the waking state is anything other than a less confused and better organised dream, corresponding more to nature and to the order of the first ideas that we received? Could not man's reason be always dreaming, for it deceives us so often, and doubts itself and its evidence in good faith; it creates the happy or unhappy uncertainty of the Pyrrhonians and Sceptics and, as Montaigne says, is not even free to make its will do what it wants.[8]

[c] Like that man who suffered from vertigo in Horace, whose illusions I have described in my *Treatise on Vertigo*[9]

[8] *Essays*, Bk. I, ch. 21. (*Complete Essays*, trans. Screech, p. 116).

[9] Horace, *Epistles*, II.ii.129–30. La Mettrie's *Traité du vertige* was published in Rennes in 1737.

If, as no-one who has any knowledge of animal economy can doubt, so much dreaming is imperfect waking, there is without doubt an infinite amount of waking that is only imperfect dreaming. We often reflect when we are asleep as we do when we are awake, and sometimes better. Sometimes we are very clever in our dreams; the preacher perorates, the poet writes verses, the miser saves up money, etc. Such is the power of habits of thought that a man who is used to calculating will solve an arithmetical problem, as has been seen, in the moments leading up to death, when one cannot remind the dying man of his wife, children, religion or any of his other less familiar ideas.[d]

But again, when awake we continually surprise ourselves dreaming so well that if that state lasted a century it would be a century spent imagining nothing, or with no ideas. We are like those dogs which listen only when they prick up their ears. When our attention does not link similar ideas or those which usually go together, they march in disorder and rush on so quickly and lightly that we can neither feel them nor distinguish them from each other. It is like certain dreams accompanied by too deep a sleep, when we remember nothing about them.

Such is the power of feelings; they can never deceive us and they are never false in relation to ourselves, within the illusion itself. For they show us and make us feel ourselves as we are really are at the moment we feel them: sad or happy, contented or discontented; for they affect our whole being as far as it is sentient, or rather they constitute it.[e] From which it follows: (1) whether life is a dream or possesses some reality, the effect on one's well-being or ill-being is the same; (2) contrary to Descartes' opinion, an unpleasant reality is less welcome than one of those charming illusions so well described by Fontenelle in his *Eclogues* :

> Often, pursuing vain phantoms, our seduced reason permits herself to go astray with great pleasure, enjoying those objects she has herself produced; and this illusion will repay for a moment the lack of true gifts, which miserly nature has not given to humans.[10]

If being deceived by nature is to our advantage, well, let her always deceive us! Let us use our very reason to mislead ourselves if it makes us happier. He who has found happiness has found everything.

But he who has found happiness has not sought it. We do not seek what we have, and if we do not have it, then we will never have it. Philosophy gives loud

[d] See Mr de Fontenelle's *Panegyric* on Mr de Lagny.[11]

[e] See what I say about happiness in my *Treatise on the Soul.*[12]

[10] 'Souvent en s'attachant à des fantômes vains,/Notre raison séduite avec plaisir s'égare; / Elle-même jouit des objets qu'elle a feints; / Et cette illusion pour un moment répare / Le défaut des vrais biens que la nature avare / N'a pas accordé aux humains', 'Alcandre, première eclogue' (*Poésies partorales*, Paris, 1688).

[11] For the *Eloge* of T. F. de Lagny, the mathematician, who replied automatically to a question on mathematics on his death-bed, see Fontenelle's *Œuvres* (Paris, 1818), vol. 1, p. 840.

[12] Ch. XII, §1.

praise to the advantages it owes to nature. Seneca was unhappy and he wrote about happiness as one writes for a lost dog. It is true that he was a Stoic, a sort of leper well armed against the pleasures of life. I believe that the first member of that sect must have been a hypochondriac.

The mind, learning and reason are most often useless in creating bliss, and sometimes even fatal and murderous, as La Mothe le Vayer proved by his own example; for although he was tutor to a prince, laden with literary honours and very rich for a man of learning, he would not have wanted to begin his career again. Such a rare creature is happiness! – as Bayle concludes rather flippantly on this subject![13]

At least the soul can do relatively easily without absolutely alien embellishments; thus in most people it seems to me quite consoled not to have any. They often despise and disdain them and are content with the pleasure of feeling, without tormenting themselves with the tiring task of thinking. Happiness seems completely invigorated and brought to complete perfection by feeling. By thus giving everybody the same right and the same claim to bliss, nature attaches them all to life and makes them cherish existence.

Does this mean that we cannot count on reason at all and that (if happiness depends on truth) we are all chasing an imaginary bliss along different paths, like a sick man chasing flies or butterflies? No, nothing is further from the truth. If reason deceives us, it is when it wishes to lead us less by itself than by its prejudices. But it is a good guide when it is guided by nature. Then, if the torch carried by experiment and observation lights us and makes us see further than our own eyes, we can walk with assurance along the confusing path, in the winding labyrinth of the human maze, which has a thousand avenues and a thousand entrances but scarcely one exit. We can succeed in not always losing ourselves and build a part of our happiness on the ruins of prejudice.

Of all types of happiness, I prefer the one which develops with our organs and seems to be found more or less, like feeling, strength, etc., in all animate bodies. I do not have enough self-love to be taken in. But when one's organisation is not of the best, it can be altered by education and acquire from that source those properties that it does not possess of itself. If the organisation is worthless, one can hope that it will become less bad, as the good becomes better. We should not ignore outside merit; it adds to the natural qualities which have not been lavished on us and it reduces the defects of our organs, as intelligence does in an ugly woman. We must always, following Aristotle's noble system, try to reach perfection. All things being equal, is it not true that a learned man with more knowledge will be happier than an ignoramus?

Since what can be acquired is so closely linked to our well-being, we should try to perfect our education. It is already a perfection to know one or a thousand sterile truths, which are no more important to us than all the sterile plants which cover the earth; but when this truth can calm our soul by freeing us from all worries of the

[13] In Bayle's *Dictionnaire*, 'Vayer', he discusses this attitude of the sceptic La Mothe le Vayer.

mind, then it is a source of happiness. Peace of the soul – that is the goal of a wise man! Seneca had so much respect for it that he deliberately wrote a long treatise about it. How fortunate is he who combines the health of a fool and a cheerful mind with knowledge which calms the soul!

Let us therefore do whatever can provide us with this sweet rest, and try to provide others with it. We shall proclaim it loudly to the Pyrrhonians: let us provide what we think Seneca removed from a sublime[f] definition of happiness, which he finally gave after so much boring verbiage. Yes, there is a useful, striking truth, which is that the bosom of nature, which produced us, awaits us all; we must return to the place we came from. If Seneca had not cherished this great truth (clear and completely unambiguous traces of which we find throughout his works) he would not have advised death, not only to the unhappy but also to those who were plunged in sensual pleasure, supposing that they could not shake it off otherwise. He did not, like Lucretius, say that death does not concern us at all because it is not yet there when we are and we are no longer there when it is; but this was because in all most ancient times, the complete destruction of our being was an accepted truth and so common among philosophers that a Stoic could easily dispense with the need to reassure minds on this account, and could even seem to consider it beneath him. Cicero gives the name of the first person[g] who decided to believe that our soul was immortal.

It would have been better for Seneca to tell us which truth was important for happiness in life, while calming our minds about the future. But I consider that Descartes also misinterpreted his silence by not interpreting it at all. Have I justified it by explaining it?

In any case, in a century as enlightened as ours, in which nature is so well understood that, on this subject at least, we are completely satisfied, it has finally been demonstrated by a thousand unanswerable proofs[h] that there is only one life and one bliss. The first precondition for happiness is feeling, and death removes all feeling. As the only means by which we can feel no longer exist, we can no more feel after death than we can before life. It is easier for an extinguished candle to give light than for a corpse to feel. False philosophy, like theology, can promise us eternal happiness and, lulling us with splendid fantasies, lead us there at the expense of our life or our pleasures. True philosophy, which is very different and much wiser, only admits temporal bliss; it casts roses and flowers in our path and teaches us to gather them. I have on my side all the classics, whose powerful geniuses were moulded by freedom of thought and who in turn were led by their fortunate and unprejudiced genius to discover the boldest truths. Those are the just limits within which wisdom confines itself, its wishes and its desires.

I know that Descartes says that the immortality of the soul is one of those truths

[f] The happy man is the one who, by using reason, neither fears nor desires.

[g] Pherecydes.[14]

[h] See *Machine Man*, *Treatise on the Soul* and many other better works.

[14] See Cicero, *Tusculans*, I. 38.

which we need to know in order to make it easier to be virtuous and to follow the path of happiness; but he was not then speaking as a philosopher. And as he admits that the sovereign good is not a subject he deals with willingly, it is easy to see that the author's caution was in proportion to the delicacy of the subject. He had reason to fear the publication of his *Letters* and hence those good Christians who were only waiting for a cruel opportunity to destroy him. Read those excellent letters I have referred to, and you will see all the worry and grief he suffered at the hands of holy theology, and all its agitation in order to prevent that great man from founding his philosophy. It is to that philosophy (despite its hypothetical nature) that the human mind will owe all the progress it will ever make in the very experiments which philosophy showed to be necessary, to say nothing of the way he taught us to order our thoughts.

But where we see the greatness of the man who considered animals as mere machines, knowing full well that man would one day be boldly compared to them, is when he says that we have no assurance concerning the soul's immortality, except in Hegesias's false philosophy[i][15] – those are his actual words. He adds that that philosopher's book was banned by one of the Ptolemies because several people, distressed by the miseries of this life (which he exaggerated) had killed themselves after having read it, in a hurry not so much to leave this life as to taste in the other world the eternal bliss with which he ensnared his readers. Which shows: (1) the fashions in opinions which are sometimes well and sometimes ill received in different ages; (2) the danger of those which are thought to be the most virtuous, holy and capable of sustaining humanity through the trials of life and of relieving unhappiness, at least by means of great hopes. I have noticed that those who are generally considered to be the best minds have never weighed in the same scales the advantages of the two opposing opinions. According to Seneca and reason, there is nothing more miserable and more pitiable than a mind worried and tormented about future objects, for as there is no certainty that they will accord with one's desires, they may be completely opposed to them. As a result, to what terrible uncertainty we are constantly prey! Those who believe in another life, it is true, feed their imaginations on pleasant ideas which reconcile them to dying; this is all the more true if they are less happy in this life and live with both piety and probity, which give them more hope than fear. The deception works to their advantage. The gains they are promised may be illusory, but they enable them to bear their disasters patiently and make the loss of life, which for me represents everything, something almost unreal for them. This is the sole advantage of credulity. But for one joyful idea, how many sad ones and cruel fears there are! On the contrary, in our opinion, if we do not have the fantastic roses provided by a pleasant dream, at least we are spared the real thorns that accompany them. Finally, all things considered, to restrict oneself to the present which alone is in our power, is the only choice worthy of a wise man; in this system

i Descartes, *Letters*, vol. VI; Valerius Maximus, Bk. VIII, ch. 9; Cicero, *Tusculans*, Bk. I; La Mothe le Vayer, *The Virtue of the Pagans*, vol. V, p. 155, vol. VIII, p. 153.

15 See note 3. Valerius Maximus: *Fata et dicta memorabilia*, VIII.viii.ext. 3.

there are no disadvantages, no worries about the future. We are only concerned to fill up well the narrow compass of our lives and thus we are all the happier when we live not only for ourselves, but also for our country, our king, and in general for humanity, which we glory in serving. Our own happiness contributes to that of society. All virtues consist in being worthy of society, as we shall explain.

Let others – always scratched, without feeling it, by the thorns with which the path is covered and following the edge of a precipice without falling into it – rise on the wings of Stoicism, if it has any left, up to the top of that steep rock on which Hesiod built a sublime temple to virtue![16] They may well give their name to some sect, as Icarus gave his to the seas into which he fell. But the more they abandon nature, without which morality and philosophy are equally incomprehensible, the more they abandon virtue. It was not created solely for philosophers. Any partisan feeling, sect or fanaticism turns its back on virtue. It was given, or rather taught, to everyone. If we are simply men, we shall find virtue; it does not reside in temples but in our hearts. It was not engraved there by some natural law, which nature does not recognise, but rather by the wisest of men, who laid its most solid foundations.

Men are generally born wicked. Without education not many of them would be good, and even with this assistance, there are many more of the former than the latter; such is the defect of the human make-up. Thus education alone has improved on organisation; it has directed men towards the profit and advantage of men, and has wound them up like a clock, to reach the degree of tension which could help and be most useful. This is the origin of virtue; the public good is its source and object.

Montaigne, the first Frenchman who dared to think, says that he who obeys laws because he believes them to be just, does not obey them justly according to their true worth.[17] They are only respectable as laws, otherwise people would not have followed all those with which history teems, and that so often seem unjust and cruel. They would have revolted a thousand times against the decrees of the Roman Senate. Since there have been in all ages, are now and always will be laws that go against what is called truth or what seems to be justice, how can such opposing interests be reconciled? Where should our preference go? Truth, like every right choice (this is still the idea of our charming philosopher and of nature), should be defended 'as far as the stake', but excluding it.[18] The most unjust laws have force on their side; only a madman dares to defy them. The law of nature, which was created before all other laws, tells us to give up truth to them rather than our bodies, and politics tells us to sacrifice its own laws rather than our country. As a result, one's country is as far above the laws as the laws are above justice and equity; as a result, everything is absorbed and swallowed up, as it were, in the general interest of society, for which everything was made.

It is normal for virtue to be treated like the truth. They are beings whose only

16 *Works and Days*, ll. 286–92.

17 *Essays*, Bk. III, ch. 13, 'On experience' (*Complete Essays*, trans. Screech, p. 1216).

18 The expression 'jusques au feu, mais exclusivement', used by Montaigne in *Essays*, Bk. III, ch. 1, 'On the useful and the honourable' (*Complete Essays*, trans. Screech, p. 894), was borrowed from Rabelais.

value lies in their usefulness, either to those who own them or to those for whom they are employed. You enlighten men! You serve society at your own expense! If so, it is the fruit of education and its seed is in self-love, not in nature. But for lack of such and such a virtue or such and such a truth, will science and society suffer? Probably, but if I do not deprive society of these advantages, it is I who will suffer! And have nature and reason invited me to enjoy well being for the sake of other people or for my own sake? That poor poet Autereau, who died in a charity hospital, to the shame of the town which he amused in many theatres, gives a philosophical reply in his *Democritus Taken for a Madman*: 'We are happy for ourselves but not for others.'[19]

'Kings', says Descartes, 'have their own virtues and justice; their limits are different from those of individuals. God always gave right when he gave force. The most apparently unjust paths become just when a Prince believes them so, and those which seem just are no longer so when he believes he is committing an injustice. The intention is everything.'[20] That is how that great philosopher speaks in those works in which he confides what is in his heart.

How I enjoy hearing Seleucus and Parysatis in Plutarch! The former, in order to persuade his wife to marry, despite the laws, his dear son Antiochus, who was literally dying of love for the beautiful queen, insisted that his friends impress on Stratonice's mind 'that whatever is agreeable to a king and useful to one's country is fine and just'. The latter, whose sex alone betrayed that she was a woman, showed just as much vigour when, in order to authorise an action of the same kind, she said to the king, her son, 'God gave you to the Persians as the sole rule of whatever is honest or dishonest, virtuous or wicked.'[21]

If we go up from the image of Gods to the Gods themselves, we shall certainly have a great idea of their justice and of the soundness of their decrees! If we go from there down to the people, who follow blindly whatever they find is accepted without examining anything, what opinion shall we not have of them?

How much proof of judgement was given by the Cyrenaics, when they realised that laws and customs alone had created the distinction between the just and the unjust, and that in order to weigh up and appreciate vices and virtues legitimately, all scales were inaccurate except those in which only the advantages for society were taken into account.[22]

Read from beginning to end, if you can, that clever[j] sceptic who, by dint of

j Le Vayer.[23]

19 Incorrect quotation from J. S. Autereau, *Démocrite prétendu fou*, (Paris, 1730), Act I, scene iv. The original reads: 'C'est pour autrui que brille cette pompe; / Vous croyez en jouir, et c'est ce qui vous trompe.'

20 This is a summary and partial quotation from a paragraph in a letter to Elisabeth of September 1646 (*Lettres*, I, p. 78) (*Œuvres*, ed. Adam and Tannery, Paris, 1976, vol. 4. p. 487).

21 Plutarch, *Life of Demetrios*, XXXI. 5–6; *Life of Artaxerxes*, XXIII. 5.

22 The Cyrenaics, forerunners of the Epicureans, were the followers of Aristippus, a pupil of Socrates, who held that pleasure was the criterion of the good.

23 La Mothe le Vayer wrote several opuscules and letters on travel: 'Des voyages et de la découverte des nouveaux pays', 'De l'utilité des voyages', and 'De l'inutilité des voyages'.

travelling without leaving his study, believed nothing, and he will convince you by the history of customs in different climates that everything is arbitrary and a human invention.

Open that famous new work which reveals the *Spirit of the Laws* and you will learn that men depend on laws, and the laws depend on climate; that if legislators ignore its influence they give orders in vain; that nothing is more widespread and more powerful than the influence of the air; that it affects the mind, character, customs, laws, politics, religion and government of each country.[24] This is a new subject, worthy of being discussed by a philosopher. And Mr de M. has developed it with infinite enjoyment and erudition; he seems to be crying everywhere: 'Legislators, be careful of the air you breathe and make laws that can be followed!' What a copious supplement to his little book the author of *Machine Man* could find in the one I have mentioned! But what a pity that there is even more disorder than genius in *The Spirit of the Laws*!

Listen to Saint-Evremond; that charming philosopher will tell you, with reference to Catilina, that what is a virtue on the throne is a crime on the scaffold,[25] for in morals and politics, as in medicine, we judge acording to events.

For how many centuries[k] did people not approve of voluntary death? Suicide was a great virtue for the Romans, and the English seem to have inherited it; disgust at life makes them conclude, even in the midst of prosperity, that one must free oneself from such a burden, and they soon apply the consequence with a pistol in their hand.[l]

While suicide used to imply a greatness of the soul which honoured a man, vengeance was a virtue. Today, even though it is criticised by Christianity, how many Christians, not in name but in fact, and how many pious people derive all their happiness from revenge and are unhappy if they do not succeed!

Can a divine being be so persevering in anger?[26]

What vices, says Saint Augustine,[m] have not been approved of? What virtues have not been condemned in different centuries? This Father of the Church, here more of a philosopher than a theologian, has no difficulty in inferring that human reason is too powerless, too incapable of judging the nature of things, to be able to decide the great question of vices and virtues. This, I believe, is tantamount to saying quite clearly that good and evil possess no specific signs to characterise them absolutely and that they can be distinguished from each other only by the interests of society (a truth which can never be taught enough). Remove this support, and

k See La Mothe le Vayer in his best work, *The Virtue of the Pagans*, vol. V.[27]

l Opium can help the wise man; / But in my opinion / One only needs instead / Courage and a gun.

m In the *City of God*, ch. 41.[28]

24 La Mettrie is referring here to the main ideas of Montesquieu's *Spirit of the Laws*.

25 This appears to be a mistaken reference.

26 'Tantaene animis caelestibus irae' (Virgil, *Æneid*, I. 11).

27 That is to say, in vol. V of his *Works*.

28 In fact xviii. 41.

farewell morality! Vices and virtues are absolutely indiscernible, to use Leibniz's unpleasant word. Such is natural equity. If anyone has another conception of it, I would be glad if he would give it to me.

If each person had been able to live alone and solely for himself, men would have existed but not humanity,[n] and there would have been vices – or what are called vices – but no remorse, for the same reason that there is no animality (to use this word in a barbarous sense) between animals, each of which is concerned only with its own self; they would have almost no intercourse amongst themselves were it not for sexual pleasure.

The need for contact in everyday life meant therefore the need to establish vices and virtues, whose origin is, as a result, a political creation. This foundation of society, although it is pure imagination, is so solid and necessary that without it the whole edifice is unable to stand up and collapses into ruins.

So we can say about virtues what Zeno said about vices, that they are all equal in themselves as they all come from the same, even wise, construction.[29]

But honour and glory, those seductive phantoms, have been appointed to act as a brilliant train for virtue, which they dazzle and incite, while on the contrary contempt, opprobium, ignominy and remorse have been attached to vices and crimes in order to stifle them, pursue them and be their furies. In addition, men's imaginations have been stirred up in order to take advantage of their feelings, so that what is in itself merely imaginary has been turned by these accounts into a real good, unless one excepts the self-esteem which is attached to fine actions, even when they are secret. Self-esteem is more flattered when these actions are public, for that is what constitutes honour, glory, reputation, esteem, consideration and other terms expressing merely the judgements of others which are in our favour and please us. For the rest, convention and an arbitrary value alone decide the merit or demerit of what are called vices and virtues.

Although there is no such thing as virtue properly speaking, or absolute virtue – as this word, like so many others, constitutes only a vain sound – there are virtues relative to society, whose ornament and support they are. He who possesses them in the highest degree is the happiest, with that kind of happiness which is proper to virtue. Those who neglect it and have no knowledge of the pleasure of being useful are deprived of that sort of felicity. Nature is so self-sufficient, that they perhaps make up for not living for others by the satisfaction of living for themselves alone and for being their own relatives, friends, mistress and whole universe. If they are unhappy, they will not worry about saving their lives simply because it is useful to their families and they will either free themselves from what is a burden to them or,

[n] What is humanity for Christians, etc. is not the same for idolators, whose religion consists in fattening up beautiful children of both sexes in order to sacrifice them to their Gods afterwards. Where is the innate idea of humanity?

[29] La Mettrie is perhaps following here La Mothe le Vayer's chapter on Zeno and the Stoics in *The Virtue of the Pagans*.

as I saw with the courageous Duke of G.,[30] the most fatal ambition will lead them to seek death.

For well-born people, happiness increases by sharing and communication. We are enriched by the good we do and we participate in the joy we create. It is worthy of man that this should be so.

But it was not enough for virtue to be the beauty of the soul. In order to incite us to make use of this beauty, the soul needed to flatter itself, not so much that it was beautiful, but rather that it was considered beautiful. It needed to take pleasure in it, like a pretty woman who enjoys flattery and love's caresses because of the vanity and voluptuousness which follow them, and who is forced by the very picture of her charms to love herself. Or rather it is like Alcibiades's coquette, who said that she would prefer to be much less lovely and to find someone who complimented her. Indeed, what does it matter for a woman to be ugly if she receives the tribute due to beauty? What does it matter for a man to be wicked if he is thought to be virtuous and if society does not suffer in any way? Is it not said every day in love affairs that it is enough to be careful and wary, and that it is better to be less suspected and more active? Thus we are made happy both by the opinions of others and by our own. Vanity is more useful to man than the most deserved and best controlled self-esteem. Ask that mass of bad authors who judge their worth according to their publishers' sales.

If we personify virtue, honour is the diamond she wears on her finger. Vile lovers that we are, we do not love her but her jewel, which we would like to have without undergoing her strict examination; and in fact it is often those who are least worthy of it who enjoy such good fortune. She is an ugly old woman who is coveted for the pendant that hangs from her ears or for her money, which must be earned. Such are the charms of that queen of the wise man, that epitome of beauty, that divinity of the Stoics!

Or if you prefer, virtue is the tree about which we care little, at which we scarcely glance and which we seek only for its shade, a strange shade which does not usually correspond very well to the body that produces it. It is either too small or too large according to the wind which, blowing from one direction or the other, restricts or stretches, contracts or expands it. In fact we are mostly real fops when it comes to virtue: the favours bestowed on us are worthless if they are not talked about. Almost nobody desires an obscure and unknown merit; we do everything for the sake of a glorious reputation. Aristotle considers it to be the most important external possession, while Horace says that hidden virtue is almost worthless.[31] Cicero would have liked to say the same thing if he had dared. He saw to it that his virtue was praised as loudly as his eloquence. Why? In order to acquire the glory for which he was so eager. There are few virtues which we do not show off. If, in order to be a philosopher, one has to despise being thought to be one, then there are none, or very few. It is rare to

[30] The Duke of Grammont insisted, despite being ill, on taking part in the battle in which he was killed, as La Mettrie recounts in *L'Ouvrage de Pénélope*, vol. 3, pp. 270–1.

[31] See *Odes*, IV. ix. 29.

find a Carneades or a Cato[o] who does good for good's sake, and in particular to the detriment of his own fortune; it is rare to find one who esteems virtue all the more for being hidden and all the less for having already transpired. Thus, although Carneades was the head of a sect opposed to that of Chrysippus and Diogenes,[32] who would not even have deigned to stretch out a finger in order to acquire all the glory in the world, it seems on reflection that he did not despise glory any less than those philosophers did and that he knew true worth perfectly well, while confusing glory with virtue and disdaining the pleasure of exercising it for any aim other than itself. If that is a refinement of self-esteem, and if to despise vanity is itself a sign of an excess of it (as modesty is often in fact a disguised form of pride), then I consider the perfection of virtue and the most noble cause of heroism to lie in that strange and splendid vanity. While judging oneself is delicate, due to the traps laid by our own self-esteem, it is no less fine to be forced to esteem ourselves even when we are despised by others. Happiness should come from ourselves rather than from others. It shows greatness to have the goddess with a hundred mouths in one's service and to reduce them to silence, to forbid them to open, to despise their incense and to be one's own renown. According to Descartes, someone who was sure that he alone was worth as much as his whole town could esteem and respect himself as much as he could be esteemed and respected by the whole town, and he would lose nothing by being deprived of so much despised applause. Anyway, what is so flattering about most praise that we should seek it so much? Those who bestow it are so unworthy of giving it that it is often not worth listening to. It is, as Regnard's madwoman says of men, 'inferior merchandise'.[33] A man of superior worth is only obliged to listen to it in the same way as a great king listens to bad poetry praising him.

If I may be allowed to draw a little picture of society's virtues, I would say that each person has his own. The physician does more by his art of preserving men than he would if he created new ones; the father brings up tender, grateful children and gives them a second life which is more precious than the first; the husband full of attention and care respects himself in his spouse and tries to fashion her a chain of flowers; the lover can never feel too strongly what a charming mistress, who owes him nothing and sacrifices all to him, does for him; the true friend, understanding but not obsequious, true but not harsh, prudent, discreet and obliging, defends his friend, gives him good advice and receives only the same from him.

There are virtues for every situation. The faithful, zealous citizen makes wishes

o Cato the Younger, about whom Velleius said (Bk. II, ch. 35): 'He did nothing right in order to be seen doing it, but because he could not do otherwise.'[34]

32 Carneades was an opponent of the Stoics, of whom Chrysippus was a follower; Diogenes was a Cynic. All these philosophers are mentioned by Cicero in the *Tusculans*, which discuss suffering and happiness; see especially Bk. V.

33 J. F. Regnard, *Les folies amoureuses*, Act III, scene IV.

34 'Nunquam recte fecit, ut facere videretur, sed quia aliter facere non poterat', See Velleius Paterculus, *Res gestae divi Augusti*, Bk. II, ch. 35.

for his country and his prince; the brave, enlightened officer leads the intrepid, ferocious soldier; the sensible moralist provides good principles taken from politics; the historian provides us with the greatest examples from the most ancient past. Sensuality, the charm of life, flows from the pens which it inspires; they are rare pens, which nature gives only to its favourites, or rather to Venus's. The comic spreads both wit and joy; the one excites the mind, which it pricks with pleasure, while the other does good to the heart, which it expands. The tragedian, the novelist, etc. arouse feelings of tenderness and grandeur, which the transfigured poet heightens to the point of enthusiasm.

To appreciate worth is worthy, and to reward it is divine. Kings: imitate the hero of the North and be the heroes of humanity, as you are its leaders. When you lower yourselves to become patrons, you raise yourselves. The courage of the soul is as far above that of the body as the polite warfare of learning is above that of weapons. Support the courage that is the glory of a state, for the other kind constitutes only its safety. Protection has the same effect on genius that the sun has on a rose; it makes it blossom.

And you, philosophers, help me: dare to speak the truth and may childhood not be man's eternal age. Do not fear men's hatred; fear only being worthy of it. Here is our virtue; everything that is useful to society constitutes one and the rest is its ghost.

What a point have we reached, cry the theologians, if there are no inherent vices or virtues, no moral good or evil, no justice or injustice? If everything is arbitrary and created by man's hand, why the remorse that racks us after a wicked action? Shall we remove the only virtue that criminals still have?

We shall leave them to make speeches and start calmly along this new path, where we are led by the best philosophy, that of physicians.

If we go back to our childhood (alas, to do that we have only too few steps to take, and the childhood of our minds is not far off), we shall find that it is the age of remorse. At first it was only a simple feeling, experienced without examination or choice, which became as deeply engraved on our brains as a seal on soft wax. Passion, the sovereign mistress of the will, can smother this feeling for a time, but it revives when passion stops, above all when the soul comes back to itself and reflects coldly; it is then that the first principles – those that form the conscience, those which it originally imbibed – return, and that is what is called 'remorse', whose effects are infinitely varied.

Remorse is thus only an unpleasant remembrance, a former habit of thought, which returns in force. It is, if you prefer, a trace that is renewed,[35] and consequently an old prejudice which sensuality and the passions cannot succeed in sending so soundly to sleep that it does not almost always reawaken sooner or later. Thus man carries his greatest enemy within himself. It follows him everywhere and as Boileau says about sorrow, following Horace, it climbs up behind and gallops with him.[36] Luckily this cruel enemy is not always the victor. Any longer-standing or stronger habit must necessarily defeat it. The most beaten track fades away, as a path is closed

[35] He means a trace made by the animal spirits in the brain.

[36] N. Boileau, 'Epître V, à M. de Guilleragues' (Paris, 1674), and Horace, *Odes*, III. i. l.40.

or a precipice filled up. Another kind of education brings another route for the spirits, other dominant traces and other feelings, which can enter our soul only on the ruins of the earlier ones, which are abolished by a new mechanism. How many physicians could I mention who have even more practice than theory in this matter!

Here are some incontrovertible facts. People dying of hunger at sea, who eat the one among their companions who is sacrificed by lot, experience no more remorse than cannibals do. Such is habit and such is need, thanks to which anything is allowed. When I see our executioners hanging, breaking on the wheel, burning and torturing their fellow beings, I can feel inside myself something which is in revolt; I seem to hear a voice groaning in the depths of my heart: 'Oh nature, Oh humanity, you are only an empty word if by these actions you are not violated – no that is not enough – if you are not torn apart while obeying the law.' But no, criminals have executioners and the executioners have none; their hearts are closed to remorse and repentance. And yet they are murderers! Yes, but stipended murderers, in the same way as idolators were and perhaps still are sacred murderers. The ones are paid and the others are revered. Is a man who, dying of hunger, is forced to slit a traveller's throat, any more guilty than a man who strangles a criminal on the orders of judges? Whether one is forced by justice or forced by misery, surely one is still forced? And surely misery itself is more pressing and more compelling than justice? But executioners are authorised and assassins are punished; the public good calls for both and is enough to justify the former and condemn the latter to death, but not to remorse, to which Pufendorf does not seem to condemn those assassins who are forced into it.[37] The law of nature, which is his foundation, should also shelter them from the laws or make men imagine laws more favourable to these poor wretches.

Another religion brings another type of remorse and other times bring other manners. In the past, only women blushed (with disappointment) at having their admirers for rivals, while the latter mocked them triumphantly, despising Cupid and the Graces. Aristotle was in favour of sodomy in order to prevent too great a number of citizens, without worrying about the precept 'go forth and multiply', etc. In the past, men had boys more openly than they have prostitutes today. That can be seen in all the classical works which freely celebrate 'the abominable action that half the world commits without the other half'. Lycurgus had weak and unhealthy children drowned and was proud of his wisdom. Look at Plutarch's account of his life,[38] and you will see that at Sparta they knew neither modesty, nor robbery,[p] nor adultery, etc. Elsewhere, women were shared[q] and were common, like bitches, or they were offered by their husbands to the first handsome well-built young man. A

p When cleverly done it was rewarded.

q Plato wanted to establish such a community of women, which others restricted. See Le Vayer, vol. VIII, p. 123.[39]

37 S. von Pufendorf, *De jure naturae ac gentium* (Lund, 1672), Bk. I, ch. 5, §IX.

38 *Lycurgus*, xvi.

39 In fact *The Virtue of the Pagans*, Pt. II, in the section on Plato.

scourge of humanity more terrible than all vices put together, which is not followed by any repentance, is the carnage of warfare. Thus it has been decreed by the ambition of princes. See how far conscience, which produces repentance, is the child of prejudice!

And yet this excellent subject, this man of rare worth who, when carried away by an instinctive movement, knocks down a bad citizen or who gives himself up to a passion which he cannot master, is tormented by remorse, which he would not have experienced if he had killed an adversary bravely or if a priest had made his feelings legitimate and given him the right to do what the whole of nature does. Ah, if pardon was created to save illustrious unfortunates, if in certain cases, as Descartes implies in his *Letters*, its exercise is more august and royal than the laws' full rigour is terrible, what is most essential, in my opinion, is to exempt him from remorse. Was man – whom nature has tried to attach to life by so many allurements, destroyed by depraved artifice – in particular the honest man, created in order to be delivered up to tormenters? No, let him use the power of his reason to provide him with what is provided for so many rogues by the force of habit. For one villain who stops being unhappy and returns to peace and tranquillity, which he did not deserve in his relations with other men, how many wise and virtuous individuals, undeservedly tormented amidst a charming and innocently delicious life, would finally throw off the yoke of an oppressive education, enjoy clear cloudless days and replace the cruel worry which devours them with sweet pleasures?

Let us learn more about the power of our organisation. Hobbes said: 'Man is a wolf to man',[40] a truth which does not surprise those who can appreciate humanity in general at its true worth. Those of us who know that without the fear of laws no wicked man would be restrained would say about the good what was said long ago about the gods: 'Fear first created good in the world.'[41]

Indeed the wise Englishman I have just quoted demonstrated that the principle of fear[r] is the first rule on which our actions are based. Who has ever used remorse as a compass? Who has ever abstained from doing what gave him pleasure or what could make his reputation or fortune, simply through fear of feeling remorse? It – or the awakening of the trace in the brain which produces it – is therefore useless before a crime. But while one is committing it and is carried away by one's passion, one thinks of nothing less than that feeling by which one is going to be racked. And when the crime has been committed and remorse rises up as if to avenge society, only those who do not need it can profit by it. The suffering of the others, whose wickedness is innate and organic, rarely (if ever) prevents them from reoffending. Thus remorse is in itself, philosophically speaking, as useless after as during and before a crime.

r See *Machine Man.*

40 The expression 'homo homini lupus' was frequently used to sum up T. Hobbes's view of the state of nature. For his view of man, and of fear as the origin of society, see in particular *De Cive* (London, 1642), ch. 1. On La Mettrie's reference to Hobbes, see also Introduction, pp. xxii–xxiii.

41 The original quotation was 'Primus in orbe deos fecit timor', Statius, *Thebaid*, III, 661.

But if it is harmful to the good and to virtue and if it corrupts their fruit without being able to limit wickedness, surely it follows that it is in general worse than useless to the human race and a harmful gift of education? Remorse seems to me to add to the problems of machines which are as much to be pitied as they are badly regulated, and which are led on towards evil as the good are towards good. These machines have enough (and perhaps even too much) fear of the laws, whose net, which is as necessary as is, in another sense, the action which leads them into it, will catch them sooner or later. If I relieve them of this heavy burden, they will experience less unhappiness but no greater impunity. Thus I am serving humanity without affecting in any way the advantages of society. For, since remorse does not make the wicked any better, to be deprived of that feeling will not inspire in them any more wickedness. Hence it is not dangerous for society to be delivered from its private executioners, provided public ones exist. Good philosophy would dishonour itself for nothing by raising spectres which frighten only honest people, for probity is usually as simple as that, instead of being solid. For honest people, the removal of an unwelcome or disgreeable feeling – which truly kills the pleasure of living by means of its poison, affecting all the other pleasures and making life a misery every day – means an increase of happiness. Let us congratulate these honest people; the sole fear of remorse cannot make their company reliable and faithful, but it can perhaps strengthen more and more their excellent morality. Let us pity the others, whom nothing can control; nature has undoubtedly treated them more as a stepmother than as a mother. In order to be happy they would need both philosophy and the certainty of impunity, which is infinitely rarer than philosophy in those who are capable of contemptible actions, wickedness and infamy.

We have seen that remorse is a vain remedy for the accidents which threaten and afflict society; that it can neither hide our ills nor tame the tigers in our species; that it even, we could say, muddies the clearest water without making muddy water any clearer; and that it depends on a conscience which, when it is not dulled at the same time as the nerves, is determined by the true or false ideas acquired in our childhood. This conscience is, as a result, only a sort of barometer, which varies according to the individual and, even more, according to the climate, and is therefore all the worse and more inaccurate as a means of measuring degrees of virtue and vice.

Let us therefore take control of these domestic enemies; let us not be at war with ourselves, at least willingly, for we are all too often unwillingly so. Let us, in short, destroy remorse. Let fools (at least among honest men) be the only ones who experience it, so that there is no longer any chaff mixed in with the wheat of life, and that cruel poison is finally banished forever, in particular from the minds of those charming people who only indulge in the wisest sort of sensuality. Indeed, if the joys found in nature are crimes, then man's pleasure and happiness is to be a criminal.

> Alas! wretched are they whose pleasures are open to censure![42]

[42] 'Heu! miseri, quorum gaudia crimen habent!' (source unknown).

Either I am very much mistaken, or the dose of antidote that I have just given will be enough to correct sometimes even the most harmful venom that prejudices have ever exhaled.

Such is nature reduced to itself and as if to its simplest expression. We think we are honouring it by wanting to decorate it with a law supposedly born with it, like many other ideas which are really acquired, but nature is not taken in by that sort of honour. It is like an honest commoner who prefers his ancient status to a recent nobility which only costs money. A well-organised soul, satisfied with what it is and with no higher aims, disdains anything attributed to it above what really belongs to it, which comes down to feeling. The art of handling the soul is provided, we might say, by the dressage of education. The fine knowledge, with which pride so lavishly gratifies our soul,[43] in fact does it harm rather than adding to its merit, because it deprives it of the merit implied by the acquisition of knowledge; for, according to the hypothesis of a supposed natural law and innate ideas, the soul, born with the capacity to discern a multitude of things and the difference between good and evil, is like those who are favoured by the accident of birth and have not merited their nobility.

In order to explain so much enlightenment that was considered to be inborn, those to whom nature seemed insufficient on its own, because they did not know it well enough, imagined several different substances and, absurdly, looked for the intelligence of reason in true beings of reason, as I have proved elsewhere.[s] But while some have gratuitously created innate ideas in order to give the words 'virtue' and 'vice' an imposing basis which made them be taken for real objects, others are no more justified in making all animate bodies feel remorse, in virtue of a particular disposition which is said to be sufficient in animals and to have as much effect as education in man. This system collapses when we consider simply that, all things being equal, some people are more subject to remorse than others and that it changes and varies according to education. That was the mistake into which I fell myself when I wrote my little *Machine Man*, but I did it on purpose, because at that time, like a bird trying out its wings and afraid of flying too far, I did not dare take arms against all prejudices at the same time.[44]

The idea of virtue was not given to us with our being, as can be seen from the fact that it is not even stable when education and time have developed and improved our organs. It is like a bird perched on a branch, always ready to fly away. The first habits are easily reformed; the organisation automatically takes back what education seemed to have stolen from it, as if perfection and artistry upset it. Who does not know the contagion of unsuitable books and the danger of bad company?

s *Treatise on the Soul.*[45]

43 La Mettrie is here referring to innate knowledge.

44 In previous editions, La Mettrie refers instead to the mistake made by *Machine Man*, without admitting that he was the author, and he praises the clandestine work *L'Examen de la religion* for its theory of remorse (see Introduction, p. xxii). In the edition of the text translated here, the reference to the *Examen* was placed in the Preface.

45 See p. 24 note 33 and p. 48 note 10.

One perverse example, a single bent conversation often destroys, so to speak, the most upright views of education, and nature is pleased to become depraved again. One might conclude that nature feels more comfortable thus, and that it enjoys limping, as if it were unbearable or painful to walk straight, if such a thing exists.

This fragile instability of even the most solidly acquired and strongly rooted virtue proves the need not only to provide good examples and good advice to maintain it, but also to flatter self-esteem by praise, rewards and gratification, which encourage it and incite it to virtue. Otherwise, unless one is stung by a particular point of honour, however much one exhorts, declaims or harangues, virtue will be a bad soldier who deserts. It is rightly said that a man who disdains life can destroy another's and it is the same for a man without self-esteem. Farewell all virtues if one reaches such an unfortunate degree of indifference! Their source has inevitably dried up. Yes, self-esteem alone can keep up the tastes to which it gives rise, and a lack of it is more dangerous than an excess. How splendid would be a society made up only of people like Diogenes, Chrysippus and other similar madmen, whom the Ancients do not make us revere enough for us not to consider them fit for Bedlam!

If the tendency to evil is such that it is easier for the good to become wicked than for the wicked to improve, we should find excuses for this inhuman inclination of humanity. We should not forget the shackles and irons we receive at birth, which follow us throughout life's slavery. Look at those trees planted at the summit and the foot of a mountain: the former are little and the latter are tall. The difference comes not only from their seeds but also from the warmer or cooler terrain in which they are planted. Man vegetates according to the same laws. He is formed by the climate in which he lives as well as the father he came from. All the elements dominate this weak machine which does not think in a damp, heavy terrain in at all the same way as it does in a pure, dry atmosphere, or when hungry in the same way as with a full stomach, etc. Thus, dependent as we are on so many external causes and above all on so many internal ones, how could we avoid being what we are? How could we regulate mechanisms that we do not know?

The human body is made up of nerves stretched to a certain point, filled with spirits which circulate with the prodigious activity of fire. Perhaps the very fire which comes out of our bodies in the form of electricity goes to make up these spirits. The tauter these nerves are, the more easily they are set in motion by the slightest cause and the faster their fluids gallop, and our thoughts with them, as one can experience in fevers. It is no more in our power to stop them or to make them move more slowly than it is in the power of a thermometer or a barometer to check the liquid that heat or air pressure must push up. If man is not a machine, why does the previously cold, dull imagination, lashed by rapidly moving blood, as the blood is by wine, become heated and brilliant and send off as many sparks as the best struck flint? Why should we turn to doctors to cure madness? For reason only returns like sight, by breaking up the clouds which hide its rays. If man is not a machine, why does a whirling ember make him dizzy and faint? Why does the touch of certain bodies, like a torpedo fish, give him such unpleasant sensations? Alas, even being tickled on the edge of the lips with a feather is unbearable, and the steadiest soul is convulsively affected by it. What transports are not caused by another sort of delicious itching! What can I say about a sound dying in the air, an unpleasant word! What anger, what fury! What a storm suddenly replaces the calmest peace! Even simply rubbing the spine can arouse both the body and the soul. If this is a sort of digression, the author of *Machine Man* can surely be pardoned. But let us return to the subject.

Who would believe it? Well being is the very motive for wickedness. It guides the rogue, the tyrant and the assassin as well as the honest man. The will is necessarily determined to desire and seek what is to the immediate advantage of the soul and the body. And how, if it is not by means of what produces the soul itself, in other words the circulation? When I do good or evil, when I am virtuous in the morning and wicked in the evening, it is the fault of my blood, which makes me cheerful, serious, lively, playful, amusing, mocking or mad, and which makes me will and determines me in everything; it is what thickens it, stops it, dissolves it or hurries it on, in the same way as when the spirits, which it has filtered in my brain matter and sent from there into the nerves, taking one path rather than another, make me turn right rather than left in a park. And yet I think that I have chosen and congratulate myself on my liberty. All our freest actions are like that one. An absolutely necessary determination carries us away, and we will not admit that we are slaves! How insane we are, and all the more unhappily insane for permanently reproaching ourselves with not having done what it was not at all in our power to do.

But since we automatically tend towards our own good and are born with this inclination and invincible disposition, it follows that each individual, when he prefers himself to all others, like those ne'er-do-wells who crawl uselessly over the earth's surface, is only following nature's order, in which he must be very odd and unreasonable not to believe he can be happy. If those who do evil can be happy, it is all the more likely that those who limit themselves to not doing good, and do not think they are obliged to keep a promise that others have made for them, can enjoy the happiness that can come from their well being and in general from their way of thinking. As Montaigne puts it very well: 'Either reason is joking or its only target should be our happiness, and all its labour should tend, in short, to make us live well, that is to say at our ease. All the opinions of the world reach the same point, that pleasure is our target. Whatever role a man may assume, he always plays his own part within it, and even in virtue, our ultimate aim is sensual pleasure.'[46]

As the pleasure of the soul is the true source of happiness, it is therefore very obvious that in relation to felicity, good and evil are totally indifferent in themselves, and that he who has greater satisfaction in doing evil will be happier than whosoever has less satisfaction in doing good. Which explains why so many

[46] *Essays*, Bk. I, ch. 20, 'To philosophise is to learn how to die'. The quotation is neither complete nor exact; see *Complete Essays*, trans. Screech, pp. 89–90.

rogues are happy in this world, and which shows us the existence of a particular individual happiness without virtue and even in crime.

Look at that courtier who has just destroyed a man whose only support was his merit; see how he congratulates himself on his odious superiority and on the favour of which he has taken advantage. What insolent pleasure glitters in his eyes and in his whole face! We should not be surprised, for amongst all the animals does not the stronger triumph when it crushes the weaker? Another has never missed an opportunity to harm you although you have always seized every chance to serve him! Pity him, despise him – you can do so, as you can a soul of clay or any vile thing – but do not hate him and let vengeance hold no pleasure for you. Feel pleasure only in doing services for even the ungrateful; they are no more guilty when they forget kindnesses than is a melancholic when, tired of life, he tries to have done with it. Remember that wickedness is the component of most men. Can gratitude be in the power of someone who is not goodness, of someone who is unhappy doing good, like a bird in a pneumatic engine,[47] and who is only satisfied when he is doing evil, which is the hateful source of pleasure in almost all men?

One source of happiness, which I do not believe to be any purer for being nobler and finer to the minds of almost everybody, is that which derives from the order of society. The more man's natural determination has seemed wicked, and as it were monstrous, in relation to society, the more it has been thought necessary to counteract it in different ways. Hence the ideas of generosity, greatness and humanity have been linked to actions which are important for men's intercourse. Esteem and consideration have been accorded to the man who would never harm anyone, however much good it might bring him; respect, honours and glory have been given to the man who would serve his country, friendship, love or even humanity to his own cost; and by means of these noble incitements, how many animals with human faces have become immortal heroes! Far from abandoning men to their own natures – which are, alas!, too sterile to allow them to bear excellent fruit – they have had to be trained and as it were grafted, in particular at an age when the sap could most easily pass into the branch which was implanted into them.

If I never tire of coming back to education, it is because education alone can give us feelings contrary to those we would have had without it. Such is the effect of the modification or change which it brings to our instinct or our way of feeling. An educated soul no longer wants, follows or does what it did before, when it was guided by instinct alone. Enlightened by a thousand new feelings, it finds bad what it used to find good, and it praises in others what it used to blame. Thus, like veritable weathercocks, we are perpetually turning in the wind of education, and we return afterwards to our first position when our organs, brought back to their natural tautness, call us back and make us follow their original dispositions. Then the old determinations come back to life and those which were artificially produced

47 The pneumatic engine or air-pump, also called Boyle's engine, created a vacuum, as was demonstrated by the fact that birds placed in it died.

fade away. So that it is not even in our power to take as much advantage of the best education as we would like, for the good of society. We degenerate despite ourselves.

This materialism deserves esteem; it should be the source of indulgence, excuse, pardon, reprieve, praise, moderation in punishment, which should only be decided regretfully, and the reward due to virtue, which cannot be accorded too wholeheartedly, as virtue is a sort of afterthought, an extraneous decoration, always ready to flee or to fall off for lack of support. One could say about princes what I have said elsewhere about physicians: that the best ones are those who have the greatest absolute knowledge of the mechanism to which our will is subjected. If someone who is guilty in relation to society is not free in his actions, it no doubt follows clearly that he was not free not to be guilty and that he is guilty as if he were not guilty; he is guilty in one sense – in the sense of arbitrary, wisely established relations – but is not at all in another, not intrinsically, in the absolute sense or philosophically speaking. To put it bluntly, he is clearly not guilty at all and only deserves compassion. Even when a philosophical prince punishes him, he groans at being forced to come to this sad extremity; he knows that legal punishment is as absolutely unjust as it is relatively necessary and that consequently the political reasons which are the basis of the law of retaliation do not prove that the man we hang is hanged with justice or equity. For, Good God, what equity is there to take the life of a miserable wretch, who is the slave of the blood galloping in his veins, as the hand of a watch is the slave of the works which make it move? And how right was the thought of that famous destroyer[t] of human liberty when he dared to say that there was more reason than justice in condemning criminals to death!

Thus, although crime is nothing in itself (as man's every action and every movement is absolutely indifferent), yet public interest deserves to be consulted and preferred in everything, for it is necessary to chain up madmen, kill mad dogs and crush serpents. Thus the only difference that exists between the wicked and the good is that for the wicked individual interest prevails over the general interest, which is immediately eclipsed in their eyes, while the good sacrifice willingly, and even with pleasure, their own interest to that of a friend or the public.

t Hobbes.[48]

48 This vague and not particularly accurate reference is perhaps inspired by Thémiseul de Saint-Hyacinthe, *Recherches philosophiques sur la nécessité de s'assurer par soi-même de la vérité* ('Londres', 1743), p. 61, which infers from Hobbes that, although criminals are punished without justice, they are punished with reason.

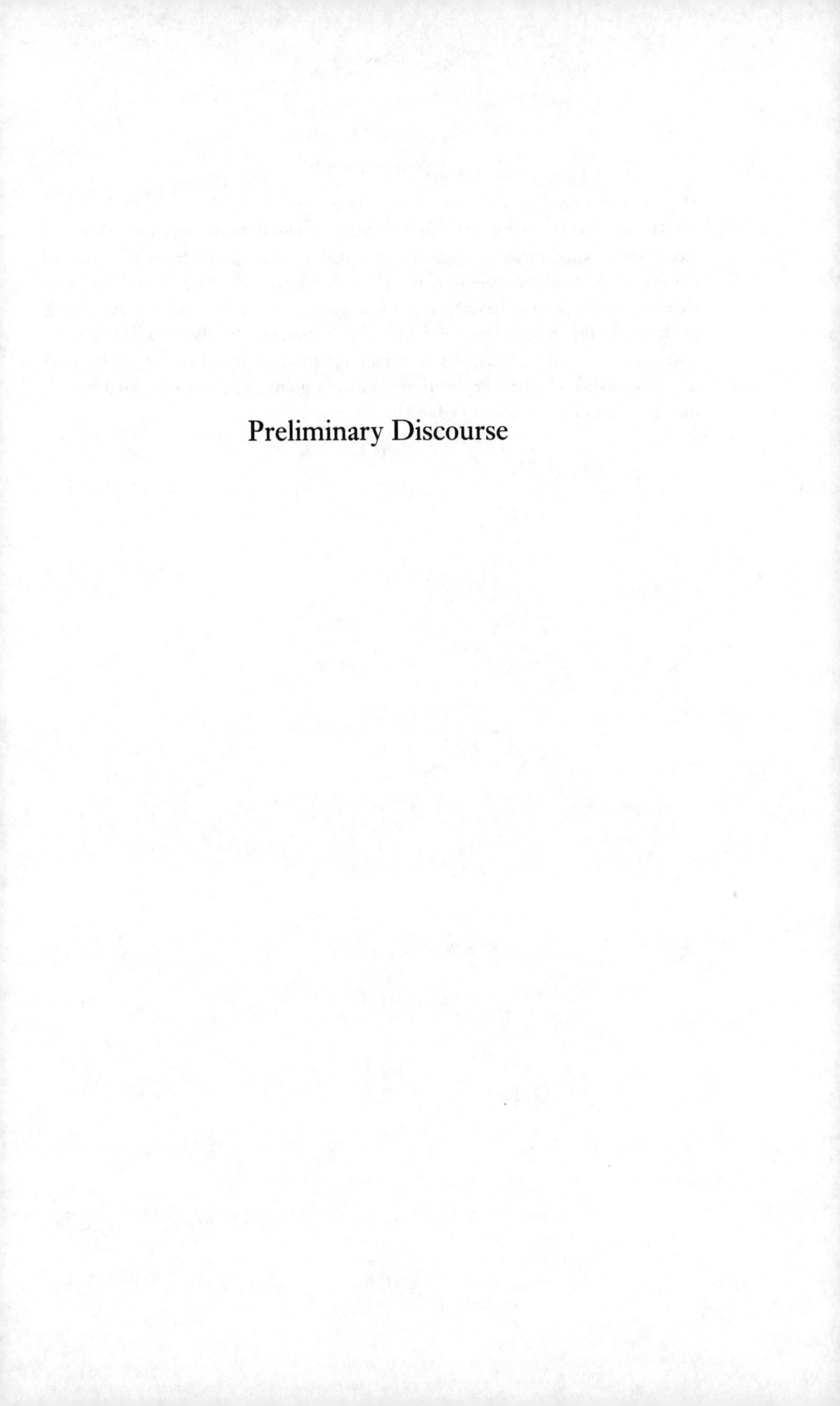

Preliminary Discourse

Note on the text

Discours preliminaire was written as an introduction to La Mettrie's *Philosophical Works*, and hence exists only in the version in which it appeared there. It incorporates some material originally included in the conclusion of the *Natural History of the Soul* and removed from the *Treatise on the Soul*, as well as some elements of self-defence developed in his *Réponse à un libelle* (*Reply to a Pamphlet*), published in the third volume of *L'Ouvrage de Pénélope* (*Penelope's Work*) in 1750. Later editions of the *Works* present minor variations in this text, but we have no way of knowing whether they were the author's doing. The text translated here is therefore that of 1750, which I edited in 1981.

I intend to prove that, however much philosophy contradicts morality and religion, not only can it not destroy these two bonds of society, as is commonly thought, but it can only tighten and strengthen them more and more. A dissertation of such great importance, if it is well done, will in my opinion be worth at least as much as one of those trite prefaces in which the author, kneeling humbly before the public, nevertheless praises himself with his customary modesty; and I hope it will not be considered out of place at the head of works like those I am daring to republish here, despite the outcry dictated by a hatred[a] which deserves only the most perfect contempt.

Open your eyes and you will see placarded everywhere:

'Proofs of the Existence of God from the Wonders of Nature'

'Proofs of the Immortality of the Soul from Geometry and Algebra'

'Religion proven by Facts'

'Physico-theology'.[1]

And so many other similar books. Read them, with no other preparation, and you will be convinced that philosophy is in itself favourable to religion and morality, and that the study of nature is the shortest route to achieve both a knowledge of its revered Creator and an understanding of moral and revealed truths. Then undertake that type of study and without taking in all the vast field of physics, botany, chemistry, natural history and anatomy, and without taking the trouble to read the best works by philosophers of every age, simply turn yourself into a physician and you will certainly become one like the others. You will see the vanity of our preachers, whether they make our temples resound with their voices or exclaim eloquently in their works on the wonders of nature. After following man step by step and seeing what he inherits from his forefathers, his different ages, his passions, his illnesses and his structure compared to that of animals, you will agree that faith alone leads us to belief in a supreme Being, and that man, organised like other animals and subject to the same laws, must, despite a few degrees more of intelligence, nevertheless meet the same fate. Thus from the summit of that glorious immortality, from the top of that magnificent theological machine, you will come down, as from the Gloria[2] at the Opera, to the physical ground from where, seeing all around you only eternal matter and forms perpetually taking each other's place and perishing, you will admit in embarrassment that all animated bodies are destined for complete destruction. And finally, once the trunk of the moral system has been totally uprooted by philosophy, all the efforts made to reconcile philosophy and morality, theology and reason, will appear trivial and futile.

[a] Theological hatred.

[1] On the first of these works, by Nieuwentijd, and the fourth, by Derham, see p. 23 note 29 above; the third is by C. F. Houtteville (*La Religion chrétienne prouvée par les faits* (Paris, 1722); and the second seems to have been invented by La Mettrie.

[2] On eighteenth-century stages, this was the highest point, in which the divinities were to be seen in heaven.

Such is the first view and plan of this discourse; now let us go further and develop all these vague general ideas.

Philosophy, to whose investigations everything is subject, is itself subject to nature, as a daughter is to her mother. In common with true medicine, it is proud of such slavery, it refuses any other and listens to no other voice. Whatever is not drawn from the very bosom of nature, whatever is not phenomena, causes, effects and, in short, the science of objects, does not concern philosophy at all and comes from an alien source.

Such is morality; it is the arbitrary fruit of politics, which can justly claim what has been unjustly usurped by others. We shall see below why it has been considered worthy of inclusion among the parts of philosophy, to which it obviously does not properly belong.

Once men had decided to live together, they needed to formulate a system of political morality to safeguard their intercourse; and as they are unruly animals, difficult to tame and spontaneously rushing after their own well being by any means, those whom wisdom and genius made worthy of leading others, wisely called on religion to second rules and laws, which are too cold and rational to be able to acquire absolute authority over the impetuous imagination of a turbulent and superficial populace. Religion appeared, its eyes covered with a sacred blindfold and soon it was surrounded by all that multitude who listen in open-mouthed amazement to the wonders for which they yearn; and, oh miracle! the less they understand these wonders, the more easily they are subdued by them.

To this twofold curb of morality and religion has prudently been added that of punishment. Good, and especially great, actions have not gone without reward, nor wicked ones without retribution, and the dread example of the guilty has restrained those who were on the point of becoming guilty. Without gibbets, wheels, gallows and scaffolds, without those vile men, the dregs of the whole of nature, who would strangle the universe for money, and despite the workings of all those wonderful machines, the weaker would not have been protected from the stronger.

Since morality, like laws and executioners, originates in politics, it follows that it is not the work of nature, nor therefore of philosophy or reason, all synonymous terms.

Hence, too, it is not surprising that philosophy does not lead us towards morality with the aim of combining with it, taking its side and supporting it with its own strength. But one should not therefore believe that philosophy leads us towards morality as against an enemy, with the aim of exterminating it. If it marches towards morality, a torch in its hand, it is in order to reconnoitre it, so to speak, and to make a dispassionate judgement about the essential difference in their interests.

Just as objects are different from behaviour, feeling from laws and truth from all arbitrary conventions, so philosophy is different from morality or, if you prefer, nature's morality (for nature has its own morality) is different from the one wisely invented by admirable craftsmanship. While the latter seems filled with respect for the celestial source whence it comes (religion), the former has no less profound a respect for the truth or for whatever even merely seems like truth, and no less an attachment to its tastes and pleasures and, in general, to sensuality. The lodestone of the one is religion and of the other is pleasure when it feels, and truth when it thinks.

Listen to religious morality: it will order you imperiously to prevail over yourself, deciding without hesitation that nothing is easier and that 'to be virtuous is only a question of will power'. Lend an ear to nature's morality: it will invite you to follow your desires, your loves and whatever gives you pleasure, or rather you will already have followed its advice. Ah! the pleasure it inspires makes us feel clearly, with no need for such superfluous reasoning, that this pleasure is the only way for us to be happy.

On the one hand, we only need to submit gently to the pleasant impulses of nature; on the other, we must stiffen ourselves, rise up against it. On the one hand it is enough to be true to ourselves, to be what we are and, as it were, be like ourselves; on the other, we must be like other people despite ourselves, we must live and almost think like them. What play-acting!

The philosopher concentrates on what seems to him to be true or false, whatever the consequences; the legislator, scarcely concerned with the truth and perhaps even (through lack of philosophy, as we shall see) afraid that it might come to light, deals only with what is just or unjust, with moral good and evil. On the one hand, whatever seems to be part of nature is called true, and whatever is not in nature, whatever is contradicted by observation and experiment, is described as false; on the other, whatever helps society is honoured by being called just, fair, etc., and whatever harms its interests is dishonoured by being called unjust. In short, so different are their aims that morality leads to equity, justice, etc., and philosophy to truth.

The morality of nature or of philosophy is thus as different from that of religion and politics – the mother of both – as nature is from art. They are so diametrically opposed that they turn their backs on one another. What should we deduce, except that philosophy is absolutely irreconcilable with morality, religion and politics, which are its triumphant rivals in society, only to be shamefully humiliated in the solitude of the study and by the light of reason's torch. They are humiliated above all by precisely those vain efforts that so many clever people have made to reconcile them.

Could nature be wrong to be made that way and could reason be wrong to speak its language, support its wishes and encourage all its tastes? On the other hand, could society be wrong in its turn not to model itself on nature? It is ridiculous to expect the one and completely unreasonable to propose the other.

How inappropriate a mould in which to cast a society is reason, so far beyond the grasp of most men that only those who have cultivated it most can appreciate its importance and value! But again, how much more inappropriate a mould in which to cast a philosopher are the prejudices and errors which constitute the basic foundations of society!

This reflection did not escape the prudence of enlightened legislators; they knew only too well the animals they had to govern.

It is easy to make men believe what they want; they can be persuaded without difficulty of what flatters their self-esteem, and they were all the more easily seduced as their superiority over other animals had already helped to dazzle them. They thought that an organised lump of clay could be immortal.

However, nature disowns this childish doctrine; it is like the flotsam it washes up and leaves far behind on the coast of the theological sea. And, if I may continue to speak metaphorically, I would even say that all the rays shining from the bosom of nature, strengthened and as though reflected by the precious mirror of philosophy, destroy and pulverise a doctrine based only on the useful moral purpose that it can supposedly serve. What proof do you want? My works themselves, since this is their sole aim, like so many other better written or more learned ones, if it is necessary to be learned to prove what is perfectly obvious everywhere, namely that there is only one life, and that the most vainglorious man with the grandest plans bases them in vain on a vanity which is mortal like he is. Yes – and no wise man would disagree – the haughty monarch dies entirely and utterly, like his meanest subject and his faithful dog. This is a terrible truth, if you like, but only for those minds whose permanent state is childhood, those minds who are frightened by a ghost. For it allows no room for either doubt or fear in those who are capable of thinking, however little, those who do not turn their eyes away from what strikes them at each moment so clearly and vividly and those who have become, so to speak, mature adults rather than adolescents.

But if philosophy goes against social conventions and the main doctrines of religion and morality, it breaks the bonds which unite men! It saps the foundations of the political structure!

Superficial and inexact minds, what panic has seized you! What hasty judgement carries you away beyond your goal and beyond truth! If those who hold the reins of empires did not reflect more soundly, what splendid honour and what a glorious reputation they would acquire! Philosophy taken for a dangerous poison, philosophy, that solid linchpin of eloquence, that nourishing lymph of reason, would be banished from our conversations and our writings. Like an imperious and tyrannical queen, we would not even dare pronounce her name without fearing to be sent to Siberia,[3] and philosophers, expelled and banished as disturbers of the peace, would suffer the same fate as the would-be physicians in Rome of old.[4]

No, it is certainly a mistake; no, philosophy does not and cannot break society's bonds. Poison is found in philosophers' writings as happiness is found in songs or

3 The Tsarina Elizabeth Petrovna of Russia, who was said to inspire fear in her subjects, introduced the punishment of banishment to Siberia.

4 It was erroneously believed that physicians had been banished from Rome by Cato.

wit in Fontenelle's shepherds.[5] We sing an imaginary happiness, we give shepherds in an eclogue a wit they do not possess and we decide that something is dangerous when it is far from being so. For the sapping we have mentioned, totally different from that of our trenches, is theoretical and metaphysical and can consequently destroy or overthrow nothing, except hypothetically. And what is the result of overthrowing in a hypothesis the accepted and accredited usages of civil life? They are not really affected but are left standing in all their strength.

I shall try to prove my thesis using irrefutable arguments.

A contradiction between principles with such diverse natures as those of philosophy and politics – principles whose aims and objects are essentially different – does not at all imply that either refutes or destroys the other. The gap between philosophical speculations, on the one hand, and socially accepted principles and the beliefs necessary (let us suppose) for the safety of men's intercourse, on the other, is not the same as that between medical theory and the practice of that art. In medicine, the one has such a direct and absolute influence on the other that woe to the patients whom some Chirac has led astray![6] In politics, however, philosophical meditations – which are as inoffensive as their authors – cannot corrupt or poison the practice of society, none of whose customs, however comical and ridiculous, which are respected by ordinary people, are not applauded, when necessary, as willingly by all philosophers as they are by those who are the least philosophical. A philosopher is certainly loth to block in any way whatever guarantees – or rather is thought to guarantee – law and order.

The reason why two apparently so contradictory objects do not harm each other in any way is that their objects have nothing in common, for their aims are as different, as far from one another and as opposed, as East and West. We shall see below that, far from destroying each other, philosophy and morality can very well contribute to, and watch over, public safety in unison. We shall see that if one influences the other it is only indirectly but always to its advantage, so that, as I said at the beginning, the bonds of society are tightened by what at first sight seems destined to break and loosen them; this paradox is even more surprising than the first and will, I hope, be just as clearly proved by the end of this discourse.

What a terrible beam would be shone by philosophy if it enlightened only so few at the cost of the destruction and ruin of the others, who make up almost the whole universe!

Perish the thought. Those who have disturbed society were far from being philosophers, as we shall see below; and philosophy, in love with truth alone, calmly contemplating the beauties of nature, incapable of temerity and usurpation, has never trespassed on the rights of politics. Indeed, what philosopher, however

5 Fontenelle also wrote eclogues depicting shepherds.

6 Pierre Chirac, from Montpellier University, was one of the leading doctors of the day and an important member of the medical establishment; La Mettrie attacked him at length in *Ouvrage de Pénélope*, (3 vols., Berlin, 1748–50, vol. I, pp. 119–25).

daring you may suppose him to be, would not admit – even when openly attacking all the principles of morality with the utmost vigour, as I dare to do in my *Anti-Seneca* – that the interests of the public are of a totally different value from those of philosophy?

Politics, surrounded by its ministers, proclaims in public, from the pulpit and almost from the roof-tops: 'the body is naught, the soul is all; mortals, save yourselves whatever the cost'. Philosophers laugh, but they do not interrupt the ceremony; they speak, as they write, calmly. Their only apostles and ministers are a small number of faithful, as gentle and peaceful as they are, who may well rejoice when they increase their flock and enrich their estate through the happy acquisition of a few fine geniuses, but who, far from wishing to overturn everything, as is commonly imagined, would profoundly regret holding up for one moment the great movement of civil affairs.

Priests hold forth and enflame people's minds with magnificent promises worthy of filling out an eloquent sermon; they prove whatever they declare without bothering to reason, and they want us to put our trust in God knows what apocryphal authorities. Their thunder is ready to strike and pulverise whoever is reasonable enough not to believe blindly whatever shocks reason most. How much more wisely do philosophers behave! They may promise nothing, but they do not get off so lightly; they pay with good sense and solid reasoning for what costs the others only their lung power and an eloquence which is as empty and as vain as their promises. Can reasoning be dangerous when it has never produced fanatics, sects or even theologians?

Let us go into greater detail and prove more clearly that the boldest philosophy does not fundamentally contradict morals and, in short, does not entail danger of any kind.

What harm, I ask the greatest enemies of the freedom of thought and expression, what harm is there in agreeing to what seems true, if one recognises just as frankly and follows just as faithfully what seems wise and useful? Of what use would be the torch of physics or all those curious observations concerning comparative anatomy and natural history? We would have to extinguish the one and neglect the others, instead of encouraging, as the greatest princes do, the men who devote themselves to such painstaking research. Can we not try to solve and explain the riddle of man? If not, the more of a philosopher one was, the worse a citizen one would be, which no-one has ever believed. And what an ill-fated gift the truth would be, if it were often better left unsaid? What an irrelevant attribute reason would be, if it were created only to be captive and subordinate! To affirm such a system is to be willing to grovel and to degrade the human race; to believe that there are truths which are better left forever buried in the bosom of nature rather than exposed to the light of day is to encourage superstition and barbarity.

He who lives like a citizen can write like a philosopher.

But to write like a philosopher is to teach materialism! Well, what harm is there in that! If this materialism is well-founded, if it is the obvious result of all the observations and experiments of the greatest philosophers and physicians; if this system is only adopted after one has attentively followed nature, assiduously taken the same steps as nature across the whole range of the animal kingdom and, so to speak, studied man closely in all his ages and in all his different states? If orthodoxy follows the philosopher more than he avoids it, if he neither seeks nor elaborates such a doctrine on purpose, if he comes across it, as it were, and if it appears as a result of his research, and as if in his wake, is it therefore a crime to publish it? Is the truth not worth enough for us to bend down, as it were, and pick it up?

Do you want any other arguments in favour of philosophy's innocence? Among the mass of those that come to mind, I shall choose only the most striking ones.

However much La Mothe le Vayer may say that death is preferable to begging,[7] not only does this not make those 'disgusting objects of public pity' tired of life (and would it be such a misfortune if those miserable people were influenced by this way of thinking and delivered society from a weight that is worse than useless to the earth!), but instead, has any unfortunate mortal, when plunged from the pinnacle of fortune into the depths of misery, ever tried to put an end to his life as a result of that philosophical statement?

However much the Stoics may cry, 'leave life if it is a burden to you; there is neither reason nor glory in remaining a prey to pain or poverty; deliver yourself from yourself, make yourself both insensible and happy, whatever the cost', people do not kill themselves, any more than they kill others. Neither are they any more likely to steal, whether they have a religion or not. Instinct, hope (a divinity which smiles on the unhappy, and the feeling which dies last in man) and the gallows have seen to that. One only takes one's life from a feeling of unhappiness, disaffection, fear, or the certainty that one is even worse off than one is, which is a dark feeling, produced by the black bile, in which philosophers and their books have no part. That is the origin of suicide, rather than any solidly reasoned system, unless you wish to add that fanaticism which made the readers of Hegesias seek death.[8]

Thus, although in cases of extreme need it is permitted, according to the law of nature and Pufendorf, to take by force a little of another's superfluity,[9] one would nevertheless not dare to take the law into one's own hands with such apparently legitimate and indispensable violence, because it is punished by the laws which are, alas, too deaf to the cries of desperate nature. It is true, by the way, that while the laws are usually right to be strict, they also sometimes find legitimate excuses for indulgence. For since the individual perpetually sacrifices himself, as it were, in order not to harm public rights, the laws which protect those rights, and the authorities, should in their turn, I believe, reduce their stern rigour, show humanity

7 In his short treatise entitled 'Des richesses et de la pauvreté', *Opuscules un Petits traictez* (Paris, 1644), no. VII. On La Mothe le Vayer, see *The System of Epicurus* and *Anti-Seneca* and p. 110 note 23.

8 On Hegesias see p. 120 note 3.

9 See Pufendorf, *De jure naturae ac gentium*, Bk. II, ch. 6, §V.

and mercy to their unhappy fellow-men, accept their mutual needs and not behave with such barbarous antagonism towards their brothers.

How can one admit to the slightest drawbacks of a science which has been deemed worthy of the approval and veneration of the greatest men of all centuries! However much the materialists may prove that man is nothing but a machine, the people will never believe it.[b] The same instinct which makes them cling to life gives them enough vanity to believe their souls immortal, and they are too unreasonable and too ignorant ever to ignore that vanity.

However much I may encourage an unhappy man no longer to feel remorse for a crime into which he was pushed, as we are above all by what is called a spontaneous reaction, he will nevertheless feel remorse and he will be pursued by it. Simply reading cannot rid us of principles which are so habitual that we take them to be natural. The conscience only shrivels through wickedness and infamy, which, far from encouraging (God forbid!), I have tried to make people regard with as much horror as I myself do. Thus all our writings are only fairytales in the eyes of the masses, and superfluous reasoning in the eyes of those who are not ready to receive their germs; and for those that are, our hypotheses likewise present no danger. Their fine penetrating genius has safeguarded their hearts from such daring and, if I dare to say so, such mental nakedness.

But wait! could not common people be seduced after all by a few gleams of philosophical light, which can easily be glimpsed among all the enlightenment that philosophy seems to be pouring forth today? And as we take much from those we live with, can we not easily adopt the bold opinions of which philosophical works are full, though less, in truth, (although the opposite is usually believed) today than in the past.

Philosophical truths are only systems, the most seductive of which is the one whose author has the most skill, wit and enlightenment, and in which each can decide for himself because, for most readers, the arguments in favour are no more proved than those against, and because a few degrees of probability more or less on one side or the other are enough to decide and force our agreement; and only well-formed minds (who are much rarer than those who are called wits) can feel or grasp these differences. How many arguments, mistakes, hatreds and contradictions have arisen from the famous question of liberty or fatalism! Yet they are only hypotheses. A narrow or fanatical mind, believing the doctrines in bad pamphlets, which he recites to us with a self-satisfied air, naturally imagines that all is lost – morality, religion, society – if it is proved that man is not free. The man of genius, on the contrary, the impartial and unprejudiced man, sees the solution to the problem, whatever it is, as completely unimportant both in itself and in relation to society. Why? Because it does not lead in practice to the delicate and dangerous

[b] And what such great harm would it do if they did believe it? Thanks to stern laws, they could be Spinozists without society having to fear the destruction of the altars to which this bold system seems to lead.

implications with which the theory seems to threaten society. I think I have proved that remorse is a prejudice created by education and that man is a machine despotically governed by absolute fatalism. I may be mistaken and I am willing to believe so. But suppose, as I sincerely believe, that it is philosophically true; what does it matter? All these issues can be put in the same class as the mathematical point, which only exists in the heads of mathematicians, and so many other geometrical and algebraic problems whose clear and ideal solutions demonstrate all the power of the human mind. This power is not the enemy of the laws and this theory is innocent, the result of pure curiosity, which is so little applicable in practice that it can no more be used than can all the metaphysical truths of the most advanced geometry.

I now move on to new reflections, naturally linked to the preceding ones, for which they can only provide more and more support.

Since polytheism was abolished by law, have we become more honest? Was Julian less worthy as an apostate than as a Christian?[10] Did it make him any less of a great man and the best of princes? Would Christianity have made Cato the Censor less stern and ferocious, or Cato the Younger less virtuous, or Cicero a less excellent citizen, etc.? In short, do we have any more virtue than the pagans? No, and they had no less religion than we. They followed theirs as we follow ours, that is to say, very badly or not at all. Superstition was left to the people and the priests, who were mercenary believers,[c] while honest people, realising that they did not need religion to make them honest, paid no attention to it. To believe in one God or many, to see nature as the blind and inexplicable cause of all phenomena, or, impressed by the wonderful order we see in them, to admit a supreme intelligence even more incomprehensible than nature, to believe that man is only an animal like any other, only more intelligent, or to consider the soul as an essentially immortal substance separate from the body – here is the battlefield on which philosophers have been at war with each other since they learnt the art of reasoning, and this war will last as long as opinion, that queen of men, reigns on earth. Here is the battlefield on which everyone can still fight and choose, from among so many colours, to follow the one which will most favour his career or prejudices, without such trivial, vain skirmishes presenting any danger. But that is what those minds who see no further than their noses cannot understand; they drown in this sea of reasoning. Here is more reasoning whose simplicity will perhaps make it more accessible to everyone.

In the same way as the silence of all the ancient authors proves the novelty of a particular foul disease,[11] so the silence of all writers concerning the ills caused by

[c] For the most part.

[10] On the Emperor Julian, see p. 115 note 26.

[11] He means venereal disease which, as La Mettrie shows in his medical works, was unknown until the end of the fifteenth century.

philosophy (supposing that it causes or can cause any) pleads in favour of its benignity and innocence.

As for the infection, or if you prefer, the contagion that is feared, I do not believe that it is possible. Each man is so strongly convinced of the truth of the principles with which he has been filled and even gorged during his childhood, and his self-respect depends so much on maintaining them without faltering, that even were I as determined as I am indifferent, I could not, even with all of Cicero's eloquence, convince anyone that he was wrong. The reason is simple. What a philosopher considers to be clear and proven is obscure and uncertain, or rather untrue, for those who are not philosophers, particularly if they are not made to become philosophers.

Therefore we need not be afraid that the minds of the people will ever model themselves on those of philosophers, who are too far above their reach. They are like those low, deep instruments which cannot go up to the high, piercing notes of some others, or like a bass which cannot rise to the ravishing sounds of the alto. It is no more possible for a mind without the slightest tincture of philosophy – however much natural penetration it may have – to adopt the turn of mind of a physician used to reflecting, than it is for the physician to adopt the turn of mind of the former and and to reason as badly. They are two physiognomies which will never be similar, two instruments, one of which is shaped, sculpted, finely wrought, while the other is rough, just as it was created by nature. And so the habit is formed and it will remain; one can no more rise than the other can descend. The ignorant man, full of prejudices, speaks and reasons to no effect; he only, as they say, beats about the bush or, which comes to the same thing, recalls and repeats (if he knows them) all the pathetic arguments of our schools and our pedants. Meanwhile the clever man follows in the steps of nature, observation and experiment, only accepts the greatest degree of probability and plausibility and only draws rigorous and direct conclusions, which strike any well-formed mind, from facts which are equally clear, and from fertile and luminous principles.

I admit that we adopt some of the ways of thinking, speaking and gesticulating of those we live with, but it happens little by little, by mechanical imitation, as our thighs move at the sight of, and in the same way as, those of certain mimes. We are gradually prepared for it and stronger habits finally overcome weaker ones.

But in this case, where shall we find that vigour and those new habits capable of defeating and uprooting the old ones? The people neither live with philosophers nor read philosophical books. If by chance one falls into their hands, they either understand nothing or, if they perceive something, they do not believe a word of it; and they rudely call philosophers madmen, like poets, and find both worthy of Bedlam.

Philosophy can only be transmitted to already enlightened minds, which have nothing to fear, as we have seen. It passes a hundred feet over other heads, where it can no more enter than can daylight into a dark dungeon.

But let us see what is the essence of the famous dispute in the field of morals between philosophers and non-philosophers. What a surprise! It is only about a simple distinction, a solid though scholastic distinction; who would have believed that this distinction alone could put an end to a sort of civil war and reconcile all our enemies? Let me explain what I mean: nothing is absolutely just, nothing absolutely unjust. There is no true equity, there are no absolute vices, no absolute greatness and no absolute crimes. Politicians and religionists, allow philosophers this truth and do not permit yourselves to be forced into a corner where you will be shamefully defeated. Admit in good faith that he who weighs justice, so to speak, against society, is just; and in their turn philosophers will allow (when have they ever denied it?) that a particular action is relatively just or unjust, honest or dishonest, wicked or virtuous, praiseworthy, vile, criminal, etc. Who denies the need for all these splendid arbitrary relations? Who says that you are wrong to have imagined another life and all that magnificent system of religion, which is a worthy subject for an epic poem? Who blames you for having taken hold of men by their weak point, sometimes by 'ensnaring' them as Montaigne[12] says, and by catching them on the hook of the most flattering of hopes, and sometimes by holding them at bay with the most terrifying of threats? We will also admit, if you wish, that all those imaginary executioners in the afterlife are the reason why ours have less work and that most ordinary people only avoid 'one of those ways of going up in the world'[d] which Dean Swift talks about,[13] because they are afraid of the torments of Hell.

Yes, you are right, magistrates, ministers and legislators, to incite men by all possible means, less to do good, about which you are perhaps very little concerned, than to act in the interests of society, which is your main point, as therein lies your safety. But why not grant us too, with the same sincerity and the same impartiality, that speculative truths are in no way dangerous and that when I have proved that the afterlife is imaginary, it will not prevent the people from continuing in the same way, respecting others' lives and wallets and believing even more in the most ridiculous prejudices than I myself believe in what seems to me to be the truth itself. Like you, we know that hydra with hundreds and thousands of mad, ridiculous and idiotic heads, and we know how difficult it is to lead an animal which does not wish to be led. We applaud your laws, your morals and even your religion, almost as much as we applaud your gallows and your scaffolds. But on seeing all the homage which we pay to the wisdom of your government, are you not tempted to pay homage in your turn to the truth of our observations, the soundness of our experiments and the wealth – and even more, the usefulness – of our discoveries?

d The gallows.

12 See, for example, *Essays*, Bk. II, ch. 12, 'An Apology for Raimond Sebond' (*Complete Essays*, trans. Screech, p. 571).

13 At the beginning of *A Tale of a Tub* (1704), J. Swift discusses the methods of exalting oneself above a crowd.

What blindness makes you refuse to open your eyes to such a dazzling light? What baseness makes you disdain to take advantage of it? Even more, what barbarous tyranny makes you disturb in their studies those peaceful men, an honour to the human mind and their country, who far from disturbing you in your public duties, can only encourage you to fulfil them properly and to set, if you can, a good example.

How little you know the philosopher if you think him dangerous!

I must paint him for you here in his truest colours. The philosopher is human and consequently is not exempt from all the passions, but they are ruled and, so to speak, circumscribed by the very compasses of wisdom. That is why they can lead him to sensuality (and why should he refuse those sparks of happiness, those honest and charming pleasures for which his senses seem obviously to have been made?), but they will never incite him to crime or debauchery. He would be sorry if his heart could be accused of being affected by the liberty or, if you prefer, licentiousness of his mind. He is usually no more ashamed of one than of the other. He is a model of humanity, frankness, gentleness and probity; while writing against the law of nature, he follows it rigorously, and while arguing about what is just, he nevertheless behaves justly in relation to society. Speak, common souls, what more do you require?

Do not accuse philosophers of immorality, of which they are almost all incapable. Truly, as the greatest wit of our time has said, it was not Bayle or Spinoza or Vanini or Hobbes or Locke or any other metaphysician of the same calibre, nor was it any of those charming, sensual philosophers like Montaigne, Saint-Evremond or Chaulieu, who brought the torch of discord into their country. It was the theologians, unruly spirits who make war on men to serve a God of peace.[14]

But let us draw a veil over the most dreadful aspects of our history and not try to compare fanaticism and philosophy. We know only too well which of them armed certain subjects against their kings; it was those monsters vomited forth from the depths of monasteries by blind superstition, a hundred times more dangerous, as Bayle has proved,[15] than deism or even atheism. These two systems are the same in relation to society and are completely blameless when they are the work not of blind debauchery but of enlightened reflection. But this is what I need to prove as I go on.

Surely it is true that a deist or an atheist, as such, will not do to others what he would not like to be done to him, whatever may be the source of this principle, which I believe is rarely natural; it is either fear, as Hobbes claimed,[16] or self-respect, which seems the chief motive for our actions. Why?

14 Voltaire, *Lettres philosophiques*, 13, on Locke. Bayle, Spinoza, Vanini, Hobbes and Locke, like Montaigne, and the seventeenth-century French writers Saint-Evremond and Chaulieu, are standard references for antireligious and Libertin writers.

15 In *Pensées diverses sur le comète* (Rotterdam, 1681), which is the inspiration for the following discussion.

16 For example in *De cive*, ch. 1; see above, p. 137 note 40.

Because there is no necessary connection between believing in only one God or believing in none, and being a bad citizen. That is why in the history of atheists I cannot find a single one who has not been a credit to others and to his country. But if humanity itself, if that innate feeling of tenderness has engraved this law in his heart, he will be humane, gentle, honest, affable, generous and unselfish; he will possess a true greatness of soul and, in a word, will combine all the qualities of a respectable member of society with all the social virtues which that implies.

Virtue can therefore grow the deepest roots in an atheist while they only, so to speak, hang by a thread on the surface of a believer's heart. That is the fate of everything that comes from a favourable organisation; the feelings which are born with us cannot be effaced, and they leave us only at death.

After that, how can one ask in good faith whether it is possible for a deist or a Spinozist to be a respectable member of society? In what way are the principles of irreligion incompatible with probity? They have no relation one with another; they are worlds apart. I might as well be surprised, like some Catholics, at a Protestant's good faith.

It is, to my mind, no more reasonable to ask whether a society of atheists could subsist. For a society not to be disturbed, what is required? For the truth of its basic principles to be recognised? Not at all. For their wisdom to be recognised? Admittedly. Their necessity? Admittedly again, if you wish, although it only affects common ignorance and stupidity. For them to be followed? Yes, yes doubtless, that is enough. Well, what deist or atheist, thinking differently from other people, does not nevertheless follow their morals? What materialist, full of, even pregnant with, his system (whether he keeps his way of thinking to himself and only speaks of it to his friends or to people like him, who are knowledgeable in the most profound sciences, or whether he has given birth and shared it with the whole universe, either in conversation or, above all, in publications), what atheist, I repeat, would immediately go and rape, burn, assassinate and immortalise himself by means of different crimes? Alas, he is too calm and his inclinations are too favourable for him to seek such an odious and horrible form of immortality, when he can equally, thanks to the beauty of his genius, leave a favourable picture in men's memories, as someone who was liked during his life for his civilised and pleasant behaviour.

But, you say, what prevents him from renouncing virtues whose practice he expects to bring him no reward? What prevents him from giving himself up to vices or crimes for which he expects no punishment after his death?

Oh! What an ingenious and admirable reflection! What prevents you yourselves, ardent spiritualists? The devil. What a splendid invention and a wonderful bugbear! The philosopher, who laughs at that very name, is restrained by another sort of fear which you share with him, when he is unlucky enough – which is rare – not to be led by the love of order. Thus, as he does not share your fears of Hell, which he tramples underfoot like Virgil[17] and the whole of wise Antiquity, he is for that very reason happier than you.

Not only do I think that a society of philosophical atheists would survive very well, but I believe that it would survive more easily than a society of believers, who are always ready to sound the alarm concerning the merit and virtue of often the gentlest and wisest men. I am not trying to encourage atheism, Heaven forbid! But, examining things as a disinterested physician, if I were a king I would lower my guard on those whose patriotic hearts could provide me with a guard, while I would double it on the others, whose prejudices are their first kings. How can one not have confidence in minds who are friends to peace and enemies of unrest and trouble, cool minds whose imagination is never overheated and who decide everything only after mature examination, like philosophers, sometimes defending the colours of truth against politics itself, sometimes supporting all its arbitrary conventions, without as a result believing themselves to be, or really being, guilty of any crime against either society or philosophy.

What, I ask, will now be our antagonists' subterfuge? The materialists' licentious and daring works, that sensuality in whose charms, I am willing to believe, most of them indulge as much as I do? But if that sensuality did not stay in the depths of their hearts but ran lasciviously into their libertine pens; if philosophers, with nature's book in their hands, climbed like modern giants onto one another's shoulders to reach the Heavens,[18] what so unpleasant conclusions could be drawn? Jupiter would no more be dethroned than Europe's customs would be destroyed by a Chinaman writing against them. Can we not give free rein to our genius or imagination without it being used as evidence against the morals of the most daring writer? We allow ourselves more freedom when, with a pen in our hand, we wish to brighten up our solitude, than we do in society, which we only want to preserve in peace.

How many writers, hiding behind their works, dare to write on virtue while their own hearts are a prey to all sorts of vices! They are like those preachers who come directly from the arms of a young female penitent whom they have converted (in their own way) and lecture on continence and chastity in speeches which are less florid than their own complexions. How many others, who hardly believe in God, have made their fortunes by writing pious books in defence of apocryphal works, which they make fun of themselves in the evening with their friends at the tavern. They laugh at their poor readers, whom they have tricked, as Seneca perhaps did, for he is suspected of not having had a heart as pure and virtuous as his pen. When one is laden with vices and wealth, surely it is ridiculous and villainous to plead in favour of virtue and poverty?

But – to come on to more commendable examples which are more closely

[17] See the *Georgics*, II.490–2, the first line of which is quoted in *The System of Epicurus* and on the title page of the *Anti-Seneca*.

[18] A reference to the myth of the giants attacking the heavens, in Ovid's *Metamorphoses*, I.150ff.

connected with my subject – the wise Bayle, whose wisdom is known to so many trustworthy people still alive, scattered throughout his works quite a large number of obscene passages and equally obscene reflections. Why? To cheer up and amuse a tired mind. Behaving somewhat like our prudes, he allowed his imagination a pleasure that he refused to his senses, an innocent pleasure, which awakens the soul and keeps it engrossed much longer. Thus gaiety in objects, on which ours most often depends, is necessary for poets; it is that gaiety which leads to the burgeoning of Graces, cupids, flowers and all that charming sensuality that flows from nature's brush and is exuded by the verse of Voltaire, Arnaud or that famous king who honours them by being their rival.[19]

How many carefree, voluptuous authors have been thought sad and gloomy because they appeared so in their novels or tragedies! A very charming man who is anything but sad (being a friend of the greatest of kings, married into one of the greatest German families, esteemed and loved by all who know him and enjoying so much honour, wealth and reputation, he would doubtless be greatly to be pitied if he were) appeared so to some of his readers in his famous *Essay on Moral Philosophy*.[20] Why? Because people think he experiences all the time the same feeling produced by philosophical truths, which are designed more to mortify the reader's self-esteem than to flatter or amuse him. How many satirists, in particular Boileau, were nothing but the virtuous enemies of contemporary vices! Taking arms and rising against vices, or punishing the wicked and forcing them to reflect, does not necessarily make one their virtuous enemy, any more than saying things that are neither pleasant nor flattering necessarily makes one sad. And as a happy and lively author can write on melancholy and tranquillity, a contented scholar can show that in general man is very far from being so.

If I dare to name myself after so many great men, what has not been said, good God, and what has not been written about me! What clamour has not been made by believers, doctors and even their patients, each of whom has espoused his own charlatan's cause. What bitter complaints from all sides! What journalist has ever refused a glorious asylum to my detractors, or rather has not calumnied me himself! What vile gazetteer from Göttingen, and even Berlin, has not got his teeth into me? In what pious houses have I been spared, or rather have I not been treated like another Cartouche?[21] By whom? By people who have never seen me, people upset at seeing me thinking differently from them and above all chagrined at my revived fortunes, and people who thought my heart was guilty of the same systematic itch as my mind. When self-esteem is wounded in its most baseless prejudices or its most depraved behaviour, of what indignity is it not capable! How was I, a weak

19 Frederick II. The poet Baculard d'Arnaud, a friend of La Mettrie, was, like Voltaire, at Frederick's court before falling out of favour.

20 P. L. M. de Maupertuis, *Essai de philosophie morale*. On this work, and on La Mettrie's disagreement with it, see Introduction, pp. xxi–xxii.

21 A famous highwayman executed in 1721.

reed transplanted into such turgid waters and continually bent by every opposing wind, able to put down such fine, solid roots? By what luck have I, surrounded by such powerful enemies, resisted and even risen despite them to the throne of a king, whose declared protection alone finally dissolved such cruel persecution, like an evil vapour?

Dare I say it? I am not in the least like all those portraits of me that circulate all over the world, and it would even be a mistake to judge me by my writings; indeed, what is most innocent in the most innocent among them is even less so than I am. I have no wicked heart or wicked intentions to be ashamed of, and if my mind has gone astray (it was made for that), my more fortunate heart has not gone astray with it.

Will people never undeceive themselves concerning philosophers? Will they never see that just as one's heart differs from one's mind, so one's morality can differ from what one writes in an audacious doctrine, a satire, a system or any sort of work.

What danger can there be in the rambling flights of a sceptical mind which flits from one hypothesis to another like a bird from branch to branch, carried away one day by one degree of probability and seduced the next by a stronger one?

Why should I blush to float thus between verisimilitude and uncertainty? Is the truth within the grasp of those who love it best and who seek it most sincerely and keenly? Alas, no! The fate of the best minds is to move from the cradle of ignorance in which we are all born to the cradle of Pyrrhonism in which most die.

And if I have shown little respect for vulgar prejudice, if I have not even deigned to use against them those wiles and tactics which have shielded so many authors from our Jews and their synods, it does not mean that I am a wrongdoer, a disrupting influence or a plague on society, for all this praise costs my enemies nothing. Whatever may be my speculation in the quiet of my study, my practice in society is quite different; I do not moralise in either speech or writing. At home I write what I consider to be true; with others I say what I consider to be good, salutary, useful and beneficial. In the one place, as a philosopher, I prefer the truth, while in the other, as a citizen, I prefer error. Error is more within everyone's grasp; it is the general food of minds in all ages and in all places. What indeed is more worthy of enlightening and leading the vile herd of mindless mortals! In society I never talk about all those lofty philosophical truths which were not made for the masses. To give a great remedy to a patient who is completely beyond all help is to dishonour it, and to discuss the august science of objects with those who are not initiated into its mysteries, who have eyes but do not see and ears but do not hear, is to profane and prostitute it. In a word, as a member of a body from which I derive so many advantages, it is right that I should act ungrudgingly according to principles to which (given the wickedness of our species) everyone owes the safety of his person and goods. But as a philosopher, attached with pleasure to wisdom's glorious chariot and rising above prejudices, I lament their necessity and regret that the whole world cannot be peopled with inhabitants whose behaviour is governed by reason.

Here is my soul in all its nudity. You should not believe that, because I have said freely what I think, I am the enemy of morals or that my own are bad. 'While what I write is impure, my life is honest.'[22] I am no more of a Spinozist for having created the *Man-machine* and exposed the *System of Epicurus* than I am wicked for having made a satire against the worst charlatans among my fellow doctors, or vain for having criticised our wits, or debauched for having dared to depict sensuality with delicate brush strokes.[23] And although I have, as a philosopher, abolished remorse, I would experience it myself as a citizen if my doctrine were dangerous (which I defy my most virulent enemy to prove).

Anyway, I have been willing to come down completely to the level of all those weak, narrow, meticulous minds which make up the learned public. The more they have misunderstood and misinterpreted me and the more odiously and unjustly they have presented my aims, the less I have felt obliged to lay before their eyes a work which has scandalised them so much and so inappropriately; they were doubtless led astray by the way I have philosophically dissected vices and virtues. But the proof that I do not feel any guilt towards society, which I respect and love, is that despite so many complaints and clamours I have just reprinted the same work, revised and reorganised, purely in fact in order to have the honour of placing at His Majesty's feet a complete copy of my works.[24] In the presence of such a genius, the only thing that should make us afraid of revealing ourselves completely is our own lack of genius.

Ah! If only all princes were as astute, as enlightened and as sensitive to the precious gift of intelligence, with what pleasure and success everyone would follow bravely the path of his talent and would encourage the progress of letters, science, arts and above all philosophy, their august sovereign. We would no longer meet with those unwelcome prejudices according to which, when cultivated too freely, that science can build upon the ruins of laws, morality, etc.; we would fearlessly give free rein to those fine powerful minds who are as capable of bringing honour to the arts by their enlightenment as they are incapable of harming society by their behaviour. And thus, far from hindering and distressing the only men who, by gradually dissipating the darkness of our ignorance, can enlighten the universe, we would encourage them, on the contrary, by all sorts of rewards and encouragement.

It is therefore true that, on the one hand, nature and human reason, enlightened by philosophy, and, on the other, religion supported and even propped up by morality and politics, are destined by their own constitutions to be eternally at war.

22 An inaccurate quotation from M. Valerius Martialis, I.5.8. The original reads: 'lasciva est nobis pagina, vita proba'.

23 The works referred to are, in order, *L'Ouvrage de Pénélope*; *Essais sur l'esprit et les beaux esprits* (n.p., 1744); *L'École de la volupté*.

24 The 1750 edition of his *Anti-Seneca* consisting of only twelve copies; see the Note on the text.

But it does not follow that philosophy, although theoretically opposed to morality and religion, can truly destroy those wise and sacred bonds. It has likewise been proved that all those philosophical wars would, at bottom, not be dangerous at all without the odious theological hatred which accompanies them. For it is enough to define, to distinguish and to agree (a rare enough thing, it is true!) in order to realise that the paths of philosophy and politics do not cross and that, in short, they have nothing important to argue about.

Here, if I am not mistaken, are two well pruned branches. Let us move on to the third and all the implications of my paradox will be proved.

Although the tightening of the bonds of society by the welcome hands of philosophy seems at first sight a more difficult problem to understand, I do not think, however, after all that has been said above, that very deep reflection is required in order to solve it.

Over what does it not stretch its wings? To what does it not communicate its strength and energy? And in how many ways can it not make itself useful and respectable?

Just as it is philosophy which treats the body in medicine, so it is philosophy which treats – although in a different way – the laws, the mind, the heart, the soul, etc., and which rules the art of thinking by means of the order which it puts into our ideas. It is philosophy that provides the basis for the art of speaking and that interferes usefully everywhere: in jurisprudence, morality, metaphysics, rhetoric, religion, etc. Yes, I repeat, usefully, whether it teaches truth or error.

Without its light, doctors would be reduced to the first fumblings of blind empiricism, which can be seen as the founder of the Hippocratic art.

How have people managed to give an appearance of doctrine and something resembling a sort of solid body, to the skeleton of metaphysics? By cultivating philosophy, whose magic art alone was able to change a Toricellian vacuum, if I may express myself in that way, into an apparent plenum and to make people believe that the fleeting breath, the air of life, which is so easily pumped out of the thorax's pneumatic engine, was immortal.[25]

If religion had been able to speak the language of reason, Nicole, that splendid writer from the last century who imitated it so well, would have been able to make it do so.[26] And what other help could he have found?

How many other excellent uses or lucky misuses of philosophers' hard work are there! Who erected morality in turn into a sort of science? Who introduced it, who brought it with its partner, metaphysics, into the field of wisdom of which it is now part? Philosophy itself. Yes, it was philosophy which sculpted and perfected this useful instrument, which made a wonderful compass of what would otherwise have been the rough magnet of society. It is thanks to philosophy that

[25] A reference to the air-pump (see above, p. 142 note 47), which disproved the Scholastic maxim that nature abhors a vacuum.

[26] P. Nicole, Jansenist co-author of the *Logique de Port-Royal* (Paris, 1662).

the most apparently sterile trees can sooner or later bear splendid fruit. It is thanks to philosophy that our academic works will perhaps likewise be clearly useful one day.

Why was Moses such a great legislator? Because he was a philosopher. The philosopher has such an effect on the art of governing that princes who have attended the school of wisdom are made in order to be, and actually are, better than those who have not been imbued with the principles of philosophy; look at the Emperor Julian and the now famous Philosopher-King. He realised the need to abrogate laws, to reduce punishments and to make them fit the crime; he turned on them the philosophical eye which shines out in all his works. Thus, in the states in which I am writing, justice is administered all the better for having been, so to speak, reasoned and wisely reformed by the Prince who governs them. If he has proscribed from the bar an art which delights him, as it delights his readers, it is because he knows how seductively prestigious it is; he has seen the way in which eloquence can be abused and how Cicero himself did so.[e][27]

It is true that the worst cause, when handled by a clever rhetorician, can triumph over the best one, when it is deprived of the sovereign empire of justice and reason, all too often usurped by the art of speaking.

But how is it possible to lay bare all that misuse, all that fine-sounding glitter of rounded phrases and artistically arranged expressions, all those empty words that perish pompously in the air, that brass mistaken for gold – in short all that fraudulent eloquence – and to separate so much alloy from true metal?

If the truth can sometimes be drawn from that impenetrable well at the bottom of which it was placed by a classical author,[28] philosophy can show us how. It is the touchstone of solid thought and right reasoning; it is the crucible in which everything that nature does not recognise is evaporated. In its clever hands, the most tangled ball of objects is, as it were, unrolled and spun out as easily as a great physician untangles and unmasks the most complicated illnesses.

Let rhetoric lend to laws or the most unjust actions an appearance of fairness and reason; philosophy is not taken in by it. It possesses a fixed point for judging properly what is honest or dishonest, fair or unfair, wicked or virtuous; it discovers the errors and injustices of the laws, and shelters the widow and the orphan from the traps of that siren which catches reason easily, and not without danger, with a brilliant flowery speech. Oh pure breath of nature, the best prepared poison cannot corrupt you!

But when eloquence itself – that art invented by coquetry of the mind, which is to philosophy what the most beautiful form is to the most precious substance – has to find its place, who gives it those male accents, that vehement force which makes

e See the excellent Memoirs that the King has presented to his Academy.

27 Frederick II outlined in his *Dissertation sur les raisons d'établir ou d'abroger les loix*, read to the Berlin Academy on 22 January 1750, his plans to reform the laws of Brandenburg.

28 Democritus.

Demosthenes or Bourdaloue thunder?[29] Philosophy. Without it, without the order that it puts into one's ideas, Cicero's eloquence would perhaps have been in vain; all those splendid speeches that made crime turn pale, virtue triumph and Verres, Catilina, etc. quake,[30] and all those masterpieces of the art of speaking would not have gained control over the minds of the whole Roman Senate and come down to us.

I know that a single flash of fiery, pathetic eloquence and the mere word 'fatherland' or 'French', pronounced in the right way, can incite men to heroism, bring back victory and steady the uncertainty of fate. But those cases in which one is appealing only to the imagination, and in which all is lost if it is not strongly aroused, are rare; on the other hand, it is an everyday occurrence for philosophy to act solely on our reason, and it serves a useful purpose even when it is misused by being applied to common errors.

But to come back, as I must, to an important subject whose surface I have only touched: it is reason, enlightened by the torch of philosophy, that shows us that fixed point to which I referred and from which one can start in order to learn what is just and unjust, morally good and bad. What is right is decided by the law, but this right is in itself neither a reasoned nor a just right; it is a right of force which often crushes a miserable wretch who has reason and justice on his side. What protects the weakest from the strongest may thus not be fair at all and, as a result, the laws can often need rectifying. But what will rectify, reform and weigh them up, so to speak, except philosophy? How and where, if not in the scales of wisdom and society? For there is our fixed point, from which we can judge what is just and unjust; fairness can be recognised and seen from this point of view alone. Once again, it can be weighed only in those scales, in which the laws should consequently be put. It can be said about them, as about all human actions, that only those which favour society are just and only those which harm its interests are unjust. This is, once again, the only way to judge properly their value and worth.

When philosophy finds in favour of Pufendorf rather than Grotius – famous names who chose to advance in the same direction by different paths – it admits that if the one proved to be a better philosopher than the other, when he recognised that any human action is of itself neutral, he hit the target just as directly as a lawyer or moralist by giving to the laws what should be attributed to those for whom they are made.[31] Dare I say it? Both of these great men, through lack of clear ideas and our fixed point, only beat about the bush.

[29] The Athenian orator Demosthenes was particularly renowned for his speeches against Philip of Macedonia; the Jesuit Louis Bourdaloue (1632–1704) was the most famous preacher of religious sermons of his day.

[30] Gaius Verres, corrupt Roman official, prosecuted by Cicero; fled to Missilia, where he died. Lucius Sergius Catilina, leader of a conspiracy defeated by Cicero; killed 62 BC.

[31] See Pufendorf, *De jure naturae ac gentium*, Bk. I, ch. 2, §VI; Bk. II, ch. 3, §IV. La Mettrie's rather obscure remark seems to be inspired by an article criticising the opinions of Pufendorf and H. Grotius that appeared in the *Nouvelle bibliothèque germanique* in 1750, entitled 'Examen de la question: s'il y a quelque chose de juste et d'injuste avant la loi'.

Thus philosophy teaches us that what is absolutely true does not stifle what is relatively just, and thus philosophy cannot harm morality, politics and, in short, the security of human intercourse. This is an obvious conclusion, on which we cannot insist enough in a discourse specifically designed to develop and expose it perfectly.

Now we know beyond doubt that what is true is not necessarily just and, vice versa, that what is just can very well not be true, and that what is legal does not imply any fairness at all; fairness is distinguished only by the sign and character which I have mentioned, that is to say the interests of society. Here we see the darkness of jurisprudence and the covered paths of politics finally lit up by the torch of philosophy. Thus all those vain arguments concerning moral good and evil, being ended forever for good minds, will henceforth be conducted only by those who are so stubborn and partial that they refuse to give in to the wisdom of philosophical reflections, or whose blind fanaticism makes them close their eyes to the most striking light.

It is time to look at our charming queen from a different angle. Philosophy enlarges the mind, just as fire dilates bodies; this property alone is always useful, whatever system one adopts.

If I reveal that all the proofs of God's existence are merely specious and dazzling, that those of the soul's immortality are merely scholastic and futile, that in short nothing can provide an idea of what our senses cannot feel nor our weak minds comprehend, our mystical Abadists[32] and our dusty scholars will cry vengeance and a pedant in vestments will publicly call me an atheist, in order to arouse the hostility of a whole nation. But if I am right, if I have proved a new truth, refuted an ancient mistake and investigated a superficially studied subject, I shall have extended the limits of my knowledge and my mind; what is more, I shall have increased public enlightenment and the intellectual level of society by transmitting my research and daring to publish what every timid or prudent philosopher whispers.

This does not mean that I cannot be mistaken, but even if that were true, nevertheless, by making my reader think and by sharpening his reflection, I would still extend the limits of his genius, and for that reason I cannot see why I should be so ill received by good minds.

In the same way as Descartes' most erroneous hypotheses are accepted as lucky mistakes inasmuch as they led to glimpses and discoveries of many truths that would still be unknown without them, the most ill-founded systems of morality or metaphysics are not therefore completely useless, provided that they are well-reasoned; a long series of wonderfully deduced consequences, even though they follow from false or illusory principles such as those of Leibniz or Wolff, makes it easier for a well-exercised mind to encompass afterwards a larger number of objects. And what will be the result? More excellent field glasses, a better telescope and, so to speak, new eyes, which will perhaps turn out soon to be very useful.

32 'Labadistes', not 'Abadistes' as La Mettrie wrote, were members of a protestant sect founded by Jean Labadie in the seventeenth century, not to be confused with Abbadie, a popular religious apologist.

Let the people say and believe that to use our minds and our talents to bring about the victory of doctrines opposed to generally accepted principles – or rather prejudices – is to misuse them; for it would on the contrary be a pity for a philosopher not to look in the sole direction from which he can acquire knowledge. Why? Because his strengthened and expanded genius – and after him all those to whom he can transmit his research and his enlightenment – will be more capable of judging the most difficult cases, of seeing the misuses that slip in here or the advantages that can be acquired there, and of finding the most direct and efficient means of putting an end to confusion. Like a physician whose lack of theory would make him eternally fumble his way in the vast labyrinth of his art, the mind without this new addition of enlightenment, which was only lacking a better application, would have been less educated and narrower, and would never have been able to discover all these things. So true is it that, according to the different uses that can be made of the knowledge of objects by their effects (for that is how I would modestly define philosophy), it has an infinite number of branches which extend a long way and seem to be able to protect everything: nature, by drawing from her bosom a thousand treasures which her ingenious penetration puts to the best use and makes even more precious; art, by exercising genius and pushing back the boundaries of the human mind.

What would be the use of enlarging our mind's faculties if it did not bring some good to society and if an increase in genius and knowledge did not help towards this in some direct or indirect manner?

Thus nothing is truer than the maxim that the more strength and enlightenment the human mind acquires, the easier it will always be to lead the people. Consequently, just as we learn in dressage to restrain and ride a spirited horse, in the same way we learn in the school of philosophy the art of taming men and bridling them when we cannot lead them by the natural light of reason. Can we do better than to attend it assiduously? And how blindly barbaric it would be to close off even its approaches?

Thus, on all sides, and even on the side of error itself, as of truth, philosophy has once again an influence on the public good; this influence is, it is true, more often indirect, but it is so great that we can say that just as it is the key to nature and to science – the glory of the mind – it is also the torch of reason, laws and humanity.

Let us thus be proud to carry a torch which is useful both to those who carry it and to those whom it enlightens.

Legislators, judges, magistrates, you will be all the better for allowing your activities to be enlightened by right philosophy. You will commit fewer injustices, iniquities and infamies; and you will contain men better as philosophers than as orators and better by reason than by sophistry.

To misuse philosophy, like eloquence, in order to seduce and increase the soul's two main faculties by means of each other is to use it cleverly. Do you believe that religion shields the weaker from the stronger? Do you think that men's prejudices are so many bridles which hold them back, and that their good faith, probity and justice would only hold by a thread once the shackles of superstition were undone? Use all your strength to preserve a precious blindness, and may their eyes never be opened if the world's unhappiness depends on it! Use the force of specious arguments to prop up their tottering faith, bring their weak genius, by the force of your own, down to the level of their fathers' religion and, like our sacred Josses,[33] lend the most revolting absurdities an appearance of plausibility. Let the Tabernacle open, let the laws of Moses be interpreted, let the mysteries be revealed and finally everything be explained. The altar can only be more respected when showered with incense by a philosopher.

Such is the fruit of the philosophical tree, an inappropriately forbidden fruit except for the fact that, as I am glad to think and even more to see, prohibition in this case, as in so many others, incites generous minds to pick it and to distribute everywhere its delicious perfume and excellent taste.

I am not trying to imply by this that one should try by all means to indoctrinate the people and to introduce them to the mysteries of nature. I realise only too well that a tortoise cannot run, nor crawling animals fly, nor blind men see. All I desire is that those who hold the helm of the state should be a little philosophical; all I believe is that they cannot be philosophical enough.

I have already given the greatest of examples to show how beneficial it is; the more philosophical princes or their ministers are, the more capable they will be of feeling the basic difference between their whims, their tyranny, their laws, their religion, and truth, equity and justice. And thus they will be more able to serve humanity and to be worthy of their subjects, more capable of knowing that philosophy, far from being dangerous, can only be useful and salutary, and more willing to allow scholars to spread enlightenment widely. They will understand better that philosophers are the eagles of the human race, created to soar, and that if they combat the prejudices of some people philosophically, it is so that those who are capable of grasping their doctrine can use it and apply it for the good of society when they think necessary.

Thus, full of unique and boundless respect for that queen of the wise man, we shall continue to believe her to be kindly, gentle, incapable of bringing any unpleasant consequences in her wake and as simple as the truth she teaches. We shall continue to believe that the oracles of that venerable Sybil are ambiguous only to those who cannot fathom their meaning and spirit, and are always directly or indirectly useful when one knows how to make good use of them.

Let us therefore – we who are zealous followers of philosophy in order to be even more zealous patriots – leave common men to shout and let us be like the Jansenists who are not prevented by an unjust excommunication from doing what they consider their duty;[34] may all the cries of theological hatred and the powerful

[33] A character in Molière's *Amour médecin*.

[34] The Jansenists were excommunicated by the papal bull *Unigenitus* in 1713 and were persecuted in

cabal of prejudices which stoke it, instead of preventing us from doing ours, never dull the dominant taste for wisdom which characterises a philosopher.

This duty, in case you ask, is to refuse to believe like an idiot who uses his reason less than a miser does his money and, even more, to refuse to pretend to believe; for hypocrisy is a comedy unworthy of man. It is also to cultivate a science that is the key to all the others and that, thanks to this century's good taste, is more fashionable today than ever before.

Yes, philosophers, here is your duty, and yours, princes, is to remove all the obstacles that frighten timid geniuses, to remove all those theological and metaphysical bombs, which are not filled with air when they are thrown by a furious holy man : 'Can a divine being be so persevering in anger?'[35]

To encourage philosophical activity with kindness and honours while you punish those who devote sleepless nights to it, when by chance this activity leads them away from the paths of the masses and received opinions, is like refusing communion and a tomb to those whom you pay to amuse you in their theatres. It is true that the one should not surprise me any more than the other, but on seeing such contradictions, how can one not cry out, like a philosopher-poet :

> 'Shall I always see my insane nation, its wishes unsure, blame what it admires, and our laws always contradict our habits, till the weak Frenchman falls asleep under the power of superstition?'[36]

The thunder is far away; let it roll, and march with an assured step towards the truth. Nothing should chain a philosopher's liberty of thought. If it is folly, it is that of noble souls; provided they rise, they are not afraid of falling.

He who sacrifices the precious gifts of genius to political virtue – which is, like them all, trivial and narrow – can truly say that he has been given a mind of stupid instinct and a soul of sordid self-interest. Let him boast of this if he thinks fit. As for me, a disciple of nature and a friend to truth alone, who derives more pleasure from the mere mental image of truth than from all the errors which bring fortune; as for me who preferred to be condemned in public for my lack of genius rather than to be saved, and even to be made rich, in obscurity by my prudence – I am a generous philosopher and will not refuse to pay homage to the charms which seduced me. The more the sea is full of reefs and known for its shipwrecks, the grander I shall continue to think it is to seek immortality there in the midst of so many perils. Yes, I shall dare to say freely what I think and, following Montaigne's example, I shall show myself to the universe as I appear in my own eyes; those who are the true judges of things will find me more innocent than guilty in my boldest opinions and perhaps virtuous in the very confession of my vices.

35 See p. 131 note 26.

36 'Ah! verrai-je toujours ma folle nation / Incertain en ses voeux, flétrir ce qu'elle admire; / Nos moeurs avec nos lois toujours se contredire / Et le faible Français s'endormir sous l'empire / De la supersitition?' Slightly adapted from Voltaire's poem, 'La mort de Mademoiselle Le Couvreur, fameuse actrice', *Œuvres* (2 vols., Amsterdam, 1732), vol. 1.

are the true judges of things will find me more innocent than guilty in my boldest opinions and perhaps virtuous in the very confession of my vices.

So let us be free in our writings as in our behaviour; let us show the proud independence of republicans. A timid, careful writer serves neither science, nor the human spirit, nor his country, and is prevented from rising by the tethers he himself has fastened. He is like a sprinter whose shoes have lead soles or a swimmer who puts bladders full of water under his arms. A philosopher must write with noble daring or expect to crawl like those who are not philosophers.

You who are so prudent and reserved, who employ so many tricks and ruses and who disguise yourselves so cleverly behind so many veils that the simple men who are the butt of your mockery cannot understand what you mean, what is holding you back? I can see; you feel that, among so many nobles who claim to be your friends[f] and with whom you live on terms of the greatest familiarity, there is not a single one who would not abandon you if you were disgraced, no not a single one who would have the generosity to ask his King to recall a man of genius. You fear the fate of that famous young scientist whose blind man was enough to enlighten the universe and send his author to Vincennes, or that other lesser genius (Toussaint) whose pure, always respectable but sometimes odd *Morals*, invented indiscreetly in the wake of paganism, have, they say, committed to that other horrible inquisition (the Bastille).[37] Well! Don't such writings incite in you an elevation and nobility of soul which knows no danger? At the sight of so many fine works, are you bereft of courage and self-respect? At the sight of so much soul, don't you feel any yourself?

I am not saying that the freedom of the soul is preferable to that of the body, but what man who is truly a man, with any susceptibility to a glorious reputation, would not willingly be deprived for a time of the latter in return for so great a prize?

Blush, Oh tyrants of sublime reason; like polyps cut into an infinite number of pieces, the works that you condemn to the flames rise up, so to speak, infinitely more numerous from their ashes. Listen to what the wisest and most enlightened minds think of those men whom you send into exile and force to leave their country (I dare to mention this without fearing that I might be suspected of any vain application or harsh regrets), of those men whom you lock up in cruel prisons! Or rather, see how a glorious reputation carries their names in triumph to the skies, while they lie groaning in prison! Oh modern Augustuses, do not be like Augustus in everything and spare yourselves the shame of literary crimes, one of which alone

[f] 'As long as you are fortunate you will have many friends. But if times change for the worse, you will be left alone' Ovid.[38]

[37] A reference to Diderot's *Lettre sur les aveugles* for which he was imprisoned in Vincennes in the summer of 1749, and F.-V. Toussaint's *Moeurs* (Amsterdam, 1748), although the latter was not imprisoned but fled to Holland.

[38] *Tristia*, I.vii.5–6: 'Donec eris felix, multos numerabis amicos / Tempora si fuerint nubila, solus eris.'

can make all your laurels wither. Do not punish arts and letters for the rashness of those who cultivate them best, otherwise modern Ovids will pass your cruel treatment on to posterity with their sighs, and indignant posterity will accord them tears and approval. And how could it, without ingratitude, read dry-eyed the *Tristia* and the complaints of writers who were only unhappy because they worked with posterity in mind?

But is it impossible to seek immortality without causing one's own ruin? What mad intoxication carries me away? Yes, there is a just, reasonable mean ('there is a mean in all things', etc.)[39] from which prudence forbids us to stray. Authors, for whom the most attractive vengeance – I mean the applause of enlightened Europe – is not enough, do you want to write immortal works with impunity? Think out loud but hide.[g] Let posterity be your only point of view, which should never be countered by any other. Write as if you were alone in the universe or as if you had nothing to fear from men's jealousy and prejudices, or you will miss your target.

I do not flatter myself that I have hit it; I do not flatter myself that the sounds which designate me and which I share with so many other obscure men will be carried into the immensity of the ages and the air. If I consult less my modesty than my weakness, I can even believe without any difficulty that the writer, subjected to the same laws as man, perishes entirely. Who even knows whether, in carrying out a plan that is so far above my strength, such a weak reputation as mine could not founder on the same reef that has already destroyed my fortune?

Whatever the case, untroubled both by the fate of my works and by my own, I shall at least testify that I have considered most of my contemporaries to be walking prejudices, that I have no more canvassed their approval than feared their blame or their criticism, and that satisfied and only too honoured by the small number of readers spoken of by Horace,[41] which a solid mind will always prefer to the whole of the rest of the world, I have sacrificed everything to the brilliant phantom which seduced me. Indeed, if my writings contain any new and daring beauty, a certain fire or any spark of genius, I owe it all to that philosophical courage which made me conceive the highest and most audacious undertaking.

My shipwreck and all the miseries which followed it are anyway easily forgotten in such a glorious port, so worthy of a philosopher; here I can drink long draughts

g It was the need to hide which made me imagine the *Dedication to Mr Haller*. I realise that it is a double extravagance to dedicate a work as daring as *Machine Man* in a friendly way to a scientist whom I have never seen and whose fifty years have not freed from all the prejudices of childhood. But I did not think that my style had betrayed me. Perhaps I should remove a text which made the person to whom it was addressed protest, groan and deny so much, but it received such public praise from writers whose approval is infinitely flattering that I did not have the courage. I take the liberty of republishing it here just as it has already been seen in all the editions of *Machine Man*, 'with apologies to the very famous, very learned and very pedantic Professor'.[40]

39 Horace, *Satires*, I.i.106: 'est modus in rebus'.

40 On the preface and La Mettrie's dispute with Haller, see Introduction, p. xvi. The phrase in quotation marks was in Latin: 'cum bena venia celeberrimi, SAVANTISSIMI, PEDANTISSIMI professoris'.

41 *Satires*, I.iv.71ff, and *Odes*, III.i.1.

of forgetfulness of all the dangers I have undergone. How can one regret such a lucky fault as mine!

But what better invitation to lovers of the truth! Here one can follow nature alone, and one can brave prejudices and all the enemies of solid philosophy, as one laughs at the angry waves from a calm harbour. I can now only hear mine thundering from a distance, like a storm battering the ship from which I have escaped. What pleasure to have no one to court but that immortal queen alone! How shameful it is that elsewhere one cannot sail freely on a sea that leads to the acquisition of so much wealth and, as it were, to the Peru of knowledge! Writers, scholars, philosophers and geniuses of all kinds, what is keeping you in chains in your own lands? He whom you can see, he who is opening the gate so generously for you, is a hero who, at an early age, reached the temple of memory by almost all the paths that lead there. Come. What are you waiting for? He will be your guide, your model and your support; he will force you, by his illustrious example, to follow in his footsteps the difficult path of glory. 'The guide, example and instrument', as the younger Pliny says in another context.[42] If you are not destined to follow him, at least you will share with us the pleasure of admiring him from close up. Truly, I swear, it is not his crown but his mind that I envy.

You who have not been affected by the sacred disturbers of respectable rest, appear bravely under such glorious auspices. Oh protected works, you would not have been protected if you were dangerous; a philosopher would not have created you and the wisest of kings would not have allowed you to be published. A vast profound mind, used to reflecting, knows only too well that what is only philosophically true cannot be harmful.

A few years ago, wrapped in a sorry coat, you were, alas, reduced to appearing alone and, as it were, timidly, like Ovid's poetry of old, without your author whom you were even afraid of unmasking; you were like those tender children who wished to hide their father from his too cruelly pursuing creditors. Today (to parody that unhappy, charming poet),[43] free and happier, you will no longer go about town without him and you will both walk with your heads held high; you will hear the populace thundering, as a sailor (to speak like a poet), certain of Neptune's protection, hears the thundering waves.

42 'Dux et exemplum et necessitas', *Letters*, Bk.VI, §24, l. 4, (trans. W. Melmoth, London, 1915). The passage concerns a woman who incites her husband to commit joint suicide because of a disease in his sexual organs.

43 *Tristia*, I, elegy 1.

Index

Cambridge Texts in the History of Philosophy

Titles published in the series thus far

Conway *The Principles of the Most Ancient and Modern Philosophy* (edited by Allison P. Coudert and Taylor Corse)

Descartes *Meditations on First Philosophy*, with selections from the *Objections and Replies* (edited with a new introduction by John Cottingham)

Antoine Arnauld and Pierre Nicole *Logic or the Art of Thinking* (edited by Jill Vance Buroker)

La Mettrie *Machine Man and Other Writings* (edited by Ann Thomson)

Schleiermacher *On Religion: Speeches to its Cultured Despisers* (edited by Richard Crouter)

Kant *The Metaphysics of Morals* (edited by Mary Gregor with an introduction by Roger Sullivan)